Essays and Studies 2005

Series Editor: Peter Kitson
Associate Editor: Helen Lucas

The English Association

The objects of the English Association are to promote the knowledge and appreciation of the English language and its literature, and to foster good practice in its teaching and learning at all levels.

The association pursues these aims by creating opportunities of co-operation among all those interested in English; by furthering the recognition of English as essential in education; by discussing methods of English teaching; by holding lectures, conferences, and other meetings; by publishing journals, books, and leaflets; and by forming local branches.

Publications

The Year's Work in English Studies. An annual bibliography. Published by Oxford University Press.

The Year's Work in Critical and Cultural Theory. An annual bibliography. Published by Oxford University Press.

Essays and Studies. An annual volume of essays by various scholars assembled by the collector covering usually a wide range of subjects and authors from the medieval to the modern. Published by D.S. Brewer.

English. A journal of the Association, *English* is published three times a year by the Association.

The Use of English. A journal of the Association, *The Use of English* is published three times a year by the Association.

Newsletter. A *Newsletter* is published three times a year giving information about forthcoming publications, conferences, and other matters of interest.

Benefits of Membership

Institutional Membership

Full members receive copies of *The Year's Work in English Studies*, *Essays and Studies*, *English* (3 issues) and three *Newsletters*.

Ordinary Membership covers *English* (3 issues) and three *Newsletters*.

Schools Membership includes copies of each issue of *English* and *The Use of English*, one copy of *Essays and Studies*, three *Newsletters*, and preferential booking and rates for various conferences held by the Association.

Individual Membership

Individuals take out Basic Membership, which entitles them to buy all regular publications of the English Association at a discounted price, and attend Association gatherings.

For further details write to The Secretary, The English Association, The University of Leicester, University Road, Leicester, LE1 7RH.

Essays and Studies 2005

Literature and the Visual Media

Edited by
David Seed

for the English Association

D.S. BREWER

ESSAYS AND STUDIES 2005
IS VOLUME FIFTY-EIGHT IN THE NEW SERIES
OF ESSAYS AND STUDIES COLLECTED ON BEHALF OF
THE ENGLISH ASSOCIATION
ISSN 0071–1357

First published 2005
D.S. Brewer, Cambridge

D.S. Brewer is an imprint of Boydell & Brewer Ltd
PO Box 9, Woodbridge, Suffolk IP12 3DF, UK
and of Boydell & Brewer Inc.
668 Mt Hope Avenue, Rochester, NY 14620, USA
website: www.boydellandbrewer.com

ISBN 1 84384 056 1

A CIP catalogue record for this title is available
from the British Library

The Library of Congress has cataloged this serial publication:
Catalog card number 36–8431

This publication is printed on acid-free paper   ˈ

Printed in Great Britain by
Athenaeum Press Ltd., Gateshead, Tyne & Wear

Contents

Illustrations

Figures 1 to 6 and 8 are reproduced courtesy of the Bill Douglas Centre for the History of Cinema and Popular Culture, University of Exeter; Figure 7 John Plunkett, personal collection.

Notes on Contributors

Mark Bould is a Senior Lecturer in Film Studies at the University of the West of England. An editor of *Historical Materialism* and an editorial consultant for *Science Fiction Studies*, he is currently completing *Film Noir: From Fritz Lang to Fight Club* (Wallflower, 2005) and *The Cinema of John Sayles: A Lone Star* (Wallflower, 2007); and co-editing a collection of M. John Harrison's criticism (Science Fiction Foundation, 2005).

Oliver Harris teaches American literature and film at Keele University. As a critic and scholarly editor he has published widely on the work of William Burroughs and also authored numerous essays on the Beats. He has written several articles on film noir, most recently 'Film Noir Fascination: Outside History, but Historically So' in *Cinema Journal* (Fall 2003).

Deborah L. Madsen is Professor of English and Chair of American Literature at the University of Geneva, Switzerland. Before that, she was Professor of English at London South Bank University. She is currently President of the Swiss Association for North American Studies. She has published more than a dozen books on various aspects of literary theory, American Studies, and ethnic literature. Her most recent book is *Chinese American Literature* (Gale, 2002).

Judie Newman is Professor of American Studies, in the School of American and Canadian Studies, University of Nottingham and the author of *Saul Bellow and History*, 1984, *John Updike*, 1988, *Nadine Gordimer*, 1988, (ed.) *Dred: A Tale of the Great Dismal Swamp*, by Harriet Beecher Stowe, 1992, rpt 1998, *The Ballistic Bard: Postcolonial Fictions*, 1995, *Alison Lurie: A Critical Study*, 2000, *Nadine Gordimer's Burger's Daughter* (Oxford University Press, 2003), plus essays and chapters in some 60 scholarly journals and books.

John Plunkett is lecturer in Victorian Literature and Culture at the University of Exeter. He is the author of *Queen Victoria – First Media Monarch* (Oxford University Press, 2003), and co-editor of *Popular Print Media 1820–1900* (Routledge, 2004). His current project is on the popularity of nineteenth-century optical recreations, including panoramas, kaleidoscopes, peepshows, and dioramas.

David Seed   holds a chair in American literature at the University of Liverpool. He is a member of the editorial board of the *Journal of American Studies*, and of the board of consulting editors for *Science Fiction Studies*. He edits the Science Fiction Texts and Studies series for Liverpool University Press. His publications include *American Science Fiction and the Cold War* (Edinburgh University Press, 1999) and *Brainwashing: The Fictions of Mind Control* (Kent State University Press, 2004). He is a Fellow of the English Association.

Grahame Smith   retired from the University of Stirling as Professor of English Studies in 2000, having taught previously at UCLA and the University of Wales and, on secondment, at the University of Malawi. In addition to articles and short monographs, he is the author of *Dickens, Money and Society* (1968), *The Novel and Society: Defoe to George Eliot* (1984), *Charles Dickens A Literary Life* (1996), *Dickens and the Dream of Cinema* (2003), and *The Achievement of Graham Greene* (1986).

Carol Watts   lectures in the School of English and Humanities at Birkbeck, University of London, where she specialises in eighteenth-century and contemporary literature, and film. Her work on the relations between film and literature includes *Dorothy Richardson* (Northcote House, 1995) and most recently an article on the concept of adaptation in relation to the melodramatic economy of D.W. Griffith's *Broken Blossoms*. She has just completed a book entitled *Laurence Sterne and the Cultural Work of Empire*.

Preface

The essays in this collection consider the interaction between literature – primarily the novel – and the visual media. In his discussion of the connections between Dickens's urban sketches and a twentieth-century film maker Grahame Smith uses the term 'interpenetration', which helpfully applies to all these essays in varying degrees. Dialogue, encounter, interrelation; all these terms avoid the suggestion of simple linear influence. It has now become a commonplace of cultural history to argue that the cinema – the main visual medium discussed in these pages – and literary Modernism both emerged out of a common pool of narrative and representational techniques. As John Plunkett demonstrates, optical entertainments in the nineteenth century, and above all the panorama, suggested new ways of seeing that were quickly converted into verbal expression. This process involved, he argues, a two-way 'cross-over' between different media. At the beginning of the twentieth century a number of factors converged to strengthen the dominance of the visual. Literary impressionism as practised by Conrad, Ford and others privileged the individual perspective with its attendant connection between seeing and understanding. The mass production of cameras had made photography so familiar by 1905 that W.D. Howells in his *London Films* could adopt the stance of a recording sensibility working his 'mental kodak'. The study of the workings of the mind led Henri Bergson to claim that consciousness worked on cinematic lines. The emergence of the cinema and Modernism in the same period enabled experimental writers to use film as *the* sign of contemporaneity. Indeed, from the 1920s onwards an increasing number of novelists – figures as diverse as Gertrude Stein, Evelyn Waugh, and John Dos Passos – wove into their works cinematic techniques like montage and there became evident a professional involvement of novelists in screenwriting. The cinematic novel was born. 'Cinematic' here suggests a heightened visual awareness as well as the specific analogy with film techniques. Judie Newman argues that this awareness informs John Updike's novels, but the signs of this change predate the emergence of a cinema-going generation of writers. As early as *The House of Mirth* (1905) Edith Wharton dramatises the production, circulation, and consumption of visual images in New York society.

The trap in early critical discussions of the relation between novel and film was to concentrate on adaptations and to project a crude model of transposition, so-called 'fidelity' to the work. In his examination of *The Killers* here, Oliver Harris shows how Hemingway's style has been taken as a precursor of *film noir* and possibly helped shape the method of the later American movies; this method was then fed back into the Hemingway's story to produce a narrative that differs strikingly from its 'original'. Harris's detailed discussion demonstrates another keynote of this collection. Whether Dickens, Joyce, or Updike is being described, every writer displays a self-consciousness about visual representation. Indeed, this self-consciousness may be one of the defining characteristics of the cinematic novel. Mark Bould directs our attention to an equally famous work: *Fahrenheit 451*. He argues that, although Ray Bradbury's novel is built around visual oppositions that lend themselves easily to movie adaptation, Truffault's film reveals a sharper sense of method in disturbing and thus problematising realist representation. Carol Watts applies the notion of 'habitus' as a shared cultural space to demonstrate ways in which the cinema informs the performatory dimension of contemporary fiction and its disjunction of sound from image. Her account of 'mutual informing' offers another variation on the theme of encounters between media that runs throughout these essays.

David Seed

Optical Recreations and Victorian Literature

JOHN PLUNKETT

MOVING IMAGES AND PROJECTION DEVICES had a long history well before the advent of cinema. Panoramas, magic lanterns, and peepshows were ubiquitous forms of public and domestic recreation throughout the nineteenth century. This essay argues that there are significant points of convergence and crossover between nineteenth-century print media and the panoply of optical recreations. The growth of optical recreations played a key role in the development of popular entertainment as an industry. This expansion was paralleled by a comparable increase in the production of popular novels and periodicals, which was instrumental in the growth of the publishing industry. Between 1848 and 1870, the British population increased by forty per cent, yet the number of books produced increased by around four hundred per cent (Davis 202). Optical and print media enjoyed mutually beneficial yet competing roles in the growth of nineteenth-century leisure practices. The synergies between literary production and screen practice are an index of the extent to which the latter permeated nineteenth-century culture and promoted new ways of seeing.

There are two principal forms of interaction between print media and optical recreations. The first stems from the way writers employed optical devices as tropes for the working of the mind: they were particularly employed as figures to materialise processes of creativity, imagination, and memory. In a well-known article, Terry Castle (1988) has traced the way that the Phantasmagoria stood for an excessive reverie of thought during the Romantic period (26–61).[1] The troping on the Phantasamgoria, however, belongs to a larger nineteenth-century fascination with the metaphoric potential of optical devices. The kaleidoscope, diorama, and magic lantern were all deployed to describe the functioning of the imagination. Optical devices were particularly apt for materialising cognitive processes because, as Isobel Armstrong has argued (1996), many optical recreations provided a sensory experience without a sensory, tactile image (126). They had an embodied yet ideal mode of viewing.

---

[1] For earlier examples, see Crary 40–3.

Writers' intra-textual use of optical tropes constitutes part of the larger structural convergence between nineteenth-century print media, conceived of in the broadest sense, and optical recreations. Thus, in addition to being used to describe the working of perception, several writers equated the experience of reading with that of viewing an optical show. Rousseau, in a discussion of the multiple characters in the novels of Samuel Richardson, asserted that 'It is easy to awaken the attention by incessantly presenting unheard of adventures and new faces, which pass before the imagination as figures in a magic lanthorn do before the eye' (Rousseau 2: 157). Rousseau treats the audience's experience of the moving images of a magic lantern performance as analogous to a reader's imaginative experience of the passing events in a fictional narrative. The convergence between print and optical media in terms of their consumption was also repeated at the level of aesthetic form and content. There was an intermittent production of books, particularly aimed at a juvenile readership, which attempted to exploit the novelty of the latest optical device or show. Insofar as it was possible, they attempted to replicate the viewing experience of peepshows, panoramas, and dioramas. The success of optical recreations exerted a creative pressure upon the conventional material organisation of the book. The nature of this influence can be thought of in relation to Bourdieu's notion (1993) of a cultural field, where the aesthetic rules of the field are determined by the dominant position within it (29–73). In nineteenth-century popular culture, the pervasiveness of optical recreations meant that, at least to some degree, they were able to define the aesthetic mode of the field.

Although magic lanterns and peepshows were regularly exhibited during the eighteenth century, it was not until the latter decades that optical shows began to form part of an emerging industry of popular entertainment. Robert Barker, for example, first took out a patent for a panorama in June 1787; the patent described 'an entire new Contrivance or Apparatus which is called by him *La Nature à Coup d'Oeil*, for the Purpose of displaying Views of Nature at Large' (Mannoni et al. 157). Barker exhibited his first panorama, a view of Edinburgh, at locations in Glasgow and Edinburgh in 1788; he then moved on to display the same picture in London in 1789.[2] Barker's success led to the opening of a purpose-built rotunda in Leicester Square in 1793, wherein he could exhibit two enormous circular canvases at once, one of 10,000 square feet and one of around 2,700 square feet. Among the subjects in the early years

---

[2] On the history of the panorama, see Altick (1978: 120–40) and Hyde (1988).

were panoramas of the Battle of Waterloo and the Siege of Flushing, together with cityscapes of Dublin, Paris, Venice, and Rome.

The success of the panorama exemplifies why nineteenth-century screen practice was such a fertile source of inspiration for writers. The panorama provided a new way of seeing the world, and of representing the self's relationship to that world. Almost immediately after its introduction, Romantic tourists started to see sweeping landscapes or cityscapes already structured as a panorama. Thomas Malton, for example, explicitly turned to the panorama to describe a London cityscape in his A *Picturesque Tour through the Cities of London and Westminster, illustrated with the most interesting views executed in aquatinta* (1792). Malton was the author of an influential treatise on perspective (1776), and his tour was one of many published during the period, following the example set by Uvedale Price, a key proponent of the picturesque. When Malton attempted to describe his view of London from the standpoint of St Paul's, the panorama was the only form capable of encompassing the totality of the cityscape:

> but as language is incapable of conveying adequate ideas of a prospect so extensive and various, I shall not attempt to describe it: indeed the pencil cannot do justice to such as scene, except in the manner of the newly invented Panorama; a mode of representation, when the scenery is correctly drawn, and coloured with proper aerial effect, superior to all others for displaying the beauties of a prospect, seen from a commanding situation; where the spectator turns; and views the whole circle of the horizon. (Malton 1792: 59)

Fast-growing London cannot be represented by conventional linguistic or artistic means. Only a panorama is able to do justice to the vastness of the modern city, which always exceeds the spectator's attempt to encompass it from a single standpoint. The panorama's ability to go beyond the existing conventions of pen and pencil helps to explain why many writers followed the example of Malton, to the extent that 'panorama' became a generic term for any type of comprehensive standpoint.

The fascination with the panorama's new way of seeing was certainly not shared by all. In *The Prelude*, William Wordsworth attacked the panorama in terms that stressed its position within a burgeoning industry of popular entertainment. Whereas Rousseau used the magic lantern as a figure for the work of the imagination, this metaphor was taken literally by Wordsworth. Rather than regarding optical devices as figures for cognition, he criticised panoramas for actually substituting for the work of the imagination. Wordsworth regarded them as simulated versions of reality; they alienated viewers from their deepest source of spiritual nourishment by replacing the natural world with a world of images. Wordsworth's hostility to the panorama forms part of a sustained attack on popular urban entertainments in book seven of *The Prelude*, which recounts the poet's residences in London in the 1790s. The sensory excess of the London shows he finds, particularly at Bartholomew Fair, come to stand for the unreality of the whole of modern urban existence. The 'moving pageant' of London life is itself treated as a giant show.

The principal attraction of Barker's panorama was its ability to imbue a flat painted scene with three-dimensional depth and life. The panorama, which was exhibited in a rotunda carefully lit to enhance its *trompe l'oeil* effect, offered the opportunity for the spectator to become immersed in its virtual world. Numerous reviews stressed the illusory power of the scene. Yet for Wordsworth, the panorama merely aped the 'absolute presence of reality'. Its all-encompassing circularity was an index to its overweening desire to supersede the natural, corporeal world:

> And with his greedy pencil taking in
> A whole horizon with power on all sides,
> Like that of Angels or commission'd Spirits,
> Plant us upon some lofty Pinnacle,
> Or in a Ship on Waters, with a world
> Of life, and life-like mockery, to East,
> To West, beneath, behind us, and before;
> Or more mechanic Artist represent
> By scale exact, in Model, wood or clay,
> From shading colours also borrowing help,
> Some miniature of famous spots and things
> Domestic, or the boast of foreign Realms;
> The Firth of Forth, and Edinburgh throned
> On crags, fit empress of that mountain Land;
> St. Peter's Church; or, more aspiring aim,
> In microscopic vision, Rome itself;
> Or, else perhaps, some rural haunt, the Falls
> Of Tivoli, and high upon that steep
> The Temple of the Sibyl, every tree
> Through all the landscape, tuft, stone, scratch minute,
> And every Cottage, lurking in the rocks,
> All that the Traveller sees when he is there.
>
> (Wordsworth 1979: 238–40)

The elevated perspective of the panorama holds out the possibility of an all-seeing viewpoint that, according to Wordsworth, belongs only to angels and the divine. The appeal of the panorama is like that of numerous shows exhibiting models of Rome, St Peter's, and the Falls of Tivoli: all rely on a mechanical imitation of reality.

Wordsworth's hostility towards the all-seeing nature of the panorama also derived from its ability to make every part of the world available for the easy consumption of the audience. The panorama, like the shows that exhibited models, reproduced 'All that the Traveller sees when he is there.' For Wordsworth, spiritual sustenance was achieved through an interactive relationship with the natural world, and the panorama and the model provided imitations that forestalled the need to visit the places they portrayed. As *The Mirror of Literature, Amusement and Instruction* declared in 1832, 'By the aid of Mr Burford's panoramic pencil, the sight-hunter of our times may enjoy a kind of imaginary tour through the world' (Anon. 1832: 393–4). The panorama and the model encouraged a passive mode of viewing that was the antithesis to that of the peripatetic traveller.

Despite Wordsworth's dislike, the number of panoramas, cosmoramas, and magic lantern performances continued to grow rapidly during the first decades of the nineteenth century. Optical media could be found in pleasure gardens, theatres, bazaars, touring shows, and institutions devoted to popular science such as Royal Polytechnic in Regent Street (opened in 1838) and the Royal Adelaide Gallery near the Strand (opened in 1832). Coinciding with this growth, the 1830s and 1840s in particular saw an enormous expansion in popular publishing and cheap periodicals (see Altick 1998). Journals like the *Penny Magazine* (1832–45) and *Saturday Magazine* (1832–44) attempted to provide the same rational recreation as panoramas and dioramas. The simultaneous development of print and optical media led to numerous points of crossover. At it simplest this convergence is reflected in the titles of periodicals and books that attempted to feed off the success of the latest optical novelty. Relevant titles include *The Literary Panorama and National Register* (1806–19), *The Kaleidoscope: or, Literary and Scientific Mirror* (1818–31); *The Diorama, Or Amusing Sketches of Life and Manners* (1826), and *The Hibernia Magazine and Monthly Panorama* (1810–11).

The interaction between print and optical media also took place at a conceptual level in that writers used optical shows to figure either their relationship with readers or their readers' engagement with their text. These tropings emphasised contrary aspects of the reading experience. Reading was figured, alternatively, as an absorbing series of moving scenes, as a process of detached observation, or as akin to a popular show. Whereas it was the passive experience of the panorama that aroused Wordsworth's distaste, this feature of optical recreations was seized upon as a structuring model by Pierce Egan for his *Life in London* (1821). Egan's *Life in London* was an enormous publishing success. It followed the riotous adventures of Corinthian Tom and Bob Logic as the former took his country cousin, Jerry Hawthorn, on a tour of the 'fast' haunts of the metropolitan underworld. Just as the various panoramas of London attempted to encompass the expanse of the city, Egan's desire to provide a guide to London low-life was keyed into his comparable assertion that the city was 'A Complete CYCLOPÆDIA where every man of the most religious or moral habits, attached to any sect, may find something to please his palate' (Egan 24). In chapter 2, Egan claimed that the book offered a camera obscura view of London. Reading the text was made analogous to viewing London through a camera obscura, primarily because it offered a detached, voyeuristic glimpse into dangerous London haunts:

> The author, in consequence, has chosen for his readers a *Camera Obscura* view of London, not only from its safety, but because it is so *snug*, and also possesses the invaluable advantage of SEEING and not being *seen*. The author of the *Devil upon two Sticks*, it appears, preferred taking a *flight* over the houses for his remarks and views of society; but if I had adopted that mode of travelling, and perchance had fallen to the ground, an hospital might have been the reward of my presumption. (Egan 19)

Although the camera obscura was not a novel device at the beginning of the nineteenth century, it remained an instrument used to aid amateur sketching. Egan's correlation between reading and viewing exemplifies the way writers used methods inspired by optical devices, particularly when it came to narrating the fast-moving experience of city-life. Significantly, he also casts his method as an advance upon the realism of Alain René Le Sage's *Le Diable boiteux* (1707), translated as *The Devil Upon Two Sticks* (1708). In Le Sage's novel, the devil Asmodeus reveals the life of Madrid to Don Cleofas by lifting the roofs off all the houses. In contrast to this lofty approach, Egan's narrative goes down to street-level in order to reveal the secrets of London life. *Life in London* uses the camera obscura as a trope to signify a close-up realism, which yet keeps the reader at a safe distance.[3]

---

[3] The French translation of *Life in London*, *Diorama Anglais, ou Promenades pittoresques à Londres. . . .* (1823), similarly draws an analogy between optical shows and Egan's method.

Other writers similarly used optical shows to envision their readers' relationship with their texts. At the end of Henry Ellison's *Emma: A Tale* (1839), a gothic romance in verse, Ellison describes his characters as akin to those seen in a Phantasmagoria show:

> Reader, these Forms are but as Figures made
> By a Phantasmagoria, briefly thrown
> On Time's strange Canvass: with the Light and Shade
> Of Fancy wrought; or like to Portraits shown
> On some old Tapestry, and faded grown
> Thro' the long Lapse of Years: at which you gaze
> 'Till each Face seems as that of one wellknown,
> And full of Recollections; Fancy plays
> Strange Tricks with us, and Phantoms at her will can raise!
>
> (Ellison 232)

Ellison's tale included the apparition of long-dead medieval knights: the characters were thus particularly redolent of the ghostly figures that characterised the Phantasmagoria. The other principal feature of Phantasmagoria show was the way that, by using a magic lantern concealed behind a screen, ghosts could be made to appear and disappear, or made to seem to move either towards or away from the audience. Ellison equates the succession of projected figures in the Phantasmagoria with his readers' transient experience of his characters.

Whereas Ellison, like Rousseau, used optical tropes to materialise the imaginative engagement of his readers, Dickens used them to stress the way his novels functioned as popular entertainments. Dickens's fascination with London shows, particularly panoramas, is evident in several journalistic pieces. He published three articles on the London Colosseum for the *Morning Chronicle* in 1835, a piece on Banvard's American panorama for the *Examiner* in December 1848, and an article on panoramic journeys for *Household Words* in April 1850.[4] In a fulfilment of Wordsworth's fears, the latter article celebrates the adventures of Mr Booley, a panoramic traveller who is able to visit the Arctic, India, and New Zealand, without ever having to leave the comfortable environs of London.

---

[4] Charles Dickens, 'The Colosseum', *Morning Chronicle*, 7 July 1835; 'Grand Colosseum Fête', *Morning Chronicle*, 10 July 1835; 'The Reopening of the Colosseum', *Morning Chronicle*, 13 October 1835; 'The American Panorama', *Examiner*, 16 December 1848; 'Some Account of an Extraordinary Traveller', *Household Words*, 20 April 1850.

Grahame Smith (2003) has argued that Dickens's interest in optical recreations fed into his fictional technique. Yet it also produced a way of envisioning his relationship with his large readership. Nowhere is this more evident than at the end of *The Old Curiosity Shop* (1841), where Dickens uses the moving panorama as a figure for both the imaginative journey of his readers and the novel's status as a public show. At the beginning of the final chapter, the narrator declares that 'The magic reel, which, rolling on before, has led the chronicler thus far, now slackens in its pace, and stops. It lies before the goal; the pursuit is at an end' (Dickens 1913: 504). The reader's passage through the novel, the 'magic reel', is equated with viewing a moving panorama, the dominant exhibition practice for panoramas from the 1820s. Moving panoramas consisted of a large painted canvas wound between two rollers, often accompanied by a narration from an accompanying lecturer. Dickens's use of the moving panorama clearly positions him as lecturer-cum-showman, whose role is to explain the moving scene passing before his readers. The pun on the magic real/reel also stresses, in a fashion akin to Rousseau, that the scenes experienced by his readers took place as much within their imagination as on the pages of the text.

Graphic artists from the period similarly used optical shows as a motif to stress the popular attraction of their work. This convergence between print, graphic, and optical media is evident in the frontispiece to volume four of Robert Seymour's *Sketches by Seymour* (c.1836). Figure 1 shows how Seymour presents the volume as a magic lantern show, much as Egan imagines his work as a camera obscura view. Seymour was a well-known illustrator and caricaturist of the 1830s, working on *Seymour's Comic Album* (1834), the *Squib Annual of Poetry, Politics, and Personalities* (1835) and *Figaro in London* (1831–8). He was also the initial illustrator for *The Pickwick Papers* until his engravings, initially conceived of as the central attraction, were, famously, upstaged by Dickens's narrative. *Sketches by Seymour* was a five-volume work containing comic illustrations of sporting jaunts and high japes, with a brief accompanying written narrative. Seymour's presentation of volume four as a comic magic lantern show emphasises the dominance of the visual attraction of his sketches in relation to the text. The reader moves from image to image, much as a magic lantern show moves successively from slide to slide. The title of the sketch, 'Galanty Show!', also positions Seymour as a popular showman in that it refers to the tradition of travelling peepshow and magic lantern showman.

In addition to materialising the work of the imagination, optical tropes recur in discussions of memory. They expressed not simply the

Figure 1 Robert Seymour, 'Galanty Show!', *Sketches By Seymour*, vol. 4
(London: G.S. Tregear, c.1836).

ability of memory to appear before the mind's eye, but the way consciousness could move easily between different scenes from the past. The kaleidoscope, diorama, and magic lantern were all used to materialise the cognitive processes of memory. The kaleidoscope was patented by David Brewster in 1817, and was an immediate sensation. In June 1818, *Blackwood's Edinburgh Review* declared that 'In the memory of man, no invention, and no work, whether addressed to the imagination or to the understanding, ever produced such an effect' (Brewster 1818b: 337). Brewster described it as an instrument for producing 'symmetry and beauty by the creation and subsequent multiplication of *compound forms*, each of which is composed of a direct and inverted image of a single form' (Brewster 1818a: 122). It is this ability to create new forms through multiple reflections that led to the kaleidoscope being appropriated as a trope to portray the working of the mind. It was particularly used to figure the way that consciousness was always creating new perceptions by making fresh connections out of the impressions it receives. A poem by Amelia Opie (1769–1853) uses the kaleidoscope in this vein to figure the workings of memory. The poem is from her last collection of verse, *Lays of the Dead* (1833), which is made up of poems to departed relatives or friends (although Opie began her literary career with a novel, *Father and Daughter* (1802), she only published devotional verse after becoming a committed Quaker in 1825).

'On the Portraits of deceased Relatives and Friends, which Hang Around Me' meditates upon the ability of the mind to conjure up its own shifting stream-of-consciousness. Opie's reflection springs from the unbidden remembrance of a dead childhood friend, whose portrait she carries with her in a necklace:

> What art thou, madness? Living death thou art!
> Death to each purpose that can life endear –
> Thou false reality! whose fancies all
> Have some foundation in their wildest mood.
> As in kaleidoscope, all things remain,
> Foil, flowers, and gauze, as when they enter'd first;
> But, when together shaken, they assume
> Such new positions, that new semblances
> They seem to wear: so, when the awful power
> Of madness shake the brain, ideas change
> Their relative position and appear
> In such confusion, on each other cast,
> That they in useless fantasies revolve
> Now bright, now dark, but *fresh delusions still*.

> But oh! the grief of thy transforming power!
> It makes the meek perverse the humble proud,
> And blasphemous the pious! Dreadful change!   (Opie 99–100)

Opie's aversion to the imaginative presence of her former friend seems keyed into a general Quaker distrust of false images. However, it is not an external religious image but Opie's own mind that has produced the 'false reality' of her friend's presence. Opie's 'Living death' refers as much to the narrator, caught in her own reverie, as to her childhood friend who has been recalled to life though her mental image. Opie's kaleidoscope functions as a metaphor for the dynamic self-absorption of the mind. Just as the kaleidoscope is able to produce an infinite number of new forms through reflection, the restless mind works fervently upon its impressions so that, in the end, it becomes caught up in its endlessly revolving fantasies. Opie's troping on the kaleidoscope is an implicit recognition of its ability to fascinate the consciousness of the viewer, in much the same way that Wordsworth saw panorama spectators as being immersed in an illusory world.

George Eliot similarly had recourse to optical devices to describe the working of memory. Her deployment of these metaphors forms part of her well-known interest in science and the visual arts. In *Middlemarch*, after Dorothea and Casaubon have returned from their honeymoon in Italy, Dorothea looks at Casaubon's drawing-room one morning, and is reminded of the hopes she held for marriage when she first stood in the room:

> The ideas and hopes which were living in her mind when she first saw this room nearly three months before were present now only as memories; she judged them as we judge transient and departed things. All existence seemed to beat with a lower pulse than her own, and her religious faith was a solitary cry, the struggle out of an object in which every object was withering and shrinking away from her. Each remembered thing in the room was disenchanted, was deadened as an unlit transparency . . . (Eliot 1994: 275)

The narrative moves between two identical scenes. The objects in the room recall Dorothea's idealistic desires, yet their remembrance only confirms her lack of fulfilment. Contrasting past and present in terms of the difference between a lit and unlit transparency brilliantly materialises the way Dorothea's memory of the same room makes evident her current oppression.

Elsewhere in *Middlemarch*, Eliot uses the diorama as a figure for the working of memory. The diorama was introduced into London in

September 1823 by Louis Daguerre and Charles Bouton: the first shows took place in a purpose-designed building in Regent's Park (see Wood 284–95). Thereafter, dioramas were put on a numerous exhibition spaces in London and the provinces. The chief appeal of the diorama was that, through changing the play of light upon a large screen painted in transparent colours, the scene could be made to transform, often from day to night or vice versa. Eliot's used the motif of the diorama in her first novel, *Adam Bede*, to critique a condition where a passive mind has become enclosed in its own memory-work:

> Bodily haste and exertion usually leave our thoughts very much at the mercy of our feelings and imagination; and it was so tonight with Adam. While his muscles were working lustily, his mind seemed as passive as a spectator at a diorama: scenes of the sad past, and probably sad future, floating before him and giving place one to the other in swift succession.
>
> He saw how it would be to-morrow morning, when he had carried the coffin to Broxton and was at home again having his breakfast: his father perhaps would come in ashamed to meet his son's glance – would sit down, looking older and more tottering than he done the morning before, and hand down his head, examining the floor – quarries; while Lisbeth would ask him how he supposed the coffin had been got ready, that he had slinked off and left undone . . . (Eliot 1998: 57)

Adam's mind is passive while scenes from the past and future pass before his consciousness. Even though Adam's body is working, his mind is metaphorised as being as passive as the audience at a diorama. Rather than exploiting the transforming scene of the diorama, Eliot plays off the way the illusory scene of the diorama captivates the audience.

Eliot uses the diorama in a similarly critical vein in *Middlemarch*. After Bulstrode has bought Stone Court from Joshua Rigg and just before he is reacquainted with Raffles, the working of his memory is described as akin to that of a diorama:

> He was doctrinally convinced that there was a total absence of merit in himself; but that doctrinal conviction may be held without pain when the sense of demerit does not take a distinct shape in memory and revive the tingling of shame or the pang of remorse. Nay, it may be held with intense satisfaction when the depth of our sinning is but a measure for the depth of forgiveness, and a clenching proof that we are peculiar instruments of the divine intention. The memory has as many moods as the temper, and shifts its scenery like a diorama. At this moment Mr. Bulstrode felt as if the sunshine were all one with that of far-off evenings when he was a very young man and used to go out preaching beyond Highbury. (Eliot 1994: 521–2)

Eliot uses the moving image of the diorama to emphasise Bulstrode's equivocal relationship to his Evangelical beliefs. His conviction of his spiritual fall remains at the level of abstract doctrine. He does not feel the implications of his fallen nature because it has not been taken into memory. Bulstrode's memory overrides his Evangelical doctrine because, rather than dwelling on the past in terms of the sale of Stone Court and Joshua Rigg's desire to become a money-changer, the sunshine sets off involuntary memories of preaching at Highbury in his youth. Eliot uses the diorama to signify the power of memory to captivate the mind and its potential to move between very different scenes; moreover, in Bulstrode's case, the memories of Highbury provide an escape from his present moral conundrums.

Writers' intra-textual use of optical motifs was replicated by a more material crossover between optical recreations and the publishing industry. The success of the various optical shows let to many attempts to recreate the same aesthetic effect through games, books, prints, and domestic devices. One of the defining features of nineteenth-century optical recreations, which both created and sustained their appeal, was that multifarious artefacts sought to reproduce the same aesthetic affect. Large-format public shows invariably had small-scale domestic counterparts. Magic lanterns varied from sophisticated professional instruments to rudimentary versions designed for children. The success of large-scale panoramas led to hand-held versions, children's games, and miniature toy theatre panoramas that could be performed in any parlour. In the early years of the panorama's novelty small hand-held panoramas were published as luxury tourist guides-cum-commemoratives. Among the many produced were panoramas of Falmouth (1806), Brighton (1831), Sidmouth (1821), Weymouth (1820), and the Isle of Wight (1820).[5] Scrolling panoramas were also used to portray public events such as the coronations of George IV in 1818 and Queen Victoria in 1838. Numerous games based on the aesthetic form and instructional value of the panorama were also produced: examples include the *Myriorama* (1824), *Panoramacopia* (1824), and *Nautorama* (1832). The convergence between print and optical media was thus only part of the latter's capacious influence.

The most obvious material convergence between optical and print media is when the latter reproduced the way of seeing associated with a

[5] These panoramas, together with the games subsequently mentioned, form part of the collection of the Yale Centre for British Art.

particular optical form. The various small- and large-scale panoramas of the 1820s and 1830s established a set of conventions for portraying large public events and the new cityscapes of England. These conventions were subsequently taken up by the growth of pictorial journalism in the 1840s. When the *Illustrated London News* began weekly publication in May 1842, it was the first periodical to be devoted to graphic news. Prior to this, few newspapers had provided engravings of contemporary events, and then only of exceptional occasions such as the coronation of Queen Victoria. By 1855, the *Illustrated London News* was claiming circulation figures of 130,000 a week. The success of the *Illustrated London News* soon led to the advent of competitors such as the *Pictorial Times* (1843–8), *Illustrated Times* (1855–62), and *Illustrated News of the World* (1858–63).

From its first issue, the *Illustrated London News* constantly stressed the artistic and technical quality of its engravings. To demonstrate its visual spectacle to the public, the *Illustrated London News* soon announced that every subscriber who purchased the journal regularly for six months would receive a print of the Colosseum panorama of London. The Colosseum in Regent's Park, which opened in 1832, was a principal London attraction. Its central feature was an enormous panorama of London from the top of St Paul's that covered 24,000 square feet of canvas (see Altick 1978: 140–62). The Colosseum print produced by the *Illustrated London News* was attempting to make an analogy between its own visual novelty and the spectacular experience of the Regent's Park venue. Moreover, the technological realism of the *Illustrated London News*'s print was accentuated because it was based on a series of daguerreotypes taken from the top of the Duke of York's column by Antoine Claudet (the *Morning Post* compared his work at the top of the column to that of Asmodeus) (Anon. 1843: 17).

The *Illustrated London News*'s panorama, 4 ft 4 inches by 4 ft, was presented to its readers on 7 January 1844. The success of the venture was such that it was soon copied by the *Pictorial Times*. At the end of 1844, the *Pictorial Times* distributed handbills that promised the imminent publication 'for all persons, the largest engraving in the world, the Grand Panorama of London from the Thames, fourteen feet in length!' (Hyde n.d.). The panorama appeared on 11 January 1845; however, the *Illustrated London News* quickly responded with its own *Panorama of the Thames in 1845*. In addition to being available to subscribers, both panoramas were made available for general purchase. Moreover, as Ralph Hyde has shown, the *Pictorial Times*'s panorama continued to maintain its attraction (Hyde n.d.). An expanded eighteen-foot version was released in 1847, again in 1849, and finally given away in a revised form to the subscribers of *Cassell's Illustrated Family Paper* (1853–67).

Panoramas came to be regularly used by the *Illustrated London News* and the *Pictorial Times*. Their presence demonstrates that panoramas established a way of seeing that became part of everyday life. The *Illustrated London News*, for example, produced a panorama of the Great Exhibition in a supplement to its edition of 22 November 1851. As Figure 2 demonstrates, it ran over several pages: when joined together its complete length was twenty-nine feet. The panorama took the viewer through the different exhibition areas of the Crystal Palace: its scale made the world's industry available much as the expanse of Crystal Palace itself did. Subsequent large prints given away with the *Illustrated London News* included panoramas of Rome (4 May 1850); Liverpool (2 April 1865); Glasgow (26 March 1864); and New York (19 August 1876).

In the same period that the *Illustrated London News* was producing its Colosseum print, there were a series of illustrated children's gift books that were modelled as a panorama or peepshow. Readers were addressed as if they were a peepshow audience, much as Pierce Egan positioned his readers as viewers of a camera obscura. The structuring of these books reflects their visual novelty in that they were the product by the same expansion in wood and steel engraving that encouraged the advent of the *Illustrated London News* (see Darton 199–251). Optical games and toys were also often promoted as a way of instructing and amusing children, and children's gift books that used optical motifs did so in order to stress that they offered amusement rather than simply moral instruction. *Kriss Kringle's Raree Show, For Good Boys and Girls* (1846), an illustrated American Christmas gift book, is one example of a book structured as a peepshow entertainment: Kriss Kringle, the avuncular narrator, was an early American incarnation of 'Father Christmas'. (It was in 1846, the same year as *Kriss Kringle's Raree Show* was published, that a Philadelphia department store reputedly became the first to call itself 'Kriss Kringle's Headquarters'.)

The opening of the book declares that, 'It is the time of Christmas holidays. Kriss Kringle has a new species of entertainment for his young friends. It is a grand RAREE SHOW! The spectators are assembled. All eyes are on the great curtain which bears the inscription *Kriss Kringle's Raree-Show for Boys and Girls*' (Anon. 1846: 5). The book is arranged as a series of thirty-eight 'sights', in which Kriss Kringle provides a narrative to an illustrated scene framed as a peepshow image. The 'sights' consist of scenes from European and North American history, ranging

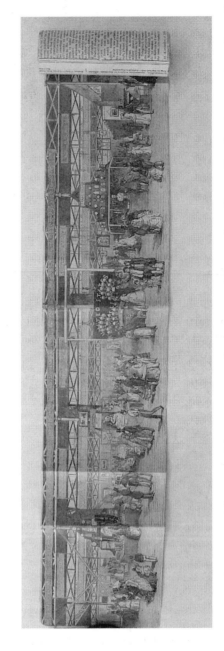

Figure 2 *Grand Panorama of the Great Exhibition: No. 1. South-East portion of the nave*, from *Illustrated London News*, 22 November 1851.

from the death of Lord Nelson to the capture of Stony Point during the American War of Independence. Kriss Kringle's role as the showman means that he is always directly addressing his readers as if they were a peepshow audience. Whereas Pierce Egan uses the camera obscura as a trope to emphasise a detachment between the reader and the scene, Kriss Kringle's persona draws the juvenile readers into the narrative.

The British equivalent to Kriss Kringle's Raree Show was Peter Parley's *Sergeant Bell and His Raree Show* (1839). Peter Parley was originally the pseudonym for Samuel Goodrich, an American writer who published around two hundred educational volumes for children, mostly under his pseudonym. The success of the Peter Parley series meant there were numerous unauthorised titles published under the name in Britain. F.J. Darton has suggested that there were at least six different British Peter Parleys (223). In *Sergeant Bell and His Raree Show*, Peter Parley follows the peepshow entertainments being performed by a travelling showman every market day in Taunton. The frontispiece by George Cruikshank shows a group of children eagerly grouped around Sergeant Bell's peepshow (see Figure 3). Like Kriss Kringle's Raree show, Peter Parley's book is structured around a series of illustrated peepshow views with an accompanying narrative. The avuncular old soldier Sergeant Bell provides a blend of amusement and instruction for his readers-cum-audience; as the narrative itself notes, 'he introduced so many proverbs, and short, pithy rhymes, and mingled so much information, cheerfulness, good sense, and good advice, in his observations, that pity was supplanted by respect' (Parley 7). Kriss Kringle's and Peter Parley's books, in both their narrative structure and their visual organisation, attempt to reproduce the mode of viewing of the peepshow. Such hybrid publications continued to appear as children's gift books for the rest of the century. *The Picture Pleasure Book* (1854), which has a picture of a peepshow on the front cover; *The Fool's Paradise: with the many wonderful adventures there as seen in the strange surprising peepshow of Professor Colley Wobble* (1878), and *Peepshow Pictures: A Novel Picture Book for Children* (1894), were all illustrated books that, to varying degrees, imitated a peepshow entertainment. Similarly, *Our Parlour Panorama* (1882), an illustrated Christmas book by the prolific children's writer, Mrs George Cupples, mimicked the numerous panorama shows that were structured in the form of a journey around the world.

Whereas Kriss Kringle and Sergeant Bell imitated the travelling showman's narrative in order to appeal to a juvenile readership, other publications more directly replicated the visual aesthetic of the different optical recreations. Children's novelty books attempted to create moving images within their covers. The conventional material organisation of the book was altered so that, insofar is it was possible, books *became* panoramas, a series of dissolving views, or a moving Punch and Judy Show. Alfred Crowquill's *Comic History of the Kings and Queens of England, from William the Conqueror to the Present Time* (c.1855), exemplifies the way that the success of optical recreations exerted a creative pressure on the materiality of the book. Crowquill presents the chronological procession of Kings and Queens in a fold-out panorama consisting of thirty-six mildly comic portraits. As Figure 4 demonstrates, the panoramic structure of the book embodies, far more successfully than consecutive pages could ever do, an unbroken national procession of English and British monarchs.

The leading publishers in children's moveable books were Dean and Son, a firm set up by Thomas Dean sometime in the late eighteenth century. They were the first children's publishing firm to use lithography extensively and their novelty books came to the fore as part of the tremendous growth in children's publishing during the 1840s (see Haining 20–6). Dean and Son's books, like many optical recreations, usually centred on the appeal of 'moving' scenes. They created 'pop-up' books that used different layers of illustration to create the illusion of scenic depth, much as various peepshows did. The firm also attempted to mimic the way that optical shows produced metamorphoses and transformations. *Dean's New Book of Magic Illuminations* (1862) consisted of a series of coloured transparencies which, when held up to the light, 'give an entirely New and surprisingly-pleasing Aspect to the Picture, – as the Scene would appear when Illuminated at Night' (Dean and Son frontispiece insert). Figure 5 demonstrates the way Dean's transparencies were centred on the play of light. The lamps on the trees and the torches held by the skaters appear translucent when held up to the light because they have been painted on to a second backing sheet, with the relevant areas of the top printed sheet being cut away. *Dean's New Book of Magic Illuminations* is an attempt to replicate the aesthetic of the diorama. The slow transformation of a day-scene to a moonlit illumination was its stock attraction.

Dean and Son also took inspiration from the magic lantern for *Dean's New Book of Dissolving Views* (1862). The origin of dissolving views went back to the Phantasmagoria shows during the 1790s; nonetheless it was not until the early 1840s that dissolving views were regularly exhibited at institutions such as the Royal Adelaide Gallery and the Royal Polytechnic (Anon. 1842: 97–101). Dissolving views slowly transformed a projected image in the same manner as the

Figure 3 George Cruikshank, frontispiece, *Sergeant Bell and His Raree Show* (London: Thomas Tegg, 1839).

diorama. The metamorphosis required two identical lanterns projecting an image on the same spot. The lanternist began by projecting an image from one of the lanterns; then, by slowly cutting off the illumination from the first lantern and simultaneously revealing the scene projected by the second, the first scene could be made to fade imperceptibly into

Figure 4 Alfred Crowquill's *Comic History of the Kings and Queens of England, from William the Conqueror to the Present Time* (London, c.1855).

The links of the skaters, and lamps, I declare,
Make the ice-covered river as gay as a fair.
While the rockets so splendid ascend to the sky,
And add to the wonders that dazzle the eye.

1

Figure 5 'Transparency of Skating Scene', *Dean's New Book of Magic Illuminations* (London: Dean and Son, 1862), 1.

Figure 6 'War-Peace', *Dean's New Book of Dissolving Views* (London: Dean and Son, 1862).

THE SERPENTINE DANCER.

INSTRUCTIONS.—Same as given for the Water Mill.

Figure 7 'Serpentine Dancer', *The Motograph Moving Picture Book* (London: Bliss, Sands, and Co., 1898).

the second. A warm pastoral summer scene could shift into a scene showing the same landscape covered with snow and frost. Dissolving views were extremely successful and became a staple component of magic lantern shows. Dean and Son attempted to provide their own dissolving views within the covers of a book. As Figure 6 demonstrates, by pulling the tab at the bottom of the page, one image would transform into another.

Dean and Son continued publishing throughout the nineteenth-century yet they produced no more novelty books based explicitly on optical shows. Children's periodicals like the *Boy's Own Annual*

Figure 8 *The Christmas Magic Motion Picture Book and Pocket Kinematograph* (London: Kinema Novelty Company, 1909).

(1879–1967) nevertheless often contained instructions on how to make your own optical toy or game. However, it was not until the advent of the cinematograph that moving image technology had a pronounced impact upon the material form of children's books. Like the earlier books structured as peepshow entertainments or dissolving views, a series of publications sought to exploit the novelty of the mutoscope and cinematograph. Flick books were produced in large numbers, while other publications included *The Motograph Moving Picture Book* (1898) and Theodore Brown's *The Christmas Magic Motion Picture Book and Pocket Kinematograph* (1909).[6] *The Motograph Moving Picture Book* consisted of a number of illustrations: when an accompanying acetate transparency was placed over the image and moved slowly up and down, it created a 3-D effect and the image itself appeared to move. Figure 7, an illustration of a serpentine dancer, exemplifies the Motograph book's reliance on early film. When the acetate transparency is moved over the drawing then she appears to dance. The shimmering motion of serpentine dancers was a favourite subject of early cinematographers, being filmed by, among others, Edison in New York and Gaumont in Paris. *The Motograph Moving Picture Book* is thus clearly exploiting both the technological novelty of the cinematograph and its subject matter. Similarly, Theodore Brown's motion picture book attempted to reproduce moving images within the covers of a book. The book stemmed from a patent Brown took out in May 1908 for a new optical device (Brown was an inveterate inventor of optical novelties; he was a notable figure in the fields of early film, magic lantern technology, and stereoscopic photography: see Herbert). *The Christmas Magic Motion Picture Book and Pocket Kinematograph* (Figure 8) consisted of a series of ten anaglyphic images showing two phases of motion, one phase printed in red, the other in green. The images were looked at through an accompanying eyepiece that could switch between red and green lenses. When an image was seen first through the red lenses and then the green lenses, the image appeared to move.

The novelty books organised as optical shows were part of an ensemble of prints, games, toys and artefacts, all of which were influenced by moving image technology. The interaction between print and optical media was only part of the latter's extensive influence. Optical

---

[6] At least two versions of the Motograph book were produced; the second had a cover by Toulouse-Lautrec and included more colour illustrations.

shows, for example, were not simply used to materialise the work of the imagination. They were also used to deploy the experience of movement and speed created by new technologies like the railways. In the late 1830s, Thomas Hood, while describing the experience of a railway journey, noted that 'There was no alternative but to watch the moving diorama that was gliding past the window' (Hood 3: 193). Although this essay has focused on the crossover from optical to print media, the interaction was always two-way. Magic lantern shows were often based on literary favourites: Dickens's novels, *Gulliver's Travels*, *Robinson Crusoe*, and the *Pilgrim's Progress*, were, unsurprisingly, among the most oft-performed. Moreover, many magic lantern slide sets either adapted or copied the original illustrations published with the novels. John Leech's illustrations for *The Christmas Carol* and John Tenniel's work for *Alice in Wonderland* often formed the basis for magic lantern slide sets. Only by tracing the multiple interactions between print, optical, and graphic media is it possible to demonstrate the hybridity characterising nineteenth-century popular culture.

Works Cited

Altick, Richard, 1978. *The Shows of London*. Cambridge, MA: Belknap Press.

Altick, Richard, 1998. *The English Common Reader: the Social History of the Mass Reading Public, 1800–1900* (1957). Columbus, OH: Ohio State University Press.

Anon., 1832. 'Fine Arts. Panorama of Milan', *The Mirror of Literature, Amusement and Instruction* (16 June), pp. 393–4.

Anon., 1842. 'Dissolving Views', *The Mirror of Literature, Amusement, and Instruction* (12 February), pp. 97–101.

Anon., 1843. 'A Few Words about our Last Number', *Illustrated London News*, (14 January), p. 17.

Anon., 1846. *Kriss Kringle's Raree Show for Boys and Girls*. Philadelphia: Walker and Gillis.

Anon., 1898. *The Motograph Moving Picture Book*. London: Bliss, Sands and Co.

Armstrong, Isobel, 1996. 'Transparency: Towards a Poetics of Glass in the Nineteenth Century', in *Cultural Babbage: Technology, Time and Invention*, eds Francis Spufford and Jenny Uglow. London: Faber & Faber, pp. 123–48.

Bourdieu, Pierre, 1993. 'The Field of Cultural Production, or: The Economic World Reversed', in *The Field of Cultural Production*, ed. Randal Johnson. Cambridge: Polity Press, pp. 29–73.

[Brewster, David] 1818a. 'Description of the Patent Kaleidoscope, Invented by Dr Brewster', *Blackwood's Edinburgh Magazine*, 3 (May), pp. 121–3.

[Brewster, David] 1818b. 'History of Dr Brewster's Kaleidoscope, With Remarks on its Supposed Resemblance to Other Combinations of Plain Mirrors', *Blackwood's Edinburgh Review*, 3 (June), pp. 331–7.

Castle, Terry, 1988. 'Phantasmagoria: Spectral Technology and the Metaphorics of Modern Reverie', *Critical Inquiry*, 15.i, pp. 26–61.

Crary, Jonathan, 1992. *Techniques of the Observer: On Vision and Modernity*. Cambridge, MA: MIT Press.

Cupples, Mrs George, 1882. *Our Parlour Panorama*. London: T. Nelson and Sons.

Darton, F.J. Harvey, 1982. *Children's Books in England: Five Centuries of Social Life*. Cambridge: Cambridge University Press.

Davis, Philip, 2002. *The Oxford English Literary History, Volume 8: The Victorians*. Oxford: Oxford University Press.

Dean and Son, 1862. *Dean's New Book of Magic Illuminations*. London: Dean and Son.

Dickens, Charles, 1913. *The Old Curiosity Shop*. London: Chapman & Hall.

Egan, Pierce, 1821. *Life in London, Or, The Day and Night Scenes of Jerry Hawthorn, ESQ, and his elegant friend Corinthian Tom, accompanied by Bob Logic, the Oxonian, in their Rambles and Sprees through the Metropolis*. London: Sherwood, Neely, and Jones.

Eliot, George, 1994. *Middlemarch*, ed. Rosemary Ashton. Harmondsworth: Penguin.

Eliot, George, 1998. *Adam Bede*, ed. Stephen Gill. Harmondsworth: Penguin.

Ellison, Henry, 1833. *Mad moments, or first verse attempts by a born natural, etc.*, vol. 1. Malta, n.p.

Haining, Peter, 1979. *Movable Books: An Illustrated History*. London: New English Library.

Herbert, Stephen, 1997. *Theodore Brown's Magic Pictures: the Art and Inventions of a Multi-Media Pioneer*. London: Projection Box.

Hood, Thomas, 1870. 'Sketches on the Road. The Railway', in *The Works: Comic and Serious, in Prose and Verse*, vol. 3. London: E. Moxon, Son, and Co., pp. 191–9.

Hyde, Ralph, 1988. *'Panoramania': The Art and Entertainment of the 'All-Embracing' View*. London: Trefoil Publications.

Hyde, Ralph, 'Comments on "The Grand Panorama of London From the Thames"'. http://www.motco.com/panoramas/001/hyde.asp.

Malton, Thomas, 1776. *A Compleat Treatise on Perspective in Theory and Practice; On the true Principles of Dr Brook Taylor*. London: Robson et al.

Malton, Thomas, 1792. *A Picturesque Tour through the Cities of London and Westminster, illustrated with the most interesting views executed in aquatinta*. London: Thomas Malton.

Mannoni, Laurent, Dorata Pesenti Campagnoni, and David Robinson, eds, 1995. *Light and Movement: Incunabula of the Moving Image*. London et al.: British Film Institute and Le Giornate del Cinema Muto.

Opie, Amelia, 1834. *Lays for the Dead*. London: Longman, Rees, Orme, Brown, Green, and Longman.

Parley, Peter, 1839. *Sergeant Bell and His Raree Show*. London: Thomas Tegg.

Rousseau, Jean-Jacques, 1790. *The Confessions of J.J. Rousseau, Part the first. To which are added, The Reveries of a Solitary Walker. Part the second. To which is added, A New Collection of Letters from the Author*. London, G.G. & J. Robinson.

Seymour, Robert, c.1836. 'Galanty Show!', *Sketches By Seymour*, vol. 4. London: G.S. Tregear.

Smith, Grahame, 2003. *Dickens and the Dream of Cinema*. Manchester: Manchester University Press.

Wood, Derek R., 1993. 'The Diorama in Great Britain the 1820s', *History of Photography*, 17.iii, pp. 284–95.

Wordsworth, William, 1979. *The Prelude, 1790, 1805, 1850*, ed. Jonathan Wordsworth, M.H. Abrams, and Stephen Gill. London and New York: W.W. Norton.

The Travelling Lanternist and the Uncommercial Traveller: An Experiment in Correspondences

GRAHAME SMITH

[For Peter Jewell]

RELENTLESSLY CLANGING MUSIC accompanies the appearance of a circle of light – the moon? – against a black ground which gradually turns to an intense blue reflecting what is now the circle's blinding intensity of light – the sun? The circle is invaded by a black disk by which it is eventually eclipsed. As the eclipse is completed the image merges into a cloudy blue sky and we move downwards to see a group of static figures dressed, somehow incongruously, in what looks like early nineteenth century women's clothing. The image jumps to a foot stamping on a pane of glass on the ground and we then focus on the destruction of a threshing machine out of which grain spills in all directions. Soldiers in bright red uniform are seen galloping: a horse rears, figures are clubbed to the ground and, in the process, revealed to be men disguised as women. A flaming torch lights a heap of hay and we are turned to the figure of what we later learn to be a traveling lanternist, his face convulsed with horror and amazement, and illuminated by the flickering reflection of flames. We see that he is looking at a number of fires in the middle distance of a darkening rural landscape. A man rolls over, his face gazing blindly at the sky. An isolated hand is held aloft, blood trickling in a long line down its palm from between its fingers. The lanternist runs fearfully away, glancing over his shoulder, and makes his escape over the Cerne Abbas Giant whose huge genitals are echoed by the enormous club he wields. One minute has passed when the word COMRADES appears before us.

This is a moment of alienating strangeness, I'd suggest, but no stranger than the following:

Once – it was after leaving the Abbey and turning my face north – I came to the great steps of Saint Martin's church as the clock was striking Three. Suddenly, a thing that in a moment more I should have trodden upon without seeing, rose up at my feet with a cry of loneliness and houselessness, struck out of it by the bell, the like of which I never heard. We then stood face to face looking at one another, frightened by one another. The creature was like a beetle-browed hare-lipped youth of twenty, and it had a loose bundle of rags on, which it held together with one of its hands. It shivered from head to foot, and its teeth chattered, and as it stared at me persecutor, devil, ghost, whatever it thought me it made with its whining mouth as if it were snapping at me, like a worried dog. Intending to give this ugly object, money, I put out my hand to stay it for it recoiled as it whined and snapped and laid my hand upon its shoulder. Instantly, it twisted out of its garment, like the young man in the New Testament, and left me standing alone with its rags in my hand. (Dickens 2000 [UC]: 154–5)

Both passages are quotations, of a kind, the second a direct extract from a literary text, the first a translation, as it were, of a visual medium into words. The aims of this essay are various, but one is the attempt to see how the works from which these passages come might relate to one another through what I want to call correspondences. There is no question of adaptation here, of course. Rather, this is a speculative exploration of how artists and works from different historical periods and in different media might illuminate one another through a kind of cultural dialogue. I've clearly made my task easier by not choosing works from such opposing ends of the cultural spectrum that they have nothing whatever in common. On the other hand, it would be fair to say that these works chose me for the purposes of this essay.

Perhaps this is the moment to identify the sources of the passages quoted. The first is from Bill Douglas's 1986 film *Comrades*, which forced itself on my attention partly because of the implications of its sub-title, 'A Lanternist's Account of the Tolpuddle Martyrs and What Became of Them', but also because it is one of the largely unrecognised and nearly forgotten great works of British, indeed of world, cinema. The second is from one of the essays, first published in Dickens's own weekly periodical, *All The Year Round*, and later collected as *The Uncommercial Traveller*. The relatively unknown film director and the hugely famous novelist might seem to have little in common, but as recently as 1985 in an article in *Essays and Studies* Philip Drew rightly argued that *The Uncommercial Traveller* had been unjustly neglected (Drew 1985). Indeed, it is only in very recent years that it has been at least partially recognised as containing some of Dickens's very greatest writing. In an ideal world I would prefer to give equal weight to both works, to show how each might be said to interpenetrate the other, despite the obvious objection that Dickens had no awareness of *Comrades* or, indeed, of the cinema itself. The general problem I face is the commonplace one in any attempt to use film in extended critical discussion, the inability to quote directly from the medium in the manner familiar from literary criticism.

Even extended use of stills is a poor substitute, as the very word itself indicates the necessity of rendering statically a medium whose nature lies in movement. But I face the added difficulty of having to assume that *Comrades* must be unknown to the vast majority of my readers. The essay's major focus, then, will be to show how Douglas's film interpene-trates Dickens's text in ways that might help us to read it in a new and illuminating manner.

Before doing this, however, I want to sketch the outlines of a method that might help to make sense of my concept of correspond-ences between, say, image and word, and the interpenetration of works from different historical periods and different media. To do this I'll turn for assistance to ideas, some of them of great antiquity, which still have currency in the field of art history, but which seem to have been largely ignored in current literary theory and criticism or in film studies. The key term I want to draw on is *paragone*, which stems directly, of course, from the Italian for comparison and which played a major role in Renaissance debates about the visual arts, the superiority of painting over sculpture, for example, and vice versa. Leonardo took an active part in this rivalry of the arts, giving the palm to painting because it more closely resembled the *disegno interno*, the design in the mind of the artist. For Leonardo the eye was 'the noblest sense', and he was also impressed by what might be called the simultaneity of painting, that it 'presents the impression which the artist wished to convey all at once'. Nonetheless, his willingness to accept that painting is mute poetry and poetry is blind painting reveals an attitude of mind that is uninterested in rigid categorisation of the arts (Richter I: 59–60). It goes without saying that I have no desire to take sides in these somewhat arcane debates concerning, from Leonardo's perspective, 'the disjointed beau-ties of literature and the transitory harmonies of musical performance' in favour of 'the simultaneity of visual harmonics' (Kemp 210). But I do wish to acknowledge, and draw from, the readiness of certain historical periods to think of the arts in holistic terms.

An example closer to our own time is Delacroix, the first great mod-ern painter, according to one of his most fervent contemporary critics, Baudelaire, who himself subscribed to what has been called a 'doctrine of Correspondences' (Baudelaire 1964: xii), which involved the ability of the great artist to play on 'the vast keyboard of nature's correspond-ences' (Baudelaire 1981: 117). Baudelaire was also committed to the view that 'the best account of a picture may well be a sonnet or an elegy' (Baudelaire 1964: ix), a mixing of forms entirely in the spirit of my own attempt to link film and literature. Delacroix's work is saturated not merely in the outstanding pictures of the past, and of his present, but in music, literature, philosophy, and the popular culture of his own period, an openness to experience that leads one critic to refer to the 'seamless interdisciplinarity of his work' (Wright 3). This interdisciplinarity stems partly from the fact that Delacroix's thinking about the arts exists very much in the tradition of Leonardo and *paragone*, as a passage from a letter of 1820 reveals: 'Painting is life itself . . . Music is vague. Poetry is vague. Sculpture requires a convention. But painting, particularly landscape painting, is the thing itself' (Steward 103). The philosophical depth of Delacroix's mind is revealed, perhaps more convincingly than in this passage, by his unvarying insistence that he painted thoughts and not objects, as he makes clear in a memorable passage in his Journal:

> In painting it is as if some mysterious bridge were set up between the spirit of the persons in the picture and the beholder . . . [who] sees . . . the external appearance of nature, but inwardly he meditates . . . proper justice is done to what is finite and what is infinite .. to what the soul finds inwardly moving in objects that are known through the senses alone. (Wellington 7–8)

In other words, the images of external reality rendered by his brush strokes are essentially a link between the mind of the painter and that of the viewer by means of which Delacroix's ideas, his primary focus of interest, are conveyed.

Delacroix's connection to my concept of correspondences, and the ways in which interrelationships between the arts can be discussed, might be illuminated by a brief analysis of one of his best-known paintings, 'Liberty Leading The People, 1831', in the context of his imaginative involvement in literature, Shakespeare in this case, although Scott and Byron loomed almost as large in Delacroix's inner world. If we draw an imaginary line through the knee of the dead soldier on the left of the painting, everything above the line is turmoil, excitement, and exhilaration. The picture's surface is organised in a number of ways, one being the attention given to the faces of two boys on opposite sides of the canvas. What they share is a joyful belief in the thrill of conflict, the intensity of gaze of the figure on the left balanced by the swagger of the boy on the right, his right leg thrust forward, brandishing his pistols in his eagerness to re-enter the fray. It is perhaps significant that Liberty's attention is focused on the slightly less eager faces of the adults. The facial expression of the top-hatted, bourgeois figure is especially problematic, the anxiety of the mature man for whom killing, and being killed, is not a game. The woman prostrate before Liberty and obviously

seeking strength from her adds another layer of complexity to the painting's vision of violence. Nonetheless, the brilliant red of Liberty's flag,
the raging crowd behind her, the tempestuous, smoke-filled sky, the
glimpse of Notre Dame, the so-called people's cathedral, all contribute
to the heady excitement of violence being perpetrated in a just cause,
what René Huyghe refers to as 'the clamour of a generation on the
march . . . a joyous and unanimous hymn' (quoted Wright 12).

But the bottom of the painting reveals the results of violence, a visual
link being provided by an ammunition pouch round the neck of the boy
on the right, a piece of equipment stolen from a government soldier. But
that is not the only thing that has been stolen from the corpses at the
foot of the painting. One of them has been stripped of his trousers revealing, and this is the essence of my analysis, his pubic hair. The shameful
horror of this degrading assault on the dead reveals the painting's cultural
profundity, rendering it Shakespearean in its complexity. An equivalent
moment in Shakespeare might be the scene in the second part of *Henry
IV* when Falstaff stabs the body of the already dead Hotspur so that he
can claim credit for his killing. Everything we thought we knew about
the Rabelaisian Falstaff and the heroic, if foolish, Hotspur is turned
around in this one action. In the spirit of this essay's general argument, I
am not suggesting that the play directly influenced the painting.
However, a letter of 1820, when Delacroix was only 22, reveals the depth
of his understanding of Shakespeare, what he refers to, in slightly frac-
tured English, as 'the tallent of the author in the living painting and
investigation of secret motions of human heart' (Steward 75). This lifelong fascination with Shakespeare, combined with the complexity of
Delacroix's own mind, is reinforced in 'Liberty Leading the People' by
echoes of his own early 'The Barque of Dante', 1822, which was, in its
turn, influenced by Géricault's 'The Raft of the Medusa', 1819. My point
is that the cultural richness I have only been able to hint at saturates the
painting, turning it from a seemingly naïve celebration of the excitement
of violence into a work that acknowledges a range of the emotions
generated by war. 'Liberty', and Delacroix's work in general, can best be
understood as a palimpsest, a multi-layered creation built on associations
drawn from the full range of human culture. And it is this that partly
justifies my attempt to rehabilitate the old concept of correspondences
as a way of discussing cultural production.

At another level, I can only hint here at the recondite nature of what
Ernst Robert Curtius refers to as the system of correspondences worked
out in his magisterial *European Literature and the Latin Middle Ages*, a
major aspect of which is 'the establishing of parallels between biblical

history and Greek mythology', which 'led to the establishment of parallels between the teachings of the Bible and pagan myths'. One example, out of a multitude, is the way in which 'Josephus had compared the fallen angels with the giants of Greek mythology', and Curtius also draws on the theology of Clement of Alexandria, which sought to harmonise 'Judaeo-Christian revelation with Greek thought', as in the following passage: '"the Greeks not only took their learning from the barbarian, but they also, in the fabulous tales of their legendary history, imitated the marvellous deeds which among us and for our salvation have been accomplished since ancient times by men of holy life supported by the power of God"' (Curtius 219). It would be grotesque to sink this essay's modest attempt at rethinking works from different periods and in different media under the weight of such exhaustive scholarship. Nonetheless, it is possible to find inspiration in one of Curtius's key analogies, in his claim that

> contemporary archaeology has made surprising discoveries by means of aerial photography at great altitudes. Through this technique it has succeeded, for example, in recognising for the first time the late Roman system of defence works in North Africa. A person standing on the ground before a heap of ruins cannot see the whole that the aerial photograph reveals.

And he goes on to remark that the 'historical disciplines will progress wherever specialisation and contemplation of the whole are combined and *interpenetrate* [my emphasis]' (Curtius ix). Seen from the ground, as it were, *Comrades* and *The Uncommercial Traveller* could not be more different, but even a slight degree of elevation may reveal connections that are worth pursuing.

I suggested early on that a major aim of my essay was to make connections between artists and works of art from different media and different historical periods. And a link from Delacroix to Dickens is provided by a misreading of Dickens by the usually perceptive Chesterton when he remarks, in connection with *The Uncommercial Traveller*, that critics 'have talked of an artist with his eye on the object. Dickens as an essayist always had his eye on an object before he had the faintest notion of a subject' (Chesterton xxvii). The suggestion here is of a kind of aimlessness, that Dickens walked the streets of London observing phenomena in a discrete manner and that he only formed them into patterns at some later stage, perhaps in the process of writing itself. That this is a mistake can be demonstrated in a number of ways. Indeed, if Delacroix painted thought rather than objects, or thought *through* objects perhaps, I would argue that the same is true of Dickens, that his urban wanderings were the vehicle of a dual process, of recording what he saw in relation to what he thought. One example is his constant rumination on the new and surprising occupations that are thrown up by the life of the city. His use of the uncommercial traveller motif is clearly relevant here, and I shall return to it later, but for the moment I shall concentrate on one of his most brilliant set-pieces, taken from a bravura *Uncommercial Traveller* essay, 'Arcadian London'. Like many of these essays, 'Arcadian London' is built on a conceit, the writer's remaining in the city during what might be called the late summer–early autumn recess when, like Paris in August, it seems largely deserted and so becomes 'the most unfrequented part of England – in a word . . . London' (UC 182). This London is a pastoral world in all kinds of interesting and amusing ways, but it creates a special need for a species of humanity whose sole function in life appears to be to look after people's homes while they are absent from them on holiday. In the traveller's case (he is temporarily a lodger in an empty house) this assistance is provided by the Klems, who 'come out of some hole when London empties itself, and go in again when it fills' (UC 184). It is impossible to do justice to the rich comedy and profound social perception of this episode in only brief quotation. The Klems possess a daughter, Miss Klem, on whose behalf the mother beseeches the traveller 'to sanction the sheltering of Miss Klem under that roof, for a single night . . . "between her takin' care of the upper part of a 'ouse in Pall Mall which the family of leaves towng termorrer"' (UC 184). There is an element of comic fantasy at work here, of course, in the fact that

> in its Arcadian time all my part of London is indistinctly pervaded by the Klem species. They creep about with beds, and go to bed in miles of deserted houses. They hold no companionship, except that sometimes, after dark, two of them will emerge from opposite houses, and meet in the middle of the road as on neutral ground, or will peep from adjoining houses over an interposing barrier of area railings, and compare a few reserved mistrustful notes respecting their good ladies or good gentlemen. (UC 185)

The literal mind might accuse Dickens of exaggeration in his portrait of the Klems and their bizarre livelihood, but is this any stranger than the modern urban phenomenon of the Scooter Man? These individuals operate between the hours of about 6 p.m. to 3 a.m. at weekends, their scooters small motorbikes that come apart into four pieces and fit into the back of a car. What gives meaning to these random details? The answer lies in the telephone calls that arrive in a central control room from people too inebriated to drive their own cars! The scooter man rides to the rescue, places his dismantled bike in the boot of the caller's vehicle, drives him or her home and then disappears off to the next job. One especially Dickensian aspect of this unusual occupation is the biker's sighting, as he finishes work in the small hours, of the next wave of workers, office cleaners and transport people, for example, who labour at unsociable hours. Oh for a Dickens, one might exclaim, to chronicle the lives of these nocturnal creatures.

When Dickens abandoned his famous periodical, *Household Words* in 1859, in favour of a new weekly publication, *All The Year Round*, his declared ambition for it was that it contain 'some sustained works of imagination that may become part of English Literature' (UC xii). In doing so he was referring to the serialised fiction, his own included, that was a distinctive feature of the new venture. But from the vantage point of 1866 he also claimed that the periodical contained materials 'that form the social history of the past eight years' (UC xii). It is my contention that the best of the *Uncommercial Traveller* essays fulfil both of these criteria, in that they unite imagination and thought with observation in a way that conveys deep insights into the nature of urban living, although these insights are almost always conveyed with humour and a charming lightness of touch. Also, as Slater and Drew point out, these writings also gave Dickens the opportunity to 'observe and reflect on himself' (UC xx), an observation that provides an opportunity to return to Bill Douglas. For Andrew Noble, Douglas exemplifies 'Blake's dictum that the imaginatively good is achieved by way of minute particulars' (Dick 13), an observation that holds equally true of Dickens. Douglas and Dickens were also alike in sharing a special attitude to the world of popular entertainment. For Douglas this was what he would have called the pictures: 'It was paradise sitting there in the cosy dark being hypnotised by the play of light. Up there was the best of all possible worlds. To enter this world, that was the dream' (Dick 16). For Dickens the theatre was a 'delightful dream', which provided the experience 'of having for an hour or two quite forgotten the real world, and of coming out into the street with a kind of wonder that it should be so wet, and dark, and cold, and full of jostling people and irreconcilable cabs' (Fielding 316). Another link between the two is their essentially imaginative presentation of what might seem, at first glance, to be purely autobiographical material. A superficial view of Douglas's first great work, the *Trilogy*, would suggest that it is a documentary record of an almost unbearably bleak childhood. But, as Andrew Noble suggests, this would be a radical error:

> It should be pointed out as an important aside that, although the Trilogy is often seen as autobiography, this is too simplistic a response. Certainly

many of the events occurred. If one relates Bill's life to the films, however, it soon becomes apparent that he either radically changed chronological sequence or that several key elements did not happen to him at all. Bill constantly reiterated Chekhov's maxim that memory was a creative filter employed not for total factual recall but to make art, and that such art, deeply aware of its own formal means, should speak to and for our common condition. (Dick 24)

This passage applies, with almost uncanny accuracy, to *The Uncommercial Traveller*. The hilariously pre-Freudian 'Nurse's Stories' is a case in point in which the main subject is introduced by way of one of Dickens's favourite devices, the manipulation of an idiom or figure of speech for his own purposes:

> If we all knew our own minds (in a more enlarged sense than the popular acceptation of that phrase), I suspect we should find our nurses responsible for most of the dark corners we are forced to go back to, against our wills. (UC 173)

At least one dark corner of the traveller's mind is occupied by his nurse's retelling of the legends of Captain Murderer,

> which she used to begin, I remember, as a sort of introductory overture by clawing the air with both hands, and uttering a long low hollow groan. So acutely did I suffer from this ceremony in combination with the infernal Captain, that I sometimes used to plead I thought I was hardly strong enough and old enough to hear the story again just yet. But she never spared me one word of it, and indeed commended the awful chalice to my lips as the only preservative known to Science against 'The Black Cat' – a weird and glaring-eyed supernatural Tom, who was reputed to prowl about the world by night, sucking the breath of infancy, and who was endowed with a special thirst (as I was given to understand) for mine. (UC 175)

The link from this to the darker aspects of Dickens's imagination, in works such as *Bleak House* and *Our Mutual Friend*, seems clear but, as the editors of the Dent edition of *The Uncommercial Traveller* point out, the traveller is a fictional persona whose nurse is almost certainly equally fictitious, a caution that has often gone unheeded. This has not discouraged biographers from taking Dickens's references to be, as Peter Ackroyd puts it, 'true transcripts from memory, considerably enlivening Dickens's childhood as a result . . . Michael Slater provides a full summary of such biographical interpretations . . . and cautions against the "tendency to read *The Uncommercial Traveller* as though it contained straight-forward chunks of autobiography"' (UC 170–1).

Douglas and Dickens are, then, both using art at least partly as a way of exploring their own inner lives but also their responses to the external world of social reality, and this is made possible by their adoption of an artistic method that is at once intensely personal and rigorously objectified. Neither is interested in an art that modestly hides its light under a bushel. Both seek to make viewers and readers self-consciously aware that they are involved with images of reality, not the thing itself.

But it is time to attempt a closer examination of the relationship between Douglas and Dickens, to show how *Comrades* might be said to interpenetrate synchronically with *The Uncommercial Traveller*, a concept that owes something to Jung's use of synchronicity as 'a kind of simultaneity' or 'a *meaningful coincidence* of two or more events' (Jung 520: italics in original). A good starting point would be the concept of art attributed to Douglas by Andrew Noble in the passage just quoted, his belief in an art that is 'deeply aware of its own formal means'. *Comrades* does, in fact, combine artistic self-consciousness with profound humanity in a peculiarly rich manner, a combination that also distinguishes some of the greatest literary artists, Dickens himself it goes without saying, in works such as *Little Dorrit*. The film's artistry is rooted in its manipulation of a whole range of visual devices that predate the cinema and which remind us that the world we see depicted in the film is filtered through the consciousness of its creator and the medium in which he embodies his vision. It is worth stressing at this point that Douglas is a true auteur rather than a collaborator. Indeed, his 'insistence on meticulous control over every detail of the production' of *Comrades* was undoubtedly a factor in the paucity of his output (Dick 178). Again there is a link with Dickens, who took the opportunity presented by his abandonment of *Household Words* for *All The Year Round* to acquire 'virtually complete control of the new journal' (UC xi). And it is well known that Dickens demanded absolute domination over his periodical down to rewriting the material provided by his contributors.

Comrades is, then, a lanternist's account of a mythically famous historical event. As a contemporary review puts it, *Comrades* is 'less a historical film than a film about history . . . essentially a film about seeing', one that records 'the development of popular, industrial entertainment'. How is all this brought about? Firstly, by making the lanternist, as we saw in the film's opening minute, the key observer of events and, in fact, their transmitter to us. It might be useful at this point to be clear as to what a travelling lanternist is. His was a new trade created by the invention and refinement of optical toys, in this case in the eighteenth century and above all the magic lantern. The evidence suggests that it was an occupation of paupers, of people no better off than the peasant characters of *Comrades*, peddlers or show-men who carried their show in a box strapped to their backs. All that was required was a light source, a collection of slides, however few and crude, and a surface on which the image could be projected. These entertainments were 'shown in every corner of Europe' and in the 'eighteenth and nineteenth centuries, only a blind person would have been unaware of their charms and effects' (Mannoni 79, 103). But, brilliantly, Douglas goes beyond this in having the actor who plays the lanternist, Alex Norton, appearing in another twelve guises, all of them connected with the world of pre-cinematic visual entertainment. We see him, to take only a few examples, as Sergeant Bell and his Raree Show, an image from a print of 1839; as a Diorama man, wearing a John Bull waistcoat; as a French manipulator of cut-out silhouettes; as a half-mad Italian photographing aborigines in a surreal Australian interior landscape; as a witch presenting a Phantasmagoria. His face even appears as the laughing cavalier in a painting in the house of Frampton, a wealthy landowner.

But *Comrades* exceeds even this degree of self-conscious artifice by constantly reminding us of ways of seeing as the film's narrative unfolds, an aspect of Douglas's work that exemplifies the mixture of art forms highlighted in the earlier discussion of *paragone*:

> Douglas did not like the idea of discrete scenes and preferred to construct a narrative which flowed more like a musical score, a unified elliptical structure. The narrative links and recurring motifs ('echoes' as Douglas called them) in this construction are fundamental to the unity of the whole hence his reluctance to cut sequences at the editing stage. (Dick 190–1)

One of these echoes is the presentation of the film's world through visual techniques that form what might be called the musical pattern of variations on a theme. When, for example, the lanternist visits the home of the wealthy Frampton the consequences of his request to perform for the household are depicted as a shadow play cast by candlelight on the drawn blinds of the mansion's windows. Having, we assume, failed in his attempt we see the lanternist himself as a silhouette against the backdrop of a gigantic moon. A more subversive moment is Douglas's disregard for one of the fundamental tenets of classical film-making, the invisibility that is assumed to exist between viewers and the means by which a fictional world in presented to them. This takes place at one of the recurrent pay-day scenes when an outraged worker holds up seven fingers, to represent the seven shillings he has just received, displaying them twice and looking directly into the camera as he does so. The transition to Australia, when the Martyrs are transported, is accomplished not by any tediously documentary detail but by the use of a 'primitive', beautifully coloured panorama, which moves before us from right to left, the joins of its various sections showing clearly and the episode preceded by the black edge of the panorama filling the whole screen. (It is also worth pointing out that the strange beauty of this effect is reinforced by a particularly lovely example of Hans Werner Henze's sparingly used score.) As we cut to the 'reality' of the ship's boat carrying passengers ashore, the captain, Alex Norton again, sells a moving toy panorama to a wealthy, gullible passenger who will figure later as a deserved victim for a second time, the object of a violent 'accident'. The film's final scene, the welcome home to the released Martyrs, is a static image of a theatre in which the master of ceremonies gives thanks to 'Our friend the lanternist who told the story. It was almost as if he had been present throughout,' at which point the splendidly dressed Alex Norton, his lantern lecturer's pointer in hand and standing beside a magnificent three-lens lantern, bows directly into the camera with a knowing look for us, the audience. The last sequence consists of a series of slides clicking through the lantern's mechanism, giving us brief biographical information of the fate of the individual Martyrs. The final image is the one we began with, a blank disc, which now belongs to the world of technology rather than the cosmos. As the credits appear the clanging chords of the work's opening music return.

Is it possible to suggest any interesting and useful connections between *Comrades* and the often fictionalised essays that make up *The Uncommercial Traveller*? If the direction of this essay were from Dickens to Douglas, I think it would be easy to show that there are Dickensian elements in the film. There is the same passionate anger at the exploitation of the dispossessed by the rich and powerful. And a tenderness towards the poor in their condition of almost absolute deprivation is contrasted with a satirical heightening of the treatment of the local landowner and vicar, which is reinforced by a clever aspect of the film's casting. The peasant characters are played by relative unknowns (Douglas would have preferred non-professionals but union pressures forbade this) while the nobs are portrayed by stars such as Robert Stephens and Freddie Jones. The film thus subverts one of the standard procedures of British costume drama in which famous personalities often overwhelm the characters they are supposed to be embodying. Again, Douglas is unsparing in his presentation of the sheer emptiness of his peasant cottages and in the dirt that shows so clearly under the fingernails of hands condemned to unremitting physical toil. One thinks here of the nightmarish depictions of poverty in such *Uncommercial Traveller* essays as 'A Small Star in the East' and 'On An Amateur Beat'. But just as the daily round is relieved by humour and good fellowship in Dickens, and sometimes by the poetic heightening of drab reality, so Douglas transfigures the lives of his poor on occasion. This is partly achieved by the film's intense concentration on faces, which results in some hallucinatory transformations of plainness into beauty and back again. But there are more extended examples, as in the arrival of a dancing sailor, played by Michael Clark, at the Harvest Festival whose set-piece display in the centre of the village is electrifying, although his disappearance from the village, still dancing, is even more magical, watched as it is by the wistful gaze of a village girl for whom this kind of escape is impossible.

We also have some direct evidence of Douglas's knowledge of and sympathy with Dickens. A copy of *David Copperfield* figures in the *Trilogy*, for example, and one of the last books Douglas bought and read before his death in 1991 was *A December Vision*, a collection of Dickens's social journalism (Dickens 1986). And the reference to Sergeant Bell in *Comrades* draws on *Sergeant Bell and his Raree-show* of 1839 by 'Peter Parley', the pseudonym of George Mogridge, a book Dickens was originally scheduled to write. However, for reasons explained earlier, the trajectory of my essay is from Douglas to Dickens, and it is an essential part of its method not to seek refuge in biographical explanations or the anxiety of influence. What my analysis of *Comrades* might permit is the substitution of the governing trope of *The Uncommercial Traveller* with another. Of course, in lighting on the Uncommercial Traveller as the unifying persona of his essays Dickens showed his usual awareness of changing patterns in the social life of his own times. The choice reflects 'the rising importance and status of commercial travellers (formerly known merely as "bagmen")' (UC xv), a choice that Dickens clarifies in his introductory essay to the collection. In describing himself as travelling, 'figurative speaking . . . for the great house of Human Interest Brothers', he is careful to draw a distinction between his activity and that of the *commercial* traveller: 'I know nothing about prices, and should have no idea, if I were put to it, how to wheedle a man into ordering something he doesn't want'

(UC 28). Slater and Drew expand on Dickens's negative response to his commercial colleagues:

> Dickens takes pains to distance himself from the negative notions attaching to commerce, something vividly brought before the public in January 1860 with the signing of a notorious Commercial Treaty with France . . . [which] was intended to prevent all possibility of war between Britain and France, but was held by its critics to demonstrate the extent to which mercenary, economic motives, rather than ethical considerations, were now the mainspring of foreign policy. A similar critique of the dehumanising effect of 'wholesale' values on national life runs continually through the Uncommercial Traveller's reports. (UC xv)

In addition to its social implications, this persona relates directly to one of Dickens's most striking personal habits, his astonishing capacity to walk for huge distances which is generalised in *The Uncommercial Traveller* as his two kinds of walking: 'one straight on end to a definite goal at a round pace; one, objectless, loitering, and purely vagabond' (UC 119). With the second we are clearly in the territory of the *flâneur*, the domain explored with such profundity by Charles Baudelaire and Walter Benjamin and applied brilliantly by Michael Hollington specifically to Dickens. If we look for the fruits of Dickens's *flâneur*-like activity in *The Uncommercial Traveller*, as good an example as any can be found in one of the more famous essays, 'On an Amateur Beat' in which the Traveller notes 'how oddly characteristic neighbourhoods are divided from one another, hereabout, as though by an invisible line across the way':

> Here, shall cease the bankers and the money-changers; here, shall begin the shipping interest and the nautical instrument shops; here, shall follow a scarcely perceptible flavouring of groceries and drugs; here, shall come a strong infusion of butchers; now, small hosiers shall be in the ascendant; henceforth, everything exposed for sale shall have its ticketed price attached. All this, as if specially ordered and appointed . . . a single stride, and everything is entirely changed in grain and character. (UC 382)

Can there be any doubt that in such passages Dickens is anticipating what has come to be called psycho-geography? This self-demarcation by the city as if it possessed a life of its own with its own consciousness and, indeed, unconscious is precisely the realm occupied by Iain Sinclair in his *Lights Out for the Territory* and in Peter Ackroyd's *London*.

Why, then, in the face of all these riches offered by the Uncommercial Traveller should one seek to dislodge him from his deserved and

appropriate place? Perhaps happy co-existence, rather than dethrone-
ment, would be the best solution, the thought that the Traveller might
enjoy sharing his journey with a companionable lanternist! One justifi-
cation might be found in the established fact that Dickens was deeply
knowledgeable about and influenced by the visual technology of the
nineteenth century. And this is reinforced by a commonplace of Dickens
criticism, to say nothing of the experience of every perceptive reader,
that his work is distinguished by its intense visuality. We could say of the
Traveller–Lanternist what is said by the master of ceremonies at the end
of *Comrades* that it is 'as if he had been present throughout'. And not
merely present throughout but able, by what we almost have to call the
magic of art, to convince us that we are present at the scene also, so that
our duo turns into a triple relationship of Traveller–Lanternist–Reader.
The remainder of this essay might be described as an analytic celebration
of the wonders of the best of *The Uncommercial Traveller* essays, a celebration that I have tried to argue and will seek to demonstrate further is
intensified by allowing Dickens's work to be interpenetrated by a much
later one from a different medium. In doing so, the essay offers a critical
reading of *The Uncommercial Traveller* by highlighting some of its outstanding pieces and giving them a degree of attention that they seem not
previously to have received in Dickens studies. This is certainly true of
'Shy Neighbourhoods', although it is worth noting that it 'seems to have
been a personal favourite' of Dickens's most intimate friend and first
biographer, John Forster (UC 117). 'Shy' here is used in a colloquial
sense that entered the language in the 1840s, i.e. being of questionable
character, disreputable, 'shady'; indeed, the essay's title is one of the
examples cited in the *Oxford English Dictionary*.

   In a way characteristic of the studied informality of these pieces, the
Lanternist–Traveller begins with an evocation of a night walk into the
country of the kind often undertaken by Dickens himself when he hiked
the thirty miles from the *All The Year Round* offices in London to his
home at Gad's Hill in Kent. It's impossible to know precisely what direction the essay is going to take until it settles into its true subject in the
fourth paragraph: 'But, it is with the lower animals of back streets and
by-ways that my present purpose rests' (UC 119). We are then presented
with a series of set-pieces, scenes or, I'd suggest, moving lantern slides,
which focus on 'the bad company birds keep' in 'shy neighbourhoods'
(UC 119); donkeys which, like birds, have a knack for 'developing their
very best energies for the very worst company' (UC 120); the 'dogs of
shy neighbourhoods', which 'I observe to avoid play, and to be conscious
of poverty' (UC 121); the essay comes to 'a close with a word on the

fowls of the same localities' (UC 124). The unifying factor in these brilliantly realised vignettes is the generally down-at-heel and even degraded aspect of the creatures who inhabit this facet of the urban world, presented with a charm, vivacity, and humour that can only be fully experienced in extended reading. But the donkey episode is perhaps best suited to expressing the Lanternist as well the Traveller aspect of the enterprise, partly because this segment illustrates particularly clearly what might be described as the 'Roll up, roll up, come and see' aspect of the essay. It is as though the Lanternist– Traveller is so delighted with his discoveries that he is calling out to us to come and enjoy the fun, just as the Travelling Lanternist advertised his wares in town and country through the use of his own vocal powers. Here, then, is the 'shy' donkey at his most expressive:

> I have known a donkey – by sight; we were not on speaking terms – who lived over on the Surrey side of London-bridge, among the fastnesses of Jacob's Island and Dockhead. It was the habit of that animal, when his services were not in immediate requisition, to go out alone, idling. I have met him, a mile from his place of residence, loitering about the streets; and the expression of his countenance at such times was most degraded . . . The last time I ever saw him (about five years ago) he was in circumstances of difficulty . . . Having been left alone with the cart of periwinkles [his owner's livelihood], and forgotten, he went off idling. He prowled among his usual low haunts for some time, gratifying his depraved taste, until, not taking the cart into his calculations, he endeavoured to turn up a narrow alley, and became greatly involved. He was taken into custody by the Police, and the Green Yard of the district being near at hand, was backed into that place of durance. At that crisis, I encountered him; the stubborn sense he evinced of being – not to compromise the expression – a blackguard, I never saw exceeded in the human subject. A flaring candle in a paper shade, stuck in among his periwinkles, showed him, with his ragged harness broken and his cart extensively shattered, twitching his mouth and shaking his hanging head, a picture of disgrace and obduracy. I have seen boys being taken to station-houses, who were as like him as his own brother. (UC 120–1)

The hilarious images we are presented with here – the donkey stuck, because of his cart, up an alley, his whole physical being resistant to moral reproach – are rendered with an actuality that is almost dream-like. And whether the fruit of observation or imagination they constitute a definitive challenge to the passage from Chesterton quoted earlier, that 'Dickens as an essayist always had his eye on an object before he had the faintest notion of a subject'. We know that another marvelous episode in 'Shy Neighbourhoods', the goldfinch offered for sale in 'a dirty court in

Spitalfields' (UC 119), which drinks such prodigious quantities of water that it seems to be 'in a consuming fever' (UC 119) but which resolutely refuses to do so when taken to its purchaser's home is based on an incident from more than twenty years earlier. Nonetheless, it takes its place in what can be read as an allegory, a kind of Aesop's fable, in which the degraded animals of shy neighbourhoods stand for the degraded human beings who live in such circumstances. In other words, the essay's richly visualised detail is in the service of an idea whether or not its episodes are the fruits of observation, imagination, or a combination of the two.

One final example of my essay's experiment in correspondences, of the interpenetration of works from different periods and in different media, might serve as a conclusion. One of the most remarkable passages in 'Arcadian London', in *The Uncommercial Traveller*, and indeed in Dickens's work as a whole, concerns the presence of speech in the metropolis, and its absence during the city's transformation to pastoral:

> It is my impression that much of its serene and peaceful character is attributable to the absence of customary Talk. How do I know but there may be subtle influences in Talk, to vex the souls of men who don't hear it? How do I know but that Talk, five, ten, twenty miles off, may get into the air and disagree with me? If I get up, vaguely troubled and wearied and sick of my life, in the session of Parliament, who shall say that my noble friend, my right reverent friend, my right honourable friend, my honourable friend, my honourable and learned friend, or my honourable and gallant friend, may not be responsible for that effect upon my nervous system. Too much Ozone in the air, I am informed and fully believe . . . would effect me in a marvelously disagreeable way; why may not too much Talk? I don't see or hear the Ozone; I don't see or hear the Talk. And there is so much Talk; so much too much, such loud cry, and such scant supply of wool; such a deal of fleecing, and so little fleece! (UC 187)

This wonderful evocation of an absence which, even when it is a presence, cannot be heard is an extraordinarily original insight into the life of big cities, an anticipation of Baudelaire, Benjamin, Sinclair, Ackroyd, and indeed of the concept of psycho-geography itself. If we were to seek a relevant comparison to help us more fully to understand and appreciate the beauty as well as the originality of this passage it would best be found, I would suggest, not in a work of literature but in Wim Wenders' 1987 film *Wings of Desire*, in which two infinitely sympathetic but weary angels are unable to prevent themselves hearing the constant susurration of the voices they are surrounded by, the normally unspoken thoughts, hopes, desires, and fears of the millions of those who inhabit the modern equivalent of the city of God.

For some this may seem a correspondence too far. It may be one thing to link Dickens with a British film set in the nineteenth century and preoccupied with pre-cinematic visual devices. To suggest any kind of connection between him and a German film set in twentieth-century Berlin might be thought to be purely gratuitous. On the other hand, I have argued that my concept of correspondences has a basis in both theory and criticism, certainly when applied to a single artist or work of art. The palimpsest-like richness I have described in Delacroix is quite simply factually accurate and impossible to dispute. And it is also impossible to deny that his work reverberates with the echoes of correspondences with his favourite writers. Indeed, Goethe famously praised the young Delacroix's lithograph series of 1827, based on his Faust, as better than the original:

> The powerful imagination of this artist forces us to rethink the situations as perfectly as he has himself. And if I must admit that in these scenes M. Delacroix has surpassed my own vision, how much more strongly the readers will find all of it alive and superior to what they were imagining. (Wright n. 13: 191–2)

If it is a leap from Goethe's praise of his own work in another medium to bringing together works without this shared element, my essay has tried to argue that the leap is worth making if it adds to our sense of the cultural richness within which works of art exist and, crucially, if it leads to an enhanced appreciation of works from different periods and in different media.

Works Cited

Ackroyd, Peter, 2000. *London: The Biography*. London: Chatto & Windus.

Baudelaire, Charles, 1964. *The Painter of Modern Life and Other Essays*, trans. and ed. Jonathan Mayne. London: Phaidon.

Baudelaire, Charles, 1981. 'The Universal Exhibition of 1855: the Fine Arts', in *Baudelaire: Select Writings on Art and Artists*, trans. P.E. Charvet. Cambridge: Cambridge University Press.

Benjamin, Walter, 1999. *The Arcades Project*, trans. Howard Eiland and Kevin McLoughlin. Cambridge, MA: Harvard University Press.

Chesterton, G.K., 1970 (1911). *Appreciations and Criticisms of the Works of Charles Dickens*. New York: Haskell House.

Curtius, Ernst Robert, 1953. *European Literature and the Latin Middle Ages*, trans. Willard R. Trask. New York: Harper & Row.

Dick, Eddie, Andrew Noble and Duncan Petrie, eds, 1993. *Bill Douglas: A Lanternist's Account*. London: British Film Institute.

Dickens, Charles, 1986. *A December Vision: His Social Journalism*, eds Neal Philip and Victor Neuberg. London: Collins. 1987 US title: *A December Vision and Other Thoughtful Writings*.

Dickens, Charles, 2000 (1861). *The Uncommercial Traveller and Other Papers*, eds Michael Slater and John Drew. London: J.M. Dent.

Douglas, Bill, 1986. *Comrades*. Skreba Films.

Douglas, Bill, 1987. *Comrades* (the published script). London: Faber & Faber.

Douglas, Bill, Centre for the History of Cinema and Popular Culture: *EVE Everyone's Virtual Exhibition*, at www.billdouglas.org/eve.

Drew, Philip, 1985. 'Dickens and the Real World: A Reading of *The Uncommercial Traveller*', in *Essays and Studies 1985*, coll. Geoffrey Harlow. London: John Murray and Atlantic Heights, NJ: Humanities Press, pp. 66–82.

Fielding, K.J., ed., 1960. *The Speeches of Charles Dickens*. Oxford: Clarendon Press.

Hollington, Michael, 1981. 'Dickens the Flâneur', *The Dickensian*, 77.ii (Summer), pp. 71–87.

Jung, C.G., 1960. 'On Synchronicity', in *The Structure and Dynamics of the Psyche: The Collected Works*, vol. 8, trans. R.F.C. Hull. London: Routledge & Kegan Paul, pp. 520–31.

Kemp, Martin, 1981. *Leonardo da Vinci: The Marvellous Works of Nature and Man*. London: J.M. Dent.

Mannoni, Laurent, 2000. *The Great Art of Light and Shadow: Archaeology of the Cinema*. Exeter: Exeter University Press.

Monthly Film Bulletin, 1987. Review of *Comrades*. 54, no. 644 (September), p. 260.

Richter, Jean Paul, ed., 1970. *The Literary Works of Leonardo da Vinci*, 3rd edn. 3 vols. London: Phaidon.

Schlicke, Paul, ed., 1999. 'Solomon Bell the Raree Showman', in *Oxford Reader's Companion to Dickens*. Oxford: Oxford University Press.

Sight & Sound, 1986–7. Review of *Comrades*. 56, no. 1 (Winter), p. 66.

Sinclair, Iain, 1997. *Lights Out for the Territory: In Tribute to London*. London: Jonathan Cape. 1998 Granta edition: resubtitled 9 *Excursions in the Secret History of London*.

Smith, Grahame, 2003. *Dickens and the Dream of Cinema*. Manchester: Manchester University Press.

Steward, Jean, ed. and trans., 1971. *Eugène Delacroix: Selected Letters*. London: Eyre & Spottiswoode.

Wellington, Hubert, ed., 1951. *The Journal of Eugène Delacroix*, trans. Lucy Norton. London: Phaidon.

Wenders, Wim, 1987. *Wings of Desire [Der Himmel ueber Berlin]* (Argos Films, etc.).

Wright, Beth S., ed., 2001. *The Cambridge Companion to Delacroix*. Cambridge: Cambridge University Press.

British Modernists Encounter the Cinema

DAVID SEED

Introduction

IT IS NO SURPRISE THAT THERE SHOULD HAVE BEEN an approximate congruence between the emerging techniques of film and the experimental methods of novelists in the period of Modernism. As John L. Fell and other critics have argued, both grew out of a shared tradition of narrative and both were extensively preoccupied with what Joseph Conrad called the 'general fundamental condition of visuality' (Schwab 345). A number of historical factors converged early in the twentieth century to strengthen the connections between film and fiction: the appropriation of impressionism from the visual arts, the rise of photography, the reduction in discursive commentary in favour of naturalistic presentation, and a general willingness among the modernists to experiment across media. Eisenstein is an important intersecting figure here in that he acknowledges a proto-cinematic dimension to Dickens and also praised Joyce's cinematic methods.[1]

At one end of the Modernist period Joseph Conrad makes his famous statement of purpose in the Preface to *The Nigger of the 'Narcissus'* (1897): 'My task which I am trying to achieve is, by the power of the written word to make you hear, to make you feel – it is, before all, to make you *see*' (Conrad 1957: x). At the other end of the period Christopher Isherwood draws his equally famous analogy in *Goodbye to Berlin* (1940): 'I am a camera with its shutter open, quite passive, recording, not thinking. Recording the man shaving at the window opposite and the woman in the kimono washing her hair. Some day, all this will have to be developed, carefully printed, fixed' (Isherwood 13). In the first, Conrad speaks as a film director, literally directing the reader's capacity for visualisation; in the second, Isherwood poses as a recording instrument, giving the reader imagistic fragments of Berlin life that will have to be shaped or 'developed' (a verbal/photographic pun) into proper narrative subjects. Both writers concern themselves with recording visual perception: Conrad with how these visual data are refracted

---

[1] For valuable comment on this aspect of Dickens, see Grahame Smith 2003.

through the perceiving consciousness and Isherwood with the means rather than the subjectivity of that perception.

Conrad's dramatisations of the immediate process of perception have been skilfully described by Ian Watt as exercises in 'delayed decoding' where there is constantly a time-lag between the registering of visual images and their interpretation (Watt 169–80). For Watt, Conrad's impressionism gives an immediacy to his descriptions that could be translating directly into cinematic terms. For instance, in *Heart of Darkness* (1899/1902) – for Watt the supreme example of Conrad's impressionistic techniques – a visual shock occurs when Marlow is training his telescope on Kurtz's house in the African interior. In the space of a few moments a long shot of the house is replaced by a medium-distance shot of parts of a 'fence'. Then an awkward movement brings the poles with their 'knobs' into sudden close-up: 'They would have been even more impressive, those heads on the stakes, if their faces had not been turned to the house. Only one. The first I had made out, was facing my way' (Conrad 1988: 57). Marlow quietly reasserts the primacy of his own reactions here by insisting that the direction of the heads spoils the effect. Nevertheless, his gaze towards the house is physically mimicked by the head facing him although the latter has closed eyes. Indeed, throughout *Heart of Darkness* Conrad exploits the nature of the terrain, especially of the jungle, to stress the suddenness of appearances, and also the melodramatic force of the reversed gaze. Marlow's horror arises from the fact of being observed by humans so different from himself that he can scarcely bring himself to acknowledge kinship.

During his discussion of a cinematographic tradition in modern fiction dating back to Flaubert, Alan Spiegel explains the scene just examined as follows: Conrad, he tells us, 'decomposes his [Marlow's] field into an arrangement of successive views'. But Spiegel continues: 'It is an eye that seems to have momentarily separated itself from mind [. . .] an eye that is without affect; that is, a camera eye precisely' (Spiegel 60–1). What Spiegel does not recognise here is that Marlow's presumption of Western civilisation is written into *Heart of Darkness* as a reluctance to draw inferences from his sense data that contradict his faith in the civilising mission of empire. Thus, we get here a rapid montage of images, which slip from domestic stability to decoration and finally to 'barbarism'; and ironically it is only the last, most dramatic image that returns Marlow's gaze.

If the observer's capacity to interpret his visual data approaches zero, he is left in a state of relative blindness. Spiegel's explanation of the eye becoming dissociated from the mind would exactly fit what happens in Conrad's Congo story 'An Outpost of Progress'. Here two Europeans take up their posts in the interior and sink into a state of extended blindness where they are unable to interpret anything they see. Instead of 'delayed decoding', they live out a perceptual blankness where appearances have a minimal significance in bearing on themselves, but otherwise mean nothing: 'They lived like blind men in a large room [...] Even the brilliant sunshine disclosed nothing intelligible. Things appeared and disappeared before their eyes in an unconnected and aimless kind of way' (Conrad 1922: 133). Where Conrad uses mist (*Heart of Darkness*) or murk (*The Secret Agent*) to suggest the limitations to his characters' understanding, in this story visual clarity becomes ironically dissociated from any capacity of the Europeans to decode their experiences. It is as if they are living out a montage of scenes from an alien culture, which form a phantasmagoria of bewildering and incomprehensible vividness.

Although Conrad was involved in negotiations over the film rights to his fiction from as early as 1913, two documents reveal his interest in film technique: a still unpublished 'film-play' that Conrad wrote in 1920 and the notes for a talk that Conrad gave in America in 1923. The first of these, *Gaspar the Strong Man*, was an adaptation of Conrad's story 'Gaspar Ruiz', which, Gene M. Moore has argued, further develops a strong visual dimension to that story and also shows Conrad's familiarity with cinematic terms like 'close-up' (Moore 37–8). His American talk was entitled 'Author and Cinematograph' and proposes a common aim to fiction and film: 'fundamentally the creator in letters aims at a moving picture – moving to the eye, to the mind, and to our complex emotions which I will express with one word – heart (Schwab 346).[2]

The analogy between fiction and film obviously underpins Conrad's visual dynamics but this last quotation suggests that it also helped him find a pictorial method of representing thought. One of the most startlingly direct linkages between thought and film was made in Henri Bergson's *Creative Evolution* (1911) where he insisted that the processes of thought and perception were essentially cinematic. For Bergson there was an unavoidable opposition between the flux or 'becoming' of real life experience and art's tendency to freeze objects into a 'snapshot' of form. Film was a unique art form since it creates movement and transition out

---

[2] In the same talk Conrad sums up one of his main purposes: 'many of my ambitions have been concentrated on the visuality and precision of images' (Schwab 346).

of a sequence of 'stills.' Thus, 'whether we would think becoming, or express it, or even perceive it, we hardly do anything else than set going a kind of cinematograph inside us' (Bergson 323). In other words, the very workings of the mind closely resemble an internal film.

The implicit relation between literary impressionism and cinematic presentation emerges in Percy Lubbock's 1921 study *The Craft of Fiction*. Here he starts from the premise that prose narratives have a unique capacity to convey the 'moving stream of impressions' (Lubbock 14) that we experience in daily life. At every point in his study Lubbock privileges the visual over written style. His key evaluative term thus is 'scene', taken from Henry James's critical writing (which in turn was strongly influenced by the methods of the theatre) and applied by Lubbock to novelists' varying capacity to embody narrative in image. But even this does not completely explain Lubbock's main evaluative argument. Scene is crucial, but so is the disciplined use of point of view. Thus, he will praise Tolstoy for the breadth of his panoramas, but take him to task for having no consistent method of achieving point of view. Equally, although Thackeray sometimes captures powerful satirical scenes, he will then violate those scenes through his discursive commentary.

This charge more or less echoes James's criticism of Trollope, but for present purposes it is more important to note how easily Lubbock's account could be applied to the cinema. The reader's gaze is constantly referred to a visual spectacle rather than a written text. Lubbock speaks of experiencing a novel as a *visual* consumption: the narrative unfolds 'as we sit to watch' (Lubbock 14). Flaubert, the supreme master of the scenic, constructs each novel 'like a picture gradually unrolled' (Lubbock 65). In Flaubert and Maupassant, the narrative emerges with a unique inevitability as if those authors were exhibitors not writers. Maupassant, we are told, is 'behind us, out of sight, out of mind', for all the world like a movie director (Lubbock 113). For Lubbock then the overriding quality of the successful novel is explained in the following way: 'It is the method of picture-making that enables the novelist to cover his great spaces of life and qualities of experience' (Lubbock 118).

Essentially the same analogy operates within Lubbock's description of psychological fiction. Here James is his main exemplar, and once again his account revolves around a notion of viewing: 'The world of silent thought is thrown open and instead of telling the reader what happened there, the novelist uses the look and behaviour of thought as the vehicle by which the story is rendered.' Lambert Strether not only supplies a consistent point of view for *The Ambassadors*; he is also used

by James to create a kind of mind-cinema where his consciousness functions as a screen 'for the movement that flickers over the surface of his
mind' (Lubbock 157). Lubbock's explicit analogy is that between the
protagonist's mind and a stage, but the visual effects and transitions
resemble more closely those of the cinema, especially at points where he
refers to the 'flickers and flashes of thought from moment to moment'
that fill his consciousness (Lubbock 256).

When Alan Spiegel's argument about the cinematographic form of
modern fiction described above was first published in article form,
David Lodge took issue not so much with the general demonstration of
the proximity between filmic and certain novelistic effects, as with
Spiegel's concentration on symbolic fiction and his resultant exclusion
of figures like Thomas Hardy. Taking the example of *The Return of the
Native*, Lodge states: 'Hardy uses verbal description as a film director
uses the lens of his camera, to select, highlight, distort, and enhance,
creating a visualized world that is both recognizable and yet more vivid,
intense, and dramatically charged than actuality' (Lodge 249). Lodge
stresses how Hardy not only uses dramatised observers but also (like
Henry James, though the comparison is not made) focalises many
scenes through a hypothetical observer. We shall see how the gaze
recurs constantly throughout the fiction under discussion here and that
this recurrence becomes a feature of the visual self-consciousness of
modern novels.

James Joyce

The evidence of Joyce's early and continuing interest in the cinema is
specific: his ill-fated opening of the first cinema in Dublin in 1909 and
subsequent consideration of doing the same again in Zurich. It is therefore not surprising that one critic has argued that 'Joyce simply and
revealingly discovered in the cinema a source of correspondence for his
own imaginative projections' (Spiegel 80). For Alan Spiegel, Joyce is
the prime example of a Modernist employing cinematic techniques to
differentiate between the edges of objects, to evoke character through
partial glimpses of their possessions, and to convey motion through a
'phase-by-phase apprehension' (Spiegel 112). This is a valuable argument for explaining the prime importance of the visual in Joyce, but
then Spiegel too easily identifies the gaze with passivity in order to
explain a quality of estrangement he finds in Joyce's visual sequences:
'the passive affectless eye [...] a characteristic of the Joycean observer

throughout most of his work' (Spiegel 67). Far from being passive, Joyce's focalisations invite the reader to speculate about character and relation in ways that give his visual data a dynamic of their own: the fussy and extensive details of the protagonist's room in 'A Painful Case', for instance, give us plenty of information about how he has tried to organise his life statically by cutting himself off from the rest of Dublin. These details suggest, in turn, the later failure of James Duffy's relationship with a woman he meets. At the opening of the story, when the focus 'pans' round his room, more is going on than an 'establishing shot'. Joyce is briefly imitating the proprietorial gaze of Duffy as it ranges over his living space. The very nature of the gaze, therefore, gives us our first indication of his character.

There is good evidence that Joyce was a constant cinema-goer, and even his earliest work suggests comparable methods even before any direct influence might be proposed. Paul Deane makes out a plausible case that 'The Dead' in *Dubliners* demonstrates a range of filmic techniques from scenic construction to the gradual reduction in characters roughly paralleling a progression from long shot to medium shot and close-up (Deane 1969). For example, Gabriel Conroy relishes memories of his wife in a brief montage sequence of flashback images:

> Moments of their secret life together burst like stars upon his memory. A heliotrope envelope was lying beside his breakfast-cup and he was caressing it with his hand. Birds were twittering in the ivy and the sunny web of the curtain was shimmering along the floor; he could not eat for happiness. They were standing on the crowded platform and he was placing a ticket inside the warm palm of her glove. He was standing with her in the cold, looking in through a grated window at a man making bottles in a roaring furnace. (Joyce 1992: 214)

The past continuous tense locates these scenes in a continuum of retrospective duration. The moment of recollection takes place on a cold night, and that circumstance makes a strong contrast with all the flashbacks where warm interiors are counterpointed against cold exteriors. Gabriel is trying to cut these scenes out of the broader, more boring narrative of his married life. Literally and metaphorically he's trying to keep the cold out, but he doesn't succeed because the last image of the story is of snow falling. Memory scenes make an imagistic comment on the dissatisfactions of his married life.

In *A Portrait of the Artist* we get rather different sorts of contrasts, especially as we move from one section of the novel to the other. In *The Film Sense* Eisenstein explains that scenic juxtaposition always implies more than placing two elements next to each other: 'Two films of any kind, placed together, inevitably combine into a new concept, a new quality, arising out of that juxtaposition [...] We automatically combine the juxtaposed elements and reduce them to a unity.' This combination can even be verbal: 'The tendency to bring together into a unity two or more independent objects or qualities is very strong, even in the case of separate words, characterizing different aspects of some single phenomenon' (Eisenstein, *The Film Sense*, 4–5). In *A Portrait* Stephen perceives his life as a series of discontinuous phases signalled by the repeated phrase a 'new life', whereas Joyce's method of imagistic modification encourages us to read across section breaks and to register the complex continuity between scenes. For instance, Chapter 4 ends after Stephen's epiphany of the girl on the beach on an image of open space. From his position on a small hill Stephen's gaze 'pans' across the coastal scene recording the symbolic juxtaposition of the moon and the 'pale waste' of skyline. The moon functions as a metaphor of Stephen's aesthetic hopes, contrasting with its prosaic context of Dublin culture. When we move into the opening lines of the next chapter the concluding image of sea-pools has been transformed into a pool at the bottom of a jar of dripping. A metaphor of lyrical openness has become a metonym of Stephen's squalid home life. Now his gaze is downwards towards the past, not outward towards the possibilities of life.

It was, however, *Ulysses* that particularly impressed Eisenstein with Joyce's approximation to the methods of film, particularly in his 'dual-level method of writing', which combined internal and external (Eisenstein, *The Film Sense*, 184–5).[3] R. Barton Palmer has applied the analogy between Eisenstein and Joyce specifically to the 'Oxen of the Sun' episode, which he takes as a kind of disjunctive montage constantly questioning the match between style and referents (Palmer 1985).[4] A more predictable choice would have been the 'Wandering Rocks' section, where fragmentary glimpses of characters in motion are assembled. Indeed, the theme of the section could be called passing. The path of Father Conmee, the opening character, is crossed by a one-legged sailor, an M.P.'s wife, schoolboys and others. As the scenes multiply, Bloom and Stephen recede from character priority into a shifting set of spatial and

---

[3] William V. Costanzo argues that the punning in *Finnegan's Wake* resembles film montage, noting that Chapter 16 is constructed like a film scenario (Costanzo 178–9).

[4] For further comment on montage in Joyce, see Barrow 1980.

social relations. Thus we see how characters pass each other and also see them in relation to fixed places as they walk past the diverse shops, churches and bars of Dublin. The reader is positioned as a spectator to these scenes, which constantly shift point of view. The difficulty of making representational data cohere has been explained by a number of critics as an application by Joyce of the notion of parallax, a term that for Ruth Perlmutter 'epiphanizes the alternation of connections and distances, of resemblances and displacements that have informed the whole book' (Perlmutter 486). For Marilyn French parallax is a major theme in *Ulysses* as Leopold Bloom, himself in motion throughout the novel, constantly tries to establish relations with objects and people that refuse to stay fixed (French 105–6). We shall see again this mobility in the observer and the observed in Virginia Woolf and Dorothy Richardson.

Virginia Woolf

In the late 1910s Virginia Woolf began a series of experiments in representing visual perception. 'The Mark on the Wall' is typical of these sketches in challenging previous orthodoxies of representation by recording a train of thought triggered by a visually ambiguous mark. Approached from one perspective, it has one resemblance; from another perspective, it looks quite different. Similarly 'Kew Gardens' explores the visual consequences of intense heat. Human figures lose their form in green–blue 'wash': 'one couple after another [...] passed the flower-bed and were enveloped in layer after layer of green–blue vapour, in which at first their bodies their bodies had substance and a dash of colour, but later both substance and colour dissolved in the green–blue atmosphere' (Dick 95). Humans become attenuated into small colour-masses against a green ground, and then even that distinction is lost. Indeed, loss of definition and substance is one of the main themes of these sketches. 'Solid Objects' begins with a distant shot of a 'small black spot' seen along a beach. Out of this emerges shape: four legs first (is it a dog?), then the revelation that we have to consider two figures – two men. One of them picks up a piece of glass and takes it home with him, where the object exercises a growing fascination but always at a level below full consciousness. Woolf explains the process of introjection as follows: 'Looked at again and again half consciously by a mind thinking of something else, any object mixes itself so profoundly with the stuff of thought that it loses its actual form and recomposes itself a little differently in an ideal shape which haunts the brain when we least expect it' (Dick 104). The young man in 'Solid Objects' embodies this fascination with form; he takes to hunting for such *objets trouvés*, getting more and more obsessed with their combination of apparent solidity and contingent shape.

By common consent, critics have described *Mrs Dalloway* (1925) as one of Woolf's most cinematic novels.[5] For Robert Humphrey, the skywriting sequence is one of the most successful instances of spatial montage or multiple perspective. The dynamic of the scene is produced through the reader following the gaze of one character up to the plane and then shifting across to a different character's perspective. As Humphrey argues, 'the object of central focus in the montage, in this instance the skywriting plane, carries the burden of unity' (Humphrey 56). A visual unity is achieved here, just as earlier Woolf had shown passers-by gazing at a grey limousine gliding through the London streets, but there is a comic irony in the sheer variety of observer's interpretation of the letters written in the sky. Although it is literally present as a shared object, the plane tantalises the spectators by suggesting a meaning just beyond their reach, and when characters look at each other, as often as not, it is to register estrangement or puzzlement. Woolf shows consummate skill in this novel at applying a device similar to a reverse shot in film, where we are given temporary access to one character's subjectivity and shifted into the consciousness of another character within the same scene. The reversal of the gaze in such cases temporarily objectifies Clarissa Dalloway and Septimus Warren Smith as they appear to others, and in this way Woolf negotiates to and fro between subjective and social life, constantly revealing the gaps between the two.[6]

This to-and-fro alternation between inner and outer has led Alan Spiegel to argue that Woolf names objects rather than describing them, in such a way that the naming acts as a verbal trace of the objects' entry into characters' consciousness (Siegel 49–50). According to Spiegel, Woolf never grants objects the physicality that they possess in Joyce's writing, but again this is debatable. The montage techniques

---

[5] Elaine Showalter comments of *Mrs Dalloway*: 'Woolf makes use of such devices as montage, close-ups, flashbacks, tracking shots, and rapid cuts in constructing a three-dimensional story' (Woolf 1992a: xxi).

[6] This method is anticipated in *Jacob's Room* (1922), the last section of which Edward Murray compares to Joyce's 'Wandering Rocks' in conveying a 'sense of simultaneity through rapid crosscutting' (Murray 149). However, the tempo of the montage together with the external time markers evoke the bustle of London on a summer day, where all characters – especially Jacob – are revealed in tantalising glimpses. Jacob's mobility as a subject reflects his elusiveness in the novel.

described above are used to suggest relation. Thus, the different descriptions of flowers, the most recurrent objects in the novel, are similarly used to render visually characters' different priorities. They appear as commodity for Richard Dalloway, objects in the social currency of his world. By contrast, Clarissa not only relishes the appearance of flowers more in the opening sequence at the florist's, but this relish lifts them out of the commercial context and triggers a nostalgic 'freeze-frame' image of a country house before the war where Clarissa tries to prolong the remembered scene by filling it with more and more sensuous detail. The very richness of this detail then raises questions about Clarissa's possible dissatisfactions with her present life.

In *To the Lighthouse* (1927) Woolf tries to render appearance when no-one is present. The transitional section 'Time Passes' contains descriptions like the following:

> What people had shed and left – a pair of shoes, a shooting cap, some faded skirts and coats in wardrobes – these alone kept the human shape and in the emptiness indicated how once they were filled and animated [...] Now, day after day, light turned, like a flower reflected in water, its clear image on the wall opposite. Only the shadows of the trees, flourishing in the wind, made obeisance on the wall, and for a moment darkened the pool in which light reflected itself; or birds, flying, made a soft spot flutter slowly across the bedroom floor. (Woolf 1992b: 141)

We remember the characters from Book I, so the traces of their presence (the clothes, shoes and so on) are not anonymous. Rather, Woolf negotiates between the presence of these traces and the physical absence of the characters. The visual dynamics of the scene come in once the wall, then the floor become used as a screen. We identify with a non-specified point of view located inside the house and witness the movement of shadows and reflections only, not the objects themselves. Without Woolf ever referring to the supernatural, it is as if the house was haunted with presences and, as in the sketches discussed above, objects become desubstantialised.[7] In the last sentence birds become a 'soft spot.' The house itself briefly resembles a perceiving consciousness.

Despite the similarity between cinematic techniques and those of Woolf's own experimental fiction, her first public statement on film was rather dismissive. A 1918 review of Compton Mackenzie, 'The "Movie"

---

[7] Woolf's 1921 sketch 'A Haunted House' similarly evokes invisible spectators returning to a familiar house to recapture visual memories (Dick 122–3).

Novel', drew a film analogy in order to ridicule the superficially hectic pace of adventure novels: 'as in a cinema, one picture must follow another without stopping, for if it stopped and we had to look at it we should be bored' (McNeillie 1987: 290). Woolf's more substantial 1926 essay 'The Cinema' explores the relation of eye to brain. In newsreels, for instance, the spectator is presented with a discontinuous sequence of scenes, and in general, she declares, 'we see life as it is when we have no part in it' (McNeillie 1994: 349). Woolf may be developing here an account by Roger Fry in his *Vision and Design* (1920, reviewed by Woolf the following year) where he argues that film 'resembles actual life in almost every respect, except that [...] the appropriate resultant action is cut off'. Fry compares film viewing to looking at scenes in a mirror, not to infer that we get a mimetic 'reflection' of reality but rather to show that in both cases we see 'much more clearly' (Fry 18). Thus, we register the relation between different parts of the scene; and the emotions triggered by film 'visions' 'are presented more clearly to the consciousness' (Fry 19). Woolf pursues this line of enquiry when, partly in response to having seen *The Cabinet of Dr Caligari*, she reflects: 'it seems plain that the cinema has within its grasp innumerable symbols for emotions that have so far failed to find expression' (McNeillie 1994: 350). Maggie Humm has skilfully glossed this essay as a non-mimetic account of film: 'Through the juxtaposition of images, film montage can suggest contradictory realities and asymmetrical emotion within the film's diegesis' (Humm 188).

Woolf's complaint of the lack of art-films in her essay provoked a response from the *New Republic* film critic Gilbert Seldes, who insisted that important 'abstract' (i.e. surrealist or expressionist) films were being shown in Paris. Seldes drew a contrast between these and 'story-films' since 'in each of the films the most significant part was played by the variation of movement and the variation of forms' (Seldes 96). Seldes's piece was more of an extension of Woolf's argument than a refutation, however. In fact, he was entirely sympathetic to her interest in film symbolism and, like Woolf, H.D. and Dorothy Richardson, he saw the future of the cinema as depending on its creation of its own representational techniques: 'We think that the movie can be made great by ceasing to be realistic; we insist that the camera is not a mere recorder' (Seldes 96).

Dorothy Richardson

A more extensive commentary on gender issues in film was given by Dorothy Richardson, who is now recognised as a formative practitioner of cinematic fiction – her serial novel *Pilgrimage* has been described as a 'celebration of light' (Donald et al. 154). From 1927 to 1933 she contributed a series of articles under the general title 'Continuous Performance' for the film quarterly *Close Up*, co-founded by Bryher and numbering H.D. among its contributors. Here, as Laura Marcus explains, Richardson examines the 'conditions of female spectatorship' (Donald et al. 150).[8] In these essays she stresses that watching a film is a participatory, shared process, 'something for collective seeing' (Donald et al. 191). The coming of sound occasioned one of Richardson's most challenging essays, 'The Cinema Gone Male' (1932). She draws a distinction here between the female characteristics of perceptual flow, cumulative memory, and silence; as against male speech and end-directed debate. Thus for her the coming of sound risked shifting film away from contemplation towards propaganda. This is cinema's 'masculine destiny. The destiny of planful becoming rather than of purposeful being' (Donald et al. 206). Richardson's conviction that female speech in relation to men was a 'façade' helps to explain why the dynamics of her novel described below lie primarily in sight and thought, rather than dialogue. In a perceptive discussion of Richardson's *Close Up* essays, Rebecca Egger argues that her essentialist position in the piece just quoted invests silent film with a dimension of heteroglossia and inscribes the female spectator as one encountering a form of non-knowing and also experiencing an erasure of conceptual differences. In other words, Richardson ultimately excludes the very kind of curious and investigative intelligence she herself was demonstrating in her essays (Egger 1992).

In *Oberland* (1927) Miriam, the protagonist of *Pilgrimage*, travels to a Swiss ski resort for a rest and in this volume, Richardson's biographer Gloria G. Fromm has argued, we are given a 'moving picture in words, with the harmony, colour, and continuity she wanted in a film' (Fromm 210). Miriam's visual transformations of France are introduced with a montage series of earlier memory scenes. Most of this volume, however, is devoted to Miriam's train journey to the Swiss resort, her arrival by sleigh, and her subsequent excursions. The extraordinary animation of the narrative grows out of Miriam's rapt scrutiny of anything and everything on her journeys from the interiors of the night train to the different perspectives on the Swiss village.

---

[8] Laura Marcus's commentary on Richardson's relation to the cinema (Donald et al. 150–9) is invaluable, as is Maggie Humm's (Humm 177–81).

As the train approaches Oberland, objects switch from right to left of Miriam and the mountains constantly seem to move in relation to her angle of vision:

> They closed in upon the train, summitless, their bases *gliding* by, a ceaseless tawny cliff *throwing* its light into the carriage, almost within touch; *receding*, *making* space at its side for sudden blue water, a river *accompanying*, *giving* them gentleness who were its mighty edge; *broadening, broadening, becoming* a wide lake, a stretch of smooth peerless blue with mountains reduced and distant upon its hither side. With the sideways *climbing* of the train the lake dropped away, down and down until presently she stood up to see it below in the distance, a blue pool amidst its encirclement of mountain and of sky. (Richardson 1967: 21; emphasis added)

Motion here is projected on to the items within Miriam's visual field as they seem to move up and down, near and far. The reader is invited to participate in the sights by the elision of the perceiving agent as if the flow of sense-data was available to all. The continuity of her gaze is ensured by the use of participial verb forms, which renders that gaze as a constant stream of visual events. This is an effect that Richardson produces throughout *Oberland*. When Miriam goes down to dinner in her hotel, her eyes 'pan' left and right along the rows of guests; when she goes into the village, she registers which lines of perspective are open, which closed. Process is everything here. Miriam is constantly composing and recomposing scenes, mentally constructing situations that she can either observe or enter, or throwing out memory links triggered by visual similarities between present and past scenes. At one point in her reveries she questions the male promotion of 'works of art' (Richardson 1967: 93) and in contrast makes her flow of visual perceptions into an experiential serial work of art where everything is relished, but nothing fixed.

Richardson was one of the most open-minded commentators on the supposed threat posed by film to stage plays and the novel. Writing in the American journal *Vanity Fair*, she rejected this view out of hand and insisted: 'the two arts [film and novel] are visibly playing into each other's hands' through adaptations and novelisations. Citing the example of H.G. Wells's published screenplay for *The King Who Was a King*, she predicted: 'the practice of film-seeing [will] create a public for a new kind of literature – film-literature – of which Mr Wells' book, if we except the small scenarios appearing from time to time in periodicals, is, characteristically enough, the first example' (Richardson 1927). With the proviso that the material conditions of consuming each medium remained distinct, Richardson predicts a symbiotic kind of literature emerging from the interaction between fiction and film.

D.H. Lawrence

Woolf and Dorothy Richardson were far more receptive to the cinema than writers like D.H. Lawrence and (initially) Aldous Huxley because, rather than perceiving canons of high art to be under threat, they recognised the expressive potential of the new medium. In a major reinterpretation of Lawrence, *Sex in the Head* (1993), Linda Williams has argued that the negative evaluation of the cinema that occurs in *The Lost Girl* (1920) demonstrates his consistent suspicion of a medium that privileges sight, since in his writings live spectacle is invested with more authenticity than passive spectatorship (Williams 2–5). Nevertheless, she continues, Lawrence's treatment of the gaze ironically has a cinematic dimension, which is inflected by class and gender. For example, in the opening chapter of *Women in Love* Gudrun feels so estranged from the colliery town that she tries to see the life around her as a kind of spectacle, a series of pictures (or scenes from a movie). But her gaze is reversed. However much she tries to see the locals as 'aborigines' (primitives), she can't blank out the fact that they are human beings; and therefore she can't avoid the sensation of being seen herself: 'She was exposed to every stare, she passed on through a stretch of torment [...] If this were human life, if these were human beings, living in a complete world, then what was her own world, outside? She was aware of her grass-green stockings, her large grass-green velour hat, her full soft coat, of a strong blue colour' (Lawrence 58).

Gudrun tries to construct a scene where she's the observing subject, looking at a world that's so different it seems unreal. But at the same time she's conscious that she comes from this region, and this induces an agonising (and snobbish) self-consciousness where she imagines herself as the object of others' observation.

Despite Lawrence's hostility to the cinema, Williams shows how important the gaze was to him as a source of drama. And his attacks on the popularity, passivity, and superficiality of cinema-going should be off-set by Lawrence's appreciation of the montage method used in John Dos Passos' *Manhattan Transfer* (1927). Reviewing that novel, Lawrence praised its evocation of interlocking stories sweeping along at a rapid tempo: 'If you set a blank record revolving to receive all the sounds, and a film-camera going to photograph all the motions of a scattered group of individuals, at the points where they meet and touch in New York, you would more or less get Mr. Dos Passos's method [...] It is like a movie picture with an intricacy of different stories and no close-ups and no writing in between' (McDonald 363–4). The exclusion of commentary and access to characters' subjectivity led Lawrence to a rare position in his writings where he praises the evocation of varied shifting spectacle.[9]

H.G. Wells

According to H.G. Wells's biographer David C. Smith, Wells initially disliked the film medium as much as Lawrence, but then by 1927–8 had revised his opinion to the extent of collaborating in the making of a number of short films (David C. Smith 1986: 323). However, there are signs from much earlier in Wells's career that he was assimilating the importance of the new art medium. In *When the Sleeper Wakes* (1899), the time traveller Graham finds one wall of his room taken up with a screen near which stand what prove to be video cylinders of stories by Kipling, Conrad, and James. This device is named the 'kinetoscope', after Edison's 'kinetograph', which Wells saw as the mechanical proto-type of the film projector. Once a 'performance' starts – in colour and with sound – Graham finds that his attention becomes totally engrossed, and in a throw-away comment Wells anticipates the later fears of redun-dancy expressed by novelists: 'He had been so absorbed in the latter-day substitute for a novel, that he awoke to the little green and white room with more than a touch of the surprise of his first awakening' (Wells 1994b: 50). The trope of cinema-viewing as dream is used here to under-score the realism of the new medium, a realism so vivid that Graham returns to the machine to see another video. This time the subject is an updated version of the Venus and Tannhäuser story so erotic to Graham that he smashes the machine in revulsion. Here again his action only confirms the unnerving vividness of the medium. Wells speculates here on the social institutionalisation of film. Later in the novel Graham realises that the 'kinematograph' has replaced newspapers as the main news medium.

In *When the Sleeper Wakes* the cinema exists as a ubiquitous feature of Wells's future world, but the introductory frame to *A Modern Utopia*

---

[9] Similarly, in *Men Without Art* (1934) Wyndham Lewis praised Hemingway's early fiction for being a 'cinema in words' and for being prime examples of exter-ior art (Lewis 1987: 33, 103–5).

(1905) places film in the narrator's (and therefore the reader's) present. In offering the reader a preliminary hint of the hybrid nature of the book (a combination of essay and novel) Wells states: '*the image of a cinematograph exhibition is the one to grasp. There will be an effect of these two people* [the narrator and his companion] *going to and fro in front of the circle of a rather defective lantern, which sometimes jams and sometimes gets out of focus*' (Wells 1994a: 4: italics in original). The analogy de-privileges, at least potentially, Wells's surrogate in this work and shows him to be just one of two narrative voices.[10]

This comparison does not signal a special visual dimension to *A Modern Utopia* so much as act as a concrete image of how Wells's subject is delivered, whereas each of his early novels has its own characteristic visual effect: *The War of the Worlds* (1898) repeatedly freezes its charac-ters in postures of panic; *The Island of Doctor Moreau* (1896) exploits the point of view of its narrator Prendick to compose – especially in its early chapters – chiaroscuro images where part of a figure is hidden by dark-ness; and *The War in the Air* (1908) builds its subject into its visual perspectives. The latter addresses the military consequences of a 'boom in aeronautics', which catches the imagination of its protagonist and his friend: 'Grubb and Bert heard of it in a music-hall, then it was driven home to their minds by the cinematograph' (Wells 1979: 14). Music-hall, cinema, and finally fiction. The third agency for opening up the possibilities of flight is George Griffith's *The Outlaws of the Air* (1895).[11] Wells shows how this enthusiasm emerges from the popular media but, more importantly, the cinematic influence helps to explain how *The War in the Air* is an extended experiment in constructing aerial perspec-tives. The rising interest in aeronautics that grips Wells's protagonist Bert Smallways takes place against an international background of impending war. His naivete lies in his assumption that flying might be simply recreational but once he crash-lands in Germany he learns the full extent of its military potential when he is shown the imperial fleet of airships.

---

[10] Clearly Wells has in mind a production that is at least partly educational. In *The Work, Wealth and Happiness of Mankind* (1932) he comments that the cin-ema is a 'more modern and even more startling case of a new, important method of intercommunication gone very seriously astray' (Wells 1934: 157): 'astray' because the educational use of film had been so neglected.

[11] The impossibility of detaching peacetime travel in airships from their military application had been established by Ignatius Donnelly in his 1890 novel *Caesar's Column* and further developed in George Griffith's *Olga Romanoff* (1894).

In 1935 Wells wrote his own screenplays for the films *Things To Come* and *The Man Who Could Work Miracles*, both produced by Alexander Korda in 1936.[12] The first of these was described by Wells as 'spectacular' and as an imagistic rendering of the ideas discussed in *The Shape of Things to Come*. The sequence falls into three phases: the present; the period of barbarism into which society lapses after the Second World War and its sequel; and finally a millenarian age of scientific progress and rational management. Wells explicitly rejected the expressionistic methods of *Metropolis* and instead drew on John Grierson's documentary techniques to give realism to the action. Among the most powerful sequences is one where two characters walk through Everytown, a typical industrial town of the 1930s. By the 1960s it has collapsed into a wasteland, which anticipates the imagery of Aldous Huxley's *Ape and Essence*:

> A dead city. Rats flee before them – starveling dogs.
> They pass across a deserted railway station.
> Public gardens in extreme neglect. Smashed notice-boards. Fountains destroyed – railings broken down.
> Suburban road with villas empty and ruinous. In the gardens are bramble-thickets and nettle-beds. (Wells 1935: 46)

The economy of this description contrasts strikingly with Wells's common tendency to discursive looseness. Here the scene is one not of destruction but of abandonment and premature ruin. The details Wells selects are metonyms of social and domestic life now lost. Such imagery was to make an impact on another author of dystopian fiction.

Aldous Huxley

Aldous Huxley's first reactions to the cinema combined a grudging recognition of its power, horror at the scale of its images, and a snobbish distaste for its impact on the masses. In his 1925 essay 'Where Are the Movies Moving?' he admits that cinema outdoes literature in its capacity to represent the fantastic or, as he puts it, 'super-realism'. Despite his early reservations about film, even at this date Huxley was interested

---

[12] The screenplay for *The Man Who Could Work Miracles* was published in 1935 (Wells 1935a). For comment on adaptations of Wells's novels, see Don G. Smith 2002.

enough to distinguish between two broad methods of cinematic narration: the 'behaviourist' using close-ups of faces, limbs, etc., and the
'expressionist' or pictorial method using visual symbolism (Baker 2000a:
174–7). However, when Huxley went to see his first 'talky' his reaction
was one of horror, a Swiftian horror at the magnified image of the human
countenance, a racial horror at the popularisation of Jewish and African-
American subjects, and a more general horror at the very thought of
popular media. The sheer extremity of Huxley's expression verges on
hysteria. He seems to regard the cinema as an ultimate form of cultural
betrayal, reflecting the 'psychical putrefaction of those who have denied
the God of life and have abandoned their souls [...] to the life-hating
devil of the machine' (Baker 2000b: 24). The 'feelies' of *Brave New
World* are ironically extrapolated from the talkies and described as one
sign of the American entertainment industry expanding right round the
globe. In 1931 Huxley loftily pronounced: 'For the great masses there is
the cinema. Its heroes and heroines are patterns for millions' (Baker
2001: 293). Huxley leaves no room for discrimination between films
or viewers. All are lumped together in a commercial process without
aesthetic value. Where Huxley saw the cinema as a medium for popular
entertainment, Wyndham Lewis saw it as a means of controlling the
masses, no doubt influenced by the appropriation of film for propaganda
purposes by the fascist regimes in Germany and Italy.[13]

By the late 1930s Huxley's attitude to film had changed. In 1937 he
had taken up permanent residence in California and thereafter secured a
number of posts as screen-writer with MGM and Twentieth-Century
Fox, producing treatments of Madame Curie's life and *Pride and Prejudice*,
among other projects.[14] Huxley had become so enthusiastic about the
cinema that in 1945 he planned his own movie adaptation of *Brave New
World*. Two works from the 1940s demonstrate Huxley's newfound interest in applying cinematic techniques in narrative. The first is *Jacob's
Hands*, a 1944 screen story about faith healing, which Huxley wrote with
Christopher Isherwood and which was not published until 1998.[15] The

---

[13] In his 1934 essay ' "Detachment" and the Fictionist' Lewis drew a stark opposition between the experiences of cinema-going and reading a novel, arguing that
the latter was based on individualism while the cinema was a group experience.
Having drawn this contrast, however, Lewis then brings it into question by
declaring that every viewer sees films differently (Lewis 1989: 218–19).

[14] For comment on Huxley's film projects, see Clark 1987.

[15] The work was published as *Jacob's Hands: A Fable*. The present-tense narrative describes how a desert faith-healer sets up a city 'Psycho-Magnetic Medical

second work is *Ape and Essence* (1949), a post-apocalyptic narrative set
in the year 2108. The narrative is introduced by a frame section describing how a man has gone in search of a screen-writer named Tallis, but
who has only found one of his scripts, which he salvages from the incin-
erator. *Ape and Essence* is thus primarily a screenplay narrative, 'edited'
without comment by the preliminary narrator. In it Huxley shrewdly uses
a whole range of film devices (dissolves, close and distant shots, among
others) to present a retrospective autopsy, set in the Hollywood area, on
the virtual death of human reason. In the aftermath of a series of wars
the few human survivors have lapsed into a new barbarism. As David
King Dunaway explains, 'Huxley created a world of devolution where
humans no longer have the biological distinction of breeding when they
choose' (Dunaway).[16] Instead they are limited to a narrow mating season
every year. Hollywood has become a wasteland:

> The Camera comes down over a large rectangular graveyard, lying
> between the ferro-concrete towers of Hollywood and those of Wilshire
> Boulevard. We land, pass under an arched gateway, enjoy a trucking shot
> of mortuary gazebos. A baby pyramid. A Gothic sentry box [...] suddenly
> in the midst of all this desolation, here is a little group of human beings.
> There are four men, heavily bearded and more than a little dirty, and two
> young women, all of them busy with shovels in or around an opened
> grave. (Huxley 1949: 46)

The imagistic progression takes us by two familiar landmarks, along a
brief satirical sequence of the discontinuous styles of Hollywood graves,
to a final startling shot of grave scavengers. This last scene culminates
the initial effect of the narrative: a transformation of a familiar location
into eerie strangeness. The script represents *the* place of film production
as waste area; in other words, paradoxically we have before us a script
that can never be produced. Furthermore, Huxley sets up a montage of
scenes showing humanity's collapse into fanatical nationalism and the
self-destructive technology of germ warfare and atomic super-weapons
counterpointed against the running commentary of a voiceover or

---

Centre'. Apart from some satire of Californian spiritual fads, *Jacob's Hands* is
mainly a psychological study of the pursuit of security through faith healing.
Isherwood's novel about film-making in 1933 London, *Prater Violet* (1946),
gives a comic view of the film business and a vivid portrait of political naivete
in the Austrian refugee who is directing the project.
[16] Dunaway also point out the influence that Wells's film *Things To Come* had
on *Ape and Essence* (Dunaway 222).

'narrator' who clearly has retained reason and a capacity for historical analysis. Within the narrative's ironic reversals, the protagonist is a young scientist on a voyage of rediscovery from New Zealand. His function is to act as the viewer's surrogate within the narrative, struggling to apply mid-twentieth-century presumptions about technological progress to situation of primitive reversion. *Ape and Essence* thus casts itself as mock-educational script on the collapse of Western culture and at the same time plays to the medium which, Huxley suggests in his opening frame, was superseding the novel.

Evelyn Waugh

No such suspicions of the demise of the novel worried Evelyn Waugh. On the contrary, his formal experiments with the comic novel owed much to his early experience of film. In 1922 he went up to Oxford and while there acted as film critic for the university magazine *Isis*. In 1924 he collaborated in the making of a comic film called *The Scarlet Woman*, which describes the Pope's attempt to convert Britain to Catholicism. Waugh had already registered the prime importance in film of 'momentary pictures and situations', as he noted in one of his Oxford reviews (Gallagher 15). For one of his biographers, however, *The Scarlet Woman* showed Waugh the 'value of the short one-joke scene as a way of constructing a narrative' (Carpenter 138). Another influence on his method was from the fiction of Ronald Firbank. This time Waugh himself drew an analogy between fiction and film, significantly just at the point where his own career as a novelist was beginning. In an article of 1929 Waugh wrote that Firbank's

> later novels are almost wholly devoid of any attribution of cause to effect; there is the barest minimum of direct description; his compositions are built up, intricately and with a balanced alternation of the wildest extravagance and the most austere economy, with conversational nuances. They may be compared to cinema films in which the relation of caption and photograph is directly reversed; occasionally a brief, visual image flashes out to illumine and explain the flickering succession of spoken words. (Gallagher 57–8)

As an anticipatory account of Waugh's own management of pacing, the relation of dialogue to image, and alternation between tonal extremes this could hardly be improved on. Such statements confirm Waugh's respect for an emerging 'genuine and self-sufficient art'

(Gallagher 68).[17] Unlike Huxley, he did not recoil from the cinema only to modify his opinion in later years, but rather showed a consistent interest in the new medium throughout his career. 1932 saw him working on a film scenario for a story by Sapper and in 1936, after visiting Alexander Korda's studio, Waugh was invited to write a script about cabaret girls to be called *Lovelies from America*. During his 1946 visit to Hollywood Waugh disliked its commercialism but never lost his fascination with film. When discussions were going ahead for the MGM adaptation of *Brideshead Revisited*, Waugh was so anxious that the novel should not be approached as a love story that he wrote an extended memo about the novel. He insisted that its theme was theological and that such a film would be the 'first time that an attempt will have been made to introduce them [theological issues] to the screen, and they are antithetical to much of the current philosophy of Hollywood' (Heath 226). In the event the project fell through.

It is symptomatic of Waugh's interest in film that he only made real progress with his first story – 'The Balance,' begun in May 1925 – once he had taken the decision recorded in his diary: 'I am making the first chapter a cinema film' (Davie 212). This decision, this specific analogy, acted as a catalyst to his writing and can be seen operating both as method and as partial subject in *Vile Bodies* (1930). This novel opens with a montage of scenes from a stormy Channel crossing, scenes accelerating, as the novel cuts between shorter and shorter fragments, towards a communal hymn-singing organised by an American evangelist Mrs Ape. This opening sequence establishes an alternation, which runs throughout the novel, between characters coming together and then dispersing. The paradigmatic social event here is the party, a situation that Waugh's brief scenic units ironically breaks into fragments. Characters are constantly torn between participation and observation, and a circular process is established between behaviour (especially outrageous behaviour at parties) and the participants' later relish of accounts of that behaviour in gossip columns the next day. One scene makes this process farcically explicit. During a party in the Prime Minister's house a Jesuit becomes convinced that there is a spy present. When the stranger is confronted he is told to take off his beard, which he does: 'He gave some tugs at the black curls, and bit by bit they came

[17] R.M. Davis has argued that Waugh's development centred on cinematic devices that rendered ideas and action visually (Davis 1965) but Leszek Kolek has modified this account by proposing that Waugh's effects depend to a large extent on rhetorical control (Kolek 1982).

away.' Once his features are revealed the situation collapses into bathos as the Jesuit recognises him: ' "That," said Father Rothschild bitterly, "is *Mr Chatterbox*" ' (Waugh 2000: 86–7). He is in a sense a spy, but purely a social one since Mr Chatterbox is the professional name of a gossip columnist (for the moment here played by a young lord). Behind the momentary melodrama Waugh exposes the voyeuristic circularity of the London social set.

Shortly after this scene Waugh introduces film-making into the novel in order to make a further satirical comment on British society. The protagonist Adam goes to visit his future father-in-law, one Colonel Blount, who he discovers is leasing the grounds of his house to a film company who are making a 'historical' study of Wesley. When Adam sees the actors in costume this makes explicit the novel's earlier presentation of social behaviour as a masquerade – hence the significance of Mrs Ape's surname. Ironically, the commercial aspects of the film ('the most important All-Talkie super-religious film to be produced solely in this country', according to the director) are explained to Adam by a man dressed as a bishop (Waugh 2000: 122). Once the film has been developed and is viewed in the Colonel's house, it becomes clear that it mimics the pace of life of the young characters in the novel. It opens with a rapid sequence of scenes: 'There came in breathless succession four bewigged men in fancy costume, sitting round a card table [. . .] Then a highwayman holding up the coach which Adam had seen; then some beggars starving outside Doubting Church; then some ladies in fancy costume dancing a minuet' (Waugh 2000: 177). The sequence reads like a paratactic stream of scenes similar to the novel itself, and Adam notices how the film seems to accelerate at points of drama. One of his friends, Agatha Runcible, has had a driving accident leaving her with severe concussion. This is described as a cinematic replay of her racing along a road: 'There was rarely more than a quarter of a mile of the black road to be seen at one time. It unrolled like a length of cinema film' (Waugh 2000: 168). Concussion has frozen Agatha in a moment of experience that endlessly repeats itself like a film loop.

In *Vile Bodies* film is used partly to comment on the frenetic tempo of the lives of Waugh's characters. In a later story, Waugh dramatises the attractions of such a tempo within the film business. 'Excursion in Reality' describes how a young writer, Simon Lent, is invited to write for a London studio an updated version of *Hamlet*. The director tells him: 'What the public wants is Shakespeare with all his beauty of thought and character translated into the language of everyday life' (Waugh 1951: 69). Simon is completely dazzled by the exhausting pace of daily work in the studios and tells his girlfriend: 'You see, for the first time in my life I have come into contact with Real Life. I'm going to give up writing novels. It was a mug's game anyway. The written word is dead – first the papyrus, then the printed book, now the film. The artist must no longer work alone. He is part of the age in which he lives' (Waugh 1951: 71). Needless to say, these words are premature. What Simon does not realise is how expendable writers have become in the film business. As the project develops, the script gets confused more and more with that of *Macbeth*, until finally the film is abandoned and Simon is out of work. As so often happens in Waugh, 'reality' proves to be something that happens to his characters over which they have virtually no control. 'Excursion in Reality' satirises not so much the cinema per se, as the superficial appeal of the film business. Waugh was well aware from the beginning of the commercial appeal of the cinema, but this never prevented him from appropriating for his own use the methods of the new medium.

After considering examples from Virginia Woolf, Gertrude Stein, James Joyce and others, Keith Cohen has stated that 'the most dynamic aspects of the new novel form were *simultaneity*, or the depiction of the two separate points in space at a single instant of time, *multiperspectivism*, or the depiction of a single event from radically distinct points of view, and *montage*, or the discontinuous disposition in the narrative of diverse diegetic elements' (Cohen 208: emphasis in original). In short, the modernists were establishing new conventions of narrative representation, which exploited discontinuity and which incorporated the perceptual horizon of the observer and which were greatly helped if not directly suggested by the emergence of parallel conventions in the cinema. Graham Greene articulated this complementarity in 1937 when he was writing as film critic for *The Spectator*, declaring: 'There is no need to regard the cinema as a completely new art; in its fictional form it has the same purpose as the novel' (Greene 57).

Works Cited

Baker, Robert S. and James Sexton, eds, 2000a. Aldous Huxley, *Complete Essays: Volume I, 1920–1925*. Chicago: Ivan R. Dee.

Baker, Robert S. and James Sexton, eds, 2000b. Aldous Huxley, *Complete Essays: Volume II, 1926–1929*. Chicago: Ivan R. Dee.

Baker, Robert S. and James Sexton (eds), 2001. Aldous Huxley, *Complete Essays: Volume III, 1930–1935*. Chicago: Ivan R. Dee.

Barrow, Craig Wallace, 1980. *Montage in James Joyce's 'Ulysses'*. Madrid: Ediciones Jose Porrua Turanzas.

Bergson, Henri, 1914 (1911). *Creative Evolution*, trans. Arthur Mitchell. London: Macmillan.

Burkdall, Thomas L., 2001. *Joycean Frames: Film and the Fiction of James Joyce*. New York: Routledge.

Carpenter, Humphrey, 1990. *The Brideshead Generation: Evelyn Waugh and His Generation*. London and Boston: Faber & Faber.

Clark, Virginia M., 1987. *Aldous Huxley and Film*. Metuchen, NJ: Scarecrow Press.

Cohen, Keith, 1979. *Film and Fiction/ The Dynamics of Exchange*. New Haven and London: Yale University Press.

Conrad, Joseph, 1922. *Tales of Unrest*. London: Eveleigh Nash and Grayson.

Conrad, Joseph, 1957. *The Nigger of the 'Narcissus', etc.* London: J.M. Dent.

Conrad, Joseph, 1988 (1899/1902). *Heart of Darkness*, 3rd edn, ed. Robert Kimbrough. New York and London: Norton.

Costanzo, William V., 1984. 'Joyce and Eisenstein: Literary Reflections on the Reel World', *Journal of Modern Literature*, 11, 175–80.

Davie, Michael, ed., 1986. *The Diaries of Evelyn Waugh*. Harmondsworth: Penguin.

Davis, R.M., 1965. 'Evelyn Waugh's Early Work: The Formation of a Method', *Texas Studies in Literature and Language*, 7 (Spring), 97–108.

Deane, Paul, 1969. 'Motion Picture Technique in James Joyce's "The Dead"', *James Joyce Quarterly*, 6, 231–6.

Dick, Susan, ed., 1989. *The Complete Short Fiction of Virginia Woolf*, rev. edn. London: Hogarth Press.

Donald, James, Anne Friedberg and Laura Marcus, eds, 1998. *'CloseUp' 1927–1933: Cinema and Modernism*. London: Cassell.

Dunaway, David King, 1989. *Huxley in Hollywood*. New York: Harper & Row.

Egger, Rebecca, 1992. 'Deaf Ears and Dark Continents: Dorothy Richardson's Cinematic Epistemology', *Camera Obscura: A Journal of Feminism, Culture and Media*, 30, 5–33.

Eisenstein, Sergei, 1957. *Film Form and The Film Sense*. Cleveland, OH: Meridian Books.

Fell, John L., 1986. *Film and the Narrative Tradition*. Berkeley and Los Angeles: University of California Press.

French, Marilyn, 1982. *The Book as World: James Joyce's 'Ulysses'*. London: Sphere.

Fromm, Gloria G., 1994. *Dorothy Richardson: A Biography*. Athens, GA: University of Georgia Press.

Fry, Roger, 1929. *Vision and Design*. London: Chatto & Windus.

Gallagher, Donat, ed., 1983. *The Essays, Articles and Reviews of Evelyn Waugh*. London: Methuen.

Greene, Graham, 1937. 'Subjects and Stories', in Charles Davy, ed., *Footnotes to the Film*. London: Lovat Dickson, pp. 57–70.

Heath, Jeffrey, 1975. '*Brideshead*: The Critics and the Memorandum', *English Studies* 56, 223–30.

Humm, Maggie, 2002. *Modernist Women and Visual Cultures: Virginia Woolf, Vanessa Bell, Photography and Cinema*. Edinburgh: Edinburgh University Press.

Humphrey, Robert, 1972. *Stream of Consciousness in the Modern Novel*. Berkeley and Los Angeles: University of California Press.

Huxley, Aldous, 1949. *Ape and Essence*. London: Chatto & Windus.

Huxley, Aldous, and Christopher Isherwood, 1998. *Jacob's Hands: A Fable*. New York: St Martin's Press.

Isherwood, Christopher, 1940. *Goodbye to Berlin*. London: Garden City Press.

Joyce, James, 1992. *Dubliners*. Harmondsworth: Penguin.

Kolek, Leszek, 1982. '"Uncinematic Devices" in Evelyn Waugh's *A Handful of Dust*', *Literatur in Wissenschaft und Unterricht* (Kiel), 15.iv (December), 353–65.

Kumar, Krishan, ed., 1994 (1905). H.G. Wells, *A Modern Utopia*. London: J.M. Dent.

Lawrence, D.H., 1989 (1920). *Women in Love*. Harmondsworth: Penguin.

Lawton, John, ed., 1994 (1899). H.G. Wells, *When the Sleeper Wakes*. London: J.M. Dent.

Lewis, Wyndham, 1987 (1934). *Men Without Art*, ed. Seamus Cooney. Santa Rosa: Black Sparrow Press.

Lewis, Wyndham, 1989. *Creatures of Habit And Creatures of Change: Essays on Art, Literature and Society 1914–1956*, ed. Paul Edwards. Santa Rosa: Black Sparrow Press.

Lodge, David, 1974. 'Hardy and Cinematographic Form', *Novel*, 7.iii (Spring), 246–54.

Lubbock, Percy, 1924. *The Craft of Fiction*. London: Jonathan Cape.

McDonald, Edward D., ed, 1961. *Phoenix: The Posthumous Papers of D.H. Lawrence*. London: William Heinemann.

McNeillie, Andrew, ed., 1987. *The Essays of Virginia Woolf. Volume 2: 1912–1918*. London: Hogarth Press.

McNeillie, Andrew, ed., 1994. *The Essays of Virginia Woolf. Volume 4: 1925 to 1928*. London: Hogarth Press.

Moore, Gene M., 1997. 'Conrad's "film-play" *Gaspar the Strong Man*', in Gene M. Moore, ed., *Conrad on Film*. Cambridge: Cambridge University Press, pp. 31–47.

Murray, Edward, 1972. *The Cinematic Imagination: Writers and the Motion Pictures*. New York: Frederick Ungar.

Palmer, R. Barton, 1985. 'Eisensteinian Montage and Joyce's *Ulysses*: The Analogy Reconsidered', *Mosaic*, 18, 73–85.

Perlmutter, Ruth, 1978. 'Joyce and Cinema', *Boundary 2*, 6.ii, 481–502.

Richardson, Dorothy M., 1927. 'Talkies, Plays and Books', *Vanity Fair* (August), 56.

Richardson, Dorothy M., 1967. *Pilgrimage 4*. London: J.M. Dent.

Schwab, Arnold T., 1965. 'Conrad's American Speeches and His Reading from *Victory*', *Modern Philology*, 62, 342–7.

Seldes, Gilbert, 1926. 'The Abstract Movie', *The New Republic*, 48, no. 615 (15 September), 95–6.

Smith, David C., 1986. H.G. *Wells Desperately Mortal. A Biography*. New Haven and London: Yale University Press.

Smith, Don G., 2002. H.G. *Wells on Film: The Utopian Nightmare*. Jefferson, NC: Macfarland.

Smith, Grahame, 2003. *Dickens and the Dream of Cinema*. Manchester and New York: Manchester University Press.

Spiegel, Alan, 1976. *Fiction and the Camera Eye: Visual Consciousness in Film and the Modern Novel*. Charlottesville: University Press of Virginia.

Watt, Ian, 1980. *Conrad in the Nineteenth Century*. London: Chatto & Windus.

Waugh, Evelyn, 1951. *Work Suspended and Other Stories together with Scott-King's Modern Europe*. Harmondsworth: Penguin.

Waugh, Evelyn, 2000 (1930). *Vile Bodies*, ed. Richard Jacobs. Harmondsworth: Penguin.

Wells, H.G., 1934. *The Work, Wealth and Happiness of Mankind*, rev. edn. London: William Heinemann.

Wells, H.G., 1935a. *The Man Who Could Work Miracles: A Film by H.G. Wells, Based on the Short Story 'The Man Who Could Work Miracles'*. London: Cresset Press.

Wells, H.G., 1935b. *Things To Come: A Film Story Based on the Material Contained in his History of the Future 'The Shape of Things To Come'*. London: Cresset Press.

Wells, H.G., 1979 (1908). *The War in the Air*. Harmondsworth: Penguin.

Wells, H.G., 1994a (1905). *A Modern Utopia*. London: J.M. Dent.

Wells, H.G., 1994b (1899). *When the Sleeper Wakes*. London: J.M. Dent.

Williams, Linda Ruth, 1993. *Sex in the Head: Visions of Femininity and Film in D.H. Lawrence*. Hemel Hempsted: Harvester Wheatsheaf.

Woolf, Virginia, 1992a. *Mrs Dalloway*, ed. Stella McNichol. Harmondsworth: Penguin.

Woolf, Virginia, 1992b. *To the Lighthouse*, ed. Stella McNichol. Harmondsworth: Penguin.

Killing 'The Killers': Hemingway, Hollywood, and Death

OLIVER HARRIS

All stories, if continued far enough, end in death, and he is no true story teller who would keep that from you.

Ernest Hemingway, *Death in the Afternoon*

Ah, it's the job.

Reardon (Edmund O'Brien) in *The Killers*

The Bell Rang

AN HOUR INTO THE CLASSIC *FILM NOIR* THRILLER, *The Killers* (1946), the detective-figure, Reardon, walks into the office of his insurance company boss and announces, 'Well, the bell rang.' Reardon means that he has finally solved the mystery of the film's enigmatic object, a green silk handkerchief found among the effects of 'the Swede', the former boxer whose murder he has been investigating.[1] Reardon then hands his boss a newspaper report of a payroll heist from some six years earlier in which the Swede is identifiable by this 'unusual green handkerchief', worn over his face as a disguise. For a few seconds there's a close-up of the clipping while Reardon's boss reads the headline aloud, and then, as he carries on reading in voiceover, the image dissolves to the scene of the crime. What follows is a stunning, two-minute long unbroken sequence-shot, filmed in semi-documentary style without a diegetic soundtrack, that has been the subject of detailed analysis by critics arguing the scene's internal complexity and film-historical importance. But curiously, both Robert Porfirio, who hails it as 'the effective "germ" of a subsequent type of caper film' (Porfirio 179), and Tom Conley, who sees it 'providing self-reflexivity for the New Wave to take from the general conventions of noir' (Conley 1991: 165), misleadingly describe the

---

[1] For more on this handkerchief, and other aspects of *The Killers* as a *film noir*, see my 2003 article, 'Film Noir Fascination'.

scene as a *flashback*.[2] The film's narrative does feature ten conventional flashbacks (a structure adapted, like the 'Rosebud' enigma, from *Citizen Kane*), in which the spectator is given privileged access to the audiovisual representation of a remembered past initially narrated by a character. But, here, speech and image are separated from one another, are detached from the narrator (it is the other character, Reardon, whose memory is involved), and, most crucially, both speech and image are mediated by their origins in a *text*. In other words, we might begin to read this scene as a type of page-to-screen adaptation, one that foregrounds the problematics of representation by making a self-reflexive statement about the nature of textual and filmic media and the relationship between them. It offers, then, a point of departure for recognising how, as Conley has argued (albeit on finally different grounds), *The Killers* 'occupies a central niche in the history of film theory, in *film noir*, and in the relations of cinema and literature' (Conley 1997: 524).

What enables us to read this particular scene as a kind of allegory or *mise en abîme* of adaptation? Most obviously, the inevitable mismatch it demonstrates between the verbal and the visual. As the written text gives rise to a set of images, we witness an *excess*, a host of visual details not described in the verbal report that is the source of those images. In the transfer from text to screen, the spectator must always 'see too much'. However, as Porfirio has observed, the mismatch here also entails something more – a failure in synchronisation itself: as he notes, the camera 'begins to anticipate the action' while the narrator 'occasionally falls behind the visual revelations of those events' (Porfirio 180). In fact, the failure goes further, and in turn points towards a double critique of representation.

Firstly, this failure to achieve synchronisation of sound and image exposes the claim to veracity made by the documentary style, as in Bordwell's assumption that the narrator 'gives the rendition of the robbery the stamp of objective verisimilitude' (197). Indeed, although it has been overlooked by critics, the final moments of this scene stage a blatant contradiction between what the recited text states and what we are shown; even as we are informed that a security guard 'fell to the ground with a bullet in his groin', we observe him quite clearly clutching not his groin but his shoulder. And secondly, this discrepancy also

[2] Indeed, *all* critics have called it a flashback, including Maureen Turim in her full-length study, *Flashbacks and Film* (181), even though it fails to match her own definition of the technique as 'a cinematic discourse on the mind's relationship to the past and on the subject's relationship to telling his or her past' (2).

begs questions about the fidelity of image to text in the process of adaptation and about the hierarchy of representations: which version of the past should we believe is the original – the real thing – and which the false copy? Finally, we may grasp the importance of this problematising of representation by observing that, while it's true that the visual exceeds the verbal source, in this instance the opposite is also the case, since here we witness a significant *loss*. For the key detail in both this sequence and the film's larger plot – the 'green handkerchief' (a gift from the femme fatale who causes Swede's death) – is not revealed at all but effectively concealed by virtue of being filmed in black-and-white. A reminder that the essential is always lost in translation, this negation matters because the entire basis to Reardon's investigation is his recollection of this detail in the report (the 'bell' that rang signals the return of his repressed memory). We might even say that this text is the source of the film from the point, some ten minutes in, when Reardon discovers Swede's handkerchief and begins trying to decipher its mystery. In which case, the elusive – or illusive – nature of this enigmatic key to the secrets of the past is subversively inscribed by these contradictions within the very representation that is supposed to resolve it.

If this analysis suggests a subtle meditation on the generation of cinematic images and film narrative out of a written source text, it stands in for the rather more obvious process of adaptation announced by the film's full title: *Ernest Hemingway's The Killers*. As we will see, the critical response to this film has usually included some sort of comparative analysis with the Hemingway short story on which it is based. In light of the recent trend towards inter-textual theories of adaptation, the more detailed of these comparative studies now appear tainted by the various fallacies of traditional 'fidelity' criticism (an essentialist assumption of authorial intention, an implicit hierarchy that favours the literary 'original' and judges the film for being true or false to its 'letter' or 'spirit', and so on). On the other hand, adaptation theorists have also worried about the limits to an expanded field, concerned that 'use of the inter-textuality model might in some cases tend to obscure the relationship between the two works' (Mayer 6). In the case of *The Killers* and 'The Killers', I would argue that what's needed is a limited dialogic approach, because the relationship and its significance has been so *obscured* by the existing criticism.

In what follows there are, therefore, a number of significant omissions: the larger matrix of international Modernism formed by the intersection of Hemingway, existentialism, and aesthetic exchanges between

European and American culture; a fully two-way analysis that rereads 'The Killers' in light of *The Killers*; the contextualising Nick Adams short-story cycle; a comparative analysis of the 1946 film and its remake in 1964, and so on. First focused extratextually and then inter-textually, my main interests lie in a sociological and medium-specific reassessment of the film's relationship with Hemingway's story and, finally, in their representations of death.

Ernest Hemingway's *The Killers*

Criticism has overwhelmingly situated *The Killers* within one of three determining contexts: the emerging tradition of what critics (but not the studios that made the films) would call *film noir*; the oeuvre of its director, Robert Siodmak; and the field of Hollywood adaptations of Hemingway's work. These three contexts can be triangulated to form an initial framework.

Of *The Killers'* relation to *film noir* a great deal has been written – it is widely recognised as 'one of the most "complete" *films noirs*' (Walker, 135) – but, significantly, the film is almost never mentioned in context of *noir*'s relation to literary adaptation.[3] While adaptation has been a constant in Hollywood's history, *noir* is something of a special case, and not only because so many films derive from a specific range of writers, chiefly the 'hardboiled' tradition of Dashiell Hammett, Raymond Chandler, James M. Cain, and Cornell Woolrich. For this literary base has also been one of the key factors in critical efforts to define the field's very identity, its claims to coherence, ever since, in August 1946, the French cineaste Nino Frank coined the term *noir* to describe recent American crime films. In fact, only Porfirio has claimed that the film's debt to Hemingway, as the Papa of the tough guy school, makes *The Killers* a fitting illustration of some 'definitive

---

[3] An exception is R. Barton Palmer's recent essay, itself exceptional for its well-theorised engagement with Patrick Cattryse's *Pour une théorie de l'adaptation filmique: le film noir américain* (Berne: Peter Lang, 1992). Acknowledging that *The Killers'* 'narrative complexity' may have cinematic sources – he cites *Citizen Kane* – Palmer claims (without supporting evidence) that it 'can also be traced to adaptation – not of the literary text actually being reworked in this instance [i.e. "The Killers"], but of a literary norm adopted by this emerging model [i.e. *film noir*] . . . from an earlier and ground-breaking adaptation' [i.e. *Murder, My Sweet*, the 1944 adaptation of Raymond Chandler's *Farewell, My Lovely*] (275).

aspects' of *film noir* (Porfirio 177), and even this lineage has been
called 'more apparent than real' (Schickel 17). If there are no more
than passing references to Hemingway in the numerous comparative
studies of *noir* film and fiction (see in particular Marling and Abbott),
it is not just because of the lack of other Hemingway *noir* adaptations,[4]
but, I would argue, because *The Killers* does not seem to fit established
comparative paradigms.

While Abbott can discuss 'the choices these films make in regard to
the novels' of Raymond Chandler, and analyse both 'the defatalization
of the femme fatale' and the 'Hollywood makeover' of their detective
heroes in the passage from page to screen (Abbott 132, 138, 133), in the
case of *The Killers* the mismatch between film and short story seems to
leave nothing to compare: what sense does it make to speak of culturally and politically significant 'choices' in the process of adaptation
when the literary source text is less than a dozen pages long, provides
the basis for only ten minutes of the film, and features neither detective-
hero nor femme fatale? At its most elementary, this is a material problem of *length*. Since both the theory and practice of literature-to-film
adaptation criticism has always taken the novel as its standard, this
issue is typically phrased in precisely the reverse terms of *cuts*, not expansions (how to redact a text of several hundred pages into a ninety-
minute movie). And in the *noir* context, cutting has been especially
important to critics because of the determining institutional and cultural conditions of film production in 1940s America. Criticism has
often focused on how *noir* films adapted their source novels because of
the need to negotiate the ideological injunctions and moral prohibi-
tions of the Production Code, observing how the repressed (usually, but
not exclusively, sexual material) returns in displaced form through the
mise-en-scène. However, the *locus classicus* of this approach – the treatment of sexuality in Howard Hawks' 1946 adaptation of Chandler's
novel, *The Big Sleep* – does not provide the only model for the workings
of censorship and its subversion.

Although Kuhn's case is that, in the film text, 'censorship is a *pro-
ductive* operation rather than, as it is commonly conceived, a process of
excision, of cutting things out' (Kuhn 79), her comparative analysis of
The Big Sleep film and novel is based precisely on noting the presence
of material too dangerous to be left in. Another model altogether is
needed, however, to take into account the distinctive stylistics as well

---

[4] Critics sometimes include *Breaking Point* (1950), based on *To Have and
Have Not*.

as length of Hemingway's short story – to reckon, that is, with the 'iceberg' aesthetic of the *already* cut text. Paradoxically, *The Killers'* very expansions of its minimalist source can be seen to achieve a similar state of culturally significant self-contradiction by the opposed route. The processes of Hollywoodisation and its resistance that have been analysed in *noir* adaptations may be just as meaningful when narrative techniques and generic types are not reworked from a literary source but added entirely from scratch. As I will argue below, the key additions that made *The Killers* – a complex flashback structure and a plot driven by the detective's pursuit of a femme fatale – should be seen as a culturally determined response to the danger of what in Hemingway's 'The Killers' is *absent*.

This emphasis on the conditions of film production brings us to our second determining context. Whereas Hemingway has an oblique relation to the *noir* field, Robert Siodmak is widely recognised as the *noir* director *par excellence* (only his fellow German émigré, Fritz Lang, is credited with more titles). On the other hand, when critics have comparatively analysed Siodmak's film and Hemingway's text they have become snared in the problematic definition of authorship. Thus Kaminsky describes both Hemingway and Siodmak as 'an author of merit', as if writer and director exercised comparable autonomous control over their materials – and then, recognising the special importance of the film's producer, Mark Hellinger, Kaminsky undoes his comparative model by creating the hyphenated identity in 'Hellinger-Siodmak's *The Killers*' (125, 129). In fact, this issue of whether to credit the director with a film's paternity was already raised in the case of Siodmak by the French critics Borde and Chaumeton (in the first – and for twenty years, the only – study of *film noir*),[5] and the material evidence supports their suspicion about Hellinger's role in *The Killers*: it was Hellinger who had long wanted to adapt the Hemingway story and who got Universal to acquire the property for his production company, Hellinger who commissioned the screenwriters (John Huston, Richard Brooks, and Anthony Veiller), arranged the lead casting, and hired the director – and Siodmak wasn't even his first choice (this was Don Siegel, who directed the remake of *The Killers* in 1964). Despite Siodmak's creative input into all aspects of the production – including 'a tremendous hand in the final screenplay' (Alpi 154) – there are, then, strong empirical grounds for

---

[5] 'What is the producer's contribution, the scriptwriter's, the editor's? Is it pure chance that the late Mark Hellinger produced three such unmistakable films as *The Killers*, *Brute Force*, and *The Naked City?*' (3).

resisting the (in any case theoretically contested) notion of *The Killers* as the response of one author to another.

Indeed, it might be just as fruitful to discuss the film in the context of Hellinger's independent production company, which played an important role in the reorganisation of the postwar film industry generally and, in particular, reworked the gangster genre by 'sponsoring candid hard-boiled social realist treatments of modern American life' (Munby 162). Since Siodmak's main interests lay elsewhere – chiefly, psychological trauma in domestic settings and obsessive relationships – it's revealing that one critic should claim he 'did get the chance to re-do *The Killers his way*' when, 'without Hellinger at the helm' (Greco 18), he directed *Criss-Cross* (1948); ironically, greater autonomy for the director may account for why the later film lacks the kind of internal contradictions and covert textual operations that make *The Killers* especially interesting.

The Killers brought Siodmak name recognition in Hollywood and his only Oscar nominations, brought Mark Hellinger International and Universal significant financial success, and made instant stars of its two leads (Burt Lancaster, on his debut, and Ava Gardner). But publicity for the film traded emphatically on the biggest star name of all, that of Ernest Hemingway. Not only did all posters and lobby cards feature Hemingway's name in the film title, but over a dozen different poster designs used the key promotional tag line to seal the association: 'Told the Untamed Hemingway way'. The original press-book begins with an astonishingly clear, if clearly misleading, hierarchy of authorship – 'Story by Ernest Hemingway / Produced by Mark Hellinger / Directed by Robert Siodmak' – while several poster designs redoubled the emphasis by featuring references to the three Hemingway novels previously adapted by Hollywood, *To Have and Have Not* (1944), *For Whom the Bell Tolls* (1943) and *A Farewell to Arms* (1932).[6] Perhaps unsurprisingly, only the small print in such publicity clarified the actual extent of Hemingway's involvement in *The Killers*; when promotional material boasted, 'Hemingway Does It Again! Author Makes Screen History with Sensational New Hit!' the impression given is of a new, original work by Hemingway – not an adaptation, '90%' of which was an 'addendum' (Greco 86) by other writers to a twenty-year-old, very short story.

If Hemingway was, as Hellinger put it at the time, 'the biggest selling element in our advertising' (quoted in Greco 86), this was because, in

---

[6] Information about the pressbook, from the Criterion DVD edition of *The Killers* and from Laurence 1989.

the 1940s, 'he alone of his generation was both a critically successful writer of fiction and also a celebrity' (Lewis xi). On the other hand, when Hollywood used his name to pre-sell its product, it constructed a Hemingway to suit each occasion: Hemingway the Romantic novelist of sentimental love stories for *A Farewell to Arms*, or the tough guy writer of 'Tense! Taut! Terrific!' action for *The Killers*, or even, in a promotion for *The Macomber Affair* (1947) that brazenly reconstructs the earlier construction in order to trade off it, the writer of 'the love story of *The Killers*' (quoted in Laurence 1989: 24). Given the publicity departments' promiscuous makeovers of Hemingway's image, what are we to make of his name's presence in the film title? Was it meant to be taken as an act of homage – a claim to fidelity, deferring to the great author – or, quite the opposite, as an unabashed Hollywood takeover, appropriating the property as its own? Begging the question of originality, Hemingway's name in the title also begs the question of the spectator's knowledge of the original. In 1946, how many of the film's audience would have read 'The Killers', or have known it was not a novel but a short story, or have otherwise known it was by Hemingway at all? But whatever the audience's cultural competence, the title wreaks a curious epistemological confusion in thoroughly mystifying the distinction between film and story: being called *Ernest Hemingway's The Killers*, the film makes it impossible to refer to Ernest Hemingway's 'The Killers' without once again naming the film.[7] It's as if the title fantasises the erasure and replacement of both author's name and original text, insisting that this, the film, is not a substitute for the story, not some pale imitation, but the thing itself, the real thing.

He investigated Hemingway

'As is well known, Hemingway's story supplies only the first two scenes of the film,' states Michael Walker (128), effectively dividing up *The Killers* into what might be termed the opening 'adaptation' and the 'expansion' that follows and, inadvertently, begging two questions. Firstly, 'well known' to whom? To modern critics, or the film's contemporary audience? And secondly, since what's 'well known' sometimes

---

[7] The same case could be made for *To Have and Have Not* and *The Snows of Killimanjaro* (1952), which also had 'Ernest Hemingway's' before the commonly abbreviated title, although neither film promoted the name as did *The Killers*.

turns out to be wrong, is the commonplace Walker notes actually the case? Both questions turn on the reception, critical as well as popular, of Hemingway's story in the context established by the film.

First published in 1927, 'The Killers' quickly became one of the most widely anthologised and critically analysed of all Hemingway's stories. Written almost entirely in terse dialogue, it is short and striking enough for spectators already familiar with it to have recognised the largely verbatim adaptation of the first two of its three scenes: the arrival of the two hit men, Max and Al, in Henry's diner, where they verbally terrorise George, the counterman, and Nick Adams, a customer, reveal their plan to ambush the Swede, and, when he doesn't appear, leave; then Nick's visit to Swede's room to tell him about the men, and Swede's quiet insistence, lying passively on his bed, that 'There ain't anything to do' (Hemingway 1955: 67). In the third scene, not adapted for the film, Nick returns to the diner where he and George briefly speculate what Swede must have done wrong, and George, responding to Nick's horrified reaction, tells him he'd 'better not think about it' (69). For critics, this gangster hit scenario becomes an absurdist moral and philosophical drama through the story's extraordinary density of repetitive, contradictory, and enigmatic details, so that the common denominator in Hemingway criticism is to read it as a text of 'false impressions' (Fleming 41) where 'very little in the story is what it appears to be' (Carter 13).

Knowing that 'textual perplexity' (Brenner 159) wouldn't sell half so well as the hardboiled violence promised in the story's title, promotion for the film naturally passed over self-reflexive artifice and played up the angle that linked Hemingway and Hellinger: their backgrounds in journalism of urban crime. Hemingway's firsthand experience as a crime reporter in Kansas City and Chicago was echoed in Hellinger's own underworld connections and fame as a former *New York Daily News* syndicated columnist, so that it's noticeable not only how much space but what kind of credit 1946 reviewers gave the producer. James Agee, for example, described in *The Nation* the film's 'good strident journalistic feeling . . . all well manipulated by Robert Siodmak, which is probably chiefly to the credit of the producer, Mark Hellinger' (Agee 217). Ignoring Siodmak's name entirely, the *Time* magazine review gave half its space to Hellinger and an evocation of 'the '20s, when Manhattan teemed with murdering bootleggers': 'The Killers . . . is packed with scenes, characters and dialogue straight out of Hellinger's Broadway.'[8]

---

[8] *Time* (6 September 1946), 40.

Most revealing of all, there's a large picture of Hellinger, taken at the Stork Club, teasingly captioned: 'He investigated Hemingway'.

Exploiting an appearance of authenticity supported by Hemingway's biography and Hellinger's reputation, the film in effect investigated the extra-textual reality hinted at in the story, when Nick Adams and George speculate about why a pair of hit men should be looking for the former boxer: ' "He must have got mixed up in something in Chicago," ' George concludes; ' "Double-crossed somebody. That's what they kill them for" ' (Hemingway 1955: 69). In later years, Hemingway himself would speak of 'the real thing in back of "The Killers" ' (Hotchner 160), supporting the idea of a true but absent history – one that offered Hellinger (who was also drawing on his underworld reporting days) a version of the iceberg aesthetic to which the film could respond by filling out the 'missing' back-story.

The critical verdict on the relationship between the 'adaptation' and the 'expansion' of Hemingway's 'The Killers' can be divided into two broad camps, each more or less preoccupied with issues of fidelity and judgements of quality. There are those who see the film's response as inadequate or reductive: in Hollywood, more means less. Thus Borde and Chaumeton observed that 'from the first sequences onward one expects something extraordinary', but that with 'the appearance of the investigator the rhythm gets weaker, and the atmosphere more commonplace. We steal in the direction of the well-made, but classical, crime film' (Borde and Chaumeton 78). For Jack Shadoian, the film used 'Hemingway's museum piece' with 'a kind of insolent nonchalance, as a symbolic introductory gesture' (Shadoian 80), a verdict echoed by John Tusca, who refers to the 'short story by Ernest Hemingway on which [the film] was ostensibly based but to which it bears only the slightest relationship' (Tusca 184). In sum, as Burt Lancaster recalled on seeing the script: 'Well, the first sixteen pages are Hemingway verbatim, and after that you have a rather interesting whodunnit film, but nothing comparable to Hemingway' (quoted in Clinch 14). In the other camp are those who claim not just the film's fidelity to the original but a kind of parity. The 1946 New Yorker review singled it out as an adaptation, noting that 'Hollywood has so frequently botched a good story by extending it that this one instance of preserving the quality of the original is most cheering'.[9] Greco describes the film's 'addendum' as 'a perfect compliment' (Greco 86, 89), while others have gone further.

[9] John McNulty, review in New Yorker (7 September 1946), 52.

'In its extension from Hemingway's short story beginning, the '46 *Killers* looked something like what Hemingway might have written,' asserts Laurence (1981: 180), and Spencer Selby goes one better still in claiming that 'the film transforms Hemingway's short story into the detective novel he never wrote but should have' (Selby 44).[10] The issue of quality, then, is answered in terms of *The Killers'* success in *completing* 'The Killers', an analysis that is crudely reductive towards the story and that curiously elides the distinction between cinema and literature.

This idea that 'The Killers' needed completing is generally argued in plot rather than aesthetic terms, responding not to 'textual perplexity' but rather to the 'perplexing mysteries within the story' (Fleming 40). Thus, Foster Hirsch: 'Although Hemingway offers no explanation for the character's almost indifferent embrace of death, the film attempts to unravel the intriguing mystery of his submission' (Hirsch 72). We might properly invert this to say that it's not *although* but *because* of the lack of an explanation that the film unravels Hemingway's mystery, and that this is the reason for introducing its detective figure. As Selby puts it: 'The film then produces Riordan [sic] to answer the questions that the viewer must have about this story' (Selby 43). In this analysis, the spectator of *The Killers* is presumed not just to know 'The Killers' but to have been left puzzled and unsatisfied by it, so that, externalising our role as readers and acting as our surrogate, Reardon fulfills our desire to know by, in effect, producing more text. The problem with this approach is not only the reductive assumption it makes about the story's readers, that they can only read for the plot, as if this is the rest of Hemingway's iceberg. The other problem, which needs addressing here, is that in conflating reader with spectator it also fails to distinguish between the historicity of Hemingway's writing and Hollywood's filming.

As an interpretation of Hemingway's story, Reardon's investigation rehistoricises what is most problematic in it according to those cultural and historical determinations registered by *film noir* in mid-1940s America. Structurally, for example, Reardon's pursuit of the Swede's back-story proceeds through flashbacks, whose remarkable proliferation in *noir* films of this period has been understood both as the 'transcription of a literary device' (Turim 171), reflecting the number of hardboiled

---

[10] Laurence and Selby evoke the prospect of the film's novelisation, a book that could only be titled '*Ernest Hemingway's "The Killers"*', but that would have to begin with a disclaimer acknowledging that the text was *not* Ernest Hemingway's 'The Killers' (as would happen, fifty years later, for the novelisation of Francis Ford Coppola's *Bram Stoker's Dracula*).

source novels, and as a symptomatic response to a general 'postwar concern about historical recollection' (Munby 216). If the flashback affirms that the 'secrets of the past need to be told or found out' (Turim 143), then its use ten times to drive *The Killers'* narrative suggests an excessive, medium-specific reaction to 'The Killers', as if over-compensating for the absence of narrative development in Hemingway. Likewise, as the insurance investigator takes on the rationalising task of the solitary detective – Edmund O'Brien plays him as a cheapened version of Bogart in *The Maltese Falcon* (1941) – it's as if Reardon's increasingly obsessive quest to solve the Swede's mystery effectively metonymises the film's need to finish off the story. Thematically, as Krutnik has demonstrated, Reardon's active role in *The Killers* is to restore the loss of agency embodied by the former boxer in his paralysed surrender to death: the film offers a defining image of its culture's 'persistent fascination with the spectacle of the passive or emasculated man' (Krutnik 127). Introducing the femme fatale – by the mid-1940s an established generic type, albeit one individualised intriguingly here – the film takes up the clue in Hemingway about Swede's feminisation – his landlady says, 'He's just as gentle' (Hemingway 1955: 68); meaning, *as a woman* – so that his loss of potency comes to represent male fears about social and economic realignments in the postwar order. In a zero-sum game of power, Reardon avenges Swede's losses by finding and triumphing over the double-crossing woman and the double-act killers, and at the film's end he exits his boss's office with a smile that expresses job satisfaction: from unfinished business to case closed.

In effect, then, the film has read back from 'effects' in Hemingway's story to produce the 'causes', even as these causes are constructed according to historical conditions and cultural types two decades later. On a range of levels, the 1946 production responded to the horror of Swede's negativity in 1927 – 'There ain't anything to do' – by doing something: narrating his crime and allocating punishment, redeeming his defeat and achieving closure.

Finally, before returning to address the second question posed by Walker's comments (whether Hemingway 'supplies only the first two scenes of the film'), we may consider the brief but usefully theorised analysis advanced by Slavoj Žižek. Deriving his terms from Lacan, Žižek takes *The Killers* to exemplify those reconstructions of artworks that 'fill the void around which some canonical work is structured' (Žižek 19). Since this central hole denotes a 'constitutive gap between the explicit symbolic texture and its phantasmatic background' (18), when some other work fills it in, 'the effect is inevitably that of obscene vulgarity'

(19). Žižek observes: 'in its first ten minutes, the film faithfully follows the original story; what then ensues, however, is a prequel to it – an attempt to reconstruct the mysterious past traumatic experience that caused the "Swede" to vegetate as a living dead, and calmly await his death' (19). Despite offering a valuable model to theorise Hemingway's iceberg aesthetic (of which, more below), Žižek's analysis more or less sums up what I would call a 'first approach' to *The Killers*, one that sees fidelity to the letter in the adaptation of Hemingway and betrayal of it in spirit in the expansion. In each respect, I would argue that this account is fundamentally mistaken. In a 'second approach', we must recognise that Hemingway supplies both less than the first two scenes, and more.

Nothing Happens

To begin with, the problem in Walker's observation has nothing to do with the usual questions of fidelity. Laurence's objection that a detailed comparative analysis shows how the script and direction 'changed *many* important details and disregarded its meaning' (Laurence 1981: 181) is both true and (given its essentialist assumptions) beside the point. In the first instance, the problem is that critics have overlooked how these first scenes are determined by how they are *framed*.

After the Universal International logo, before the titles begin to roll and before the appearance of Henry's diner, the first shot fades in from a black screen to the dark interior of a car speeding through the night. In a tight close-up, the spectator is positioned in the backseat, looking ahead over the shoulders of two men. After ten seconds, the shot cuts to the road illuminated in the car's headlamps as seen from the driver's point of view. Only now does the camera cut to the scene of the diner, as the titles appear and Miklos Rozsa's dramatic 'Killers' theme music swells to a sudden crescendo. Paradoxically, the importance of this opening frame is suggested by its very lack of necessity: not only does it have no equivalent in Hemingway's story (first line: 'The door of Henry's lunch-room opened and two men came in'), but, as an introduction to the action that follows, the film simply does not require it. However, if we work backwards from effects to functions, and consider two other framing devices that follow, a critical purpose becomes apparent.

Firstly, these opening frames cannot be mistaken for location shots: the road beyond the windshield is obviously a back-projection, as visibly *screened* as the town, lit by a key light in the far distance that casts enormous shadows towards us, is a Universal sound stage. The film begins by literally setting its own artifice into the foreground. In this, it follows Hemingway's story, which playfully alludes to vaudeville, photography, and the movies, and whose stagy, unreal qualities critics have often noted as a counterpoint to its claims to realism.[11] However, the self-reflexive dimension in *The Killers* is emphatically and historically medium-specific: the dark interior of the car must remind spectators of their location in a cinema theatre (the silhouetted figures of the killers reproduce the shapes of those seated in the row in front), while, as Conley notes, 'the headlamps are an icon of the cinema being projected over the head of the viewer' (Conley 1991: 156). If we now cut forward to the closing seconds of the film's first movement – the moment of Swede's death – we find a second, equally self-reflexive framing device in the form of the killers' gunfire. As the gunmen 'blast away at the camera' (Phillips 71), the lighting creates an extraordinary cinematic flicker that darkens and illuminates the killers in rapid alternation, as if presenting us with positive and negative images. Put together, these instances of meta-cinematic framing that open and close the Hemingway adaptation (to be, temporarily, inexact) form a revealing contrast to the kind of frames used for the adaptation of *For Whom the Bell Tolls* three years earlier. That production began and ended with elaborate illuminated lettering, clearly intended to invoke for the spectator an association with the literary status of the film's source text (rather like the close-up shots of a leather-bound edition of *Jane Eyre* at either end of the 1944 film of Charlotte Bronte's novel). In *The Killers*, therefore, we can see how the cinematic framing of Hemingway's text – key elements of what Turim calls the film's 'covert enunciation' of its 'symbolic project, its projection of symbolization' (Turim 181) – functions to inscribe a vital, medium-specific, critical distance, achieved through visual devices that have no equivalent in the original story.

There is, finally, a second set of frames that are scripted and that relate directly to Hemingway's dialogue. This frame opens with the very first line spoken in the film, which is Nick Adams's single-word request to the counterman: 'Ketchup'. Again, it is the entirely gratuitous nature of this addition, as well as its placement, that implies its subtle but significant function. The frame closes with the key line in the whole film – the pivot point in the narrative between adaptation and expansion – or rather with its extraordinary double repetition. In the first

---

[11] Greco likewise notes that Siodmak and his cinematographer, Woody Bredell, achieved a 'remarkable authenticity' and yet, in scenes like the diner, 'there is something eerie in the way they enhance the reality of it' (96).

frame, whether the film adaptation's marking of difference is recognised or overlooked depends on whether or not the viewer knows the original text (where Nick doesn't speak until addressed by the killers). The duplication of dialogue in the second frame, however, has the effect of restaging this very structure of differentiation between original and adaptation within the film itself. Explaining his fate to Nick Adams, Swede says, in a quiet monotone and with a long, enigmatic pause: 'I did something wrong – once.' It is significant that numerous critics should have mistaken these words as Hemingway's (actually, 'I got in wrong' 1955: 67), because they generate a crucial confusion within the film. This occurs in the very next scene, when the 'adaptation' stops and the 'expansion' begins, as Reardon quotes these words over Swede's body in the morgue. What Reardon says is: 'Once I did something wrong.' Lest we miss the errors – inverting 'once' and cutting out the long pause – Reardon repeats the line, and compounds his mistake by describing them as Swede's 'last words to Nick' (actually, 'Thanks for coming'). Wrongly repeating twice last words that aren't last words about doing something wrong once – the confusion is the equal of anything in Hemingway. And, since critics have sometimes confused this key line with that in the original text and almost always overlooked its falsifying repetition within the film, it would appear as if *The Killers* correctly anticipated its own confusion *with* Hemingway. Corresponding to its failures in synchronisation elsewhere – including the sustained use of voice-off to disrupt Hemingway's dialogue in the diner scene (see Conley 1991: 159–60) – this emphatic contradiction in speech, this internal failure of fidelity between adaptation and expansion, stands in therefore for the external relationship between text and film. In short, each of these frames insist on the difference of *Ernest Hemingway's The Killers* with respect to Ernest Hemingway's 'The Killers'.

The second problem posed by the question of what is supposedly 'well known' about the adaptation concerns the most striking failure of all to differentiate *The Killers* from 'The Killers'. In the film criticism, one mistake occurs over and over again – namely, the impression that Hemingway's story ends with Swede's death. To be more precise, this error takes two forms, claiming either that the film 'begins by faithfully recording the whole of Hemingway's story of a killing' (Crowther 50), or that, for the film, we 'see Swede killed. The horror is not left to the imagination, it is explicit' (Kaminsky 50). The first error effectively rewrites the story in terms of the film, projecting backwards onto the source precisely what is absent from it: Swede's death. The second assumes that the film acts out what is implied in the story but not shown. Either way, the film has left its indelible print, as the 'false ending' in *Ernest Hemingway's The Killers* circulates a false cultural memory of Ernest Hemingway's 'The Killers'. One of the essential enigmas of Hemingway's text is therefore lost, since the killers themselves announce as they leave that they aren't now going to kill anyone ('We're through with it,' says Max (Hemingway 1955: 64)). As Paul Smith observes: 'For all the impending violence and seemingly inevitable bloodshed, nothing happens. The killers don't kill' (Smith 10).

'Nothing happens': this is not the same as saying that something *fails* to happen. For once we confront the force of what this non-event actually is – death – we might recognise that this is the non-event, the nothing, that happens, and that happens, paradoxically, precisely because the killers don't kill. The horror of the ending, in other words, is not a murder scene left to our imagination, but the interminable non-ending with which the Swede – and we – are left.

Death in 'The Killers' therefore constitutes a particular form of Hemingway's theory of omission, which he had already practised in short stories several times before. In 1923, for 'Out of Season', and in 1924, for 'Indian Camp', Hemingway left out a beginning and an ending that in each case related to death, and he implied as much when referring to 'The Killers', a text that lacks both a beginning (Swede's crime) and an ending (his punishment): 'That story probably had more left out of it than anything I ever wrote. More even than when I left the war out of Big Two-Hearted River' (quoted. in Johnston 247).[12] The idea, he famously claimed, was that 'you could omit anything if . . . the omitted part would strengthen the story and make people feel something more than they understood' (Hemingway 1986: 54). But this 'anything' is, in 'The Killers' at least, the more specific, and yet still more ambiguous, thing that is 'nothing'. One name for this kind of non-event is *trauma*, which Miriam Clark calls the 'vital other' to Hemingway's prose: 'Hemingway's omissions gain raw force not from the unsaid . . . but from the unsayable, the bodily experience outside and in excess of language and story' (Clark 169).

At this point we might conclude that *The Killers* completely negates Hemingway's aesthetic by crudely representing what can only be represented by its omission. It would then support Linda Dittmar's verdict (referring to *The Old Man and the Sea*) on the resistance of

[12] Hemingway 'clarified' this to mean he left out 'all Chicago', but I read this reference to a specific history, like his allusions to the real-life boxer behind the Swede, as a misleading literalism.

Hemingway's minimalist aesthetic to filming, since his style 'lures his adapters into excess' and because 'explication can deplete a text' (Dittmar 54). However, the paradoxical achievement of *The Killers* is to turn its very excess of explication against itself; its expansion subverts any possible fullness of representation through the Baroque excesses of its surface style and structure, as its multiple flashbacks fragment the narrative, disorder its chronology, and disorient its spectators. These disturbances not only create punctual gaps in knowledge of the past, they point towards the central absent cause that gives rise to them – the gaping hole that runs from 1940 (when the payroll heist takes place and the Swede falls victim to the femme fatale's double-cross) until 1946 (the time of Swede's death and Reardon's investigation). As 'Big Two-hearted River' omitted the First World War, so *The Killers*, like many other *noir* films, omits the Second. And this culturally determined repression of global historical trauma can indeed be felt, if not understood, in relation to the film's representation of Swede's death as an individual instance of existential trauma. For rather than showing us too much, this scene forces the spectator to confront the very emptiness that marks death's impossible alterity. This is the constitutionally 'unsayable' that informs the institutionally 'unsaid'.

In the scene of Swede's death the film stages both visually and verbally and with remarkable power the *nothing* that happens in 'The Killers'. To recall Žižek's terms, it is here that the film, in the very process of filling out the void in Hemingway's story, *creates its own void*. This is like answering a riddle with a riddle, since the scene of death in *The Killers* fills the hole in 'The Killers' with another hole, one that the rest of the film's narrative will ostensibly fill out. In Lacan's terms, what we encounter here is 'the Thing', the Real that is not repressed but foreclosed, that which cannot be represented and so 'will always be represented by emptiness': 'All art is characterized by a certain mode of organization around this emptiness' (Lacan 129, 130). And yet this void is materialised as a visceral proximity according to the force of the cinematic medium that 'brings me', as Steven Shaviro says, 'compulsively, convulsively, face to face with an Otherness that I can neither incorporate nor expel' (Shaviro 259). For the hole in vision that confronts the spectator in *The Killers* takes the form of an extraordinary sequence in which Siodmak alternates between shots of Swede's paralysed stare towards the camera and shots of the dark door behind which the killers are readying their guns. Exploiting the mirroring effect of the shot/reverse-shot structure, Siodmak forces the spectator to identify with both looks. That is to say: looking at the Swede's immobilised look, we do not see, but, as in a mirror, see only ourselves seeing; looking at what Swede sees, we see a door beyond which death waits, a sort of empty mirror. For what feels like an eternity, as we wait – wish – for it to be over, nothing happens.

This profoundly disturbing moment is the visual correlative to the verbal hole in Swede's speech, the gap that Reardon closes in his falsification of the line, 'I did something wrong – once.' Swede is not really hesitating, nor does he exactly give emphasis (to 'once') by his pause. The blank here is a paradoxical absence, because it gives voice to the unsayable, forcing us to hear, precisely, nothing. No word is missing between 'wrong' and 'once', and yet Reardon's closure of the gap in his repetition of the line falsifies it by leaving nothing out.

Swede's key line and its 'adaptation' by Reardon effectively index the structural relation between the film's opening movement and all that follows. For the words that declare Swede's identification with fate and embrace of death come to express, in Reardon's mouth, a primal truth that is repressed: consciously, despite his relentless drive to investigate, Reardon does not identify with the Swede at all. On the contrary, when the screen fades back in from Swede's death to reveal Reardon in the police station the morning after, it is as though we have awoken from a nightmare, one that Reardon does not remember. In narrative terms, we might understand this structural relation via the psychoanalytical model suggested by Thierry Kuntzel. In Altman's summary, Kuntzel proposed a two-stage division of film that produces two roles for the film spectator: 'at first analogous to the dreamer (the introductory sequence representing his dream), the spectator subsequently becomes analogous to the analyst (the remainder of the film representing an explanation of the introductory "dream" material)' (Altman 527). The value of this model here is to clarify the shift in the spectator's position that corresponds to the introduction of Reardon and our identification with him. If we put this model together with Hemingway's, the binary dream/analysis finds its exact match in feeling/understanding. Forced by Siodmak's direction to feel Swede's encounter with death, but unable to understand it, the spectator is invited to side with Reardon as the one who 'untangles the dream material, explaining it' (Altman 527) – that is, explaining it away. In terms of the cinematic medium, the film spectator is caught between the affective dimension of the image and the analytical satisfactions of narrative. This structure, in which a symptom is unravelled by analysis and causal knowledge substitutes for ethically based feeling, marks Reardon's appearance in the very next scene.

Shortly after Reardon's entry he interviews Nick Adams, evidently disturbed after witnessing Swede's refusal to save himself. In the police station morgue, Nick narrates the film's first flashback, which ends with Swede's realisation that the past has caught up with him. Not grasping the situation, Nick asks: 'What's the matter, Swede, are you sick?' Swede replies: 'Yeah, I feel kinda sick.' When the flashback ends, Reardon asks questions until Nick stops him with the line: 'Look, mister, I'm feeling kinda sick myself.'[13] At this point, Nick exits the film, effectively knowing and understanding nothing about the Swede's fate. For this, we must look to Reardon. And yet, already, the spectator's identification with the detective is divided. Just before Nick's flashback, when Reardon finishes reciting Swede's 'last words' – making the telltale errors – he lifts the sheet covering his cadaver. In close-up we see him turn over one of the boxer's enormous hands, fingering its scars. It's a casual gesture and that's what makes it such a chilling moment, for the way he holds hands with the dead proves that Reardon cannot grasp death. The detail warns us that, whereas Nick feels an embodied empathy – identifying with the Swede's feeling of sickness – Reardon feels nothing. It is an early warning, easily ignored for now, that our investment of desire in the detective will produce the wrong kind of knowledge. Thus the spectator probably follows Reardon in failing to react when, in the form of raw statistics – 'Born Philadelphia, June 23, 1908. Mother died 1909' – the film offers a tantalising glimpse of Swede's traumatic upbringing, a back-story Reardon overlooks entirely.[14] The longer the film goes on, the more it will subvert its own overt project – and the basis to its own narrative development – by distancing us from Reardon. It thereby indicts the spectator for sharing his drive to know – a drive that is steadily revealed to us as a disavowal, of his own sickness, of his own death-drive, of that which cannot be grasped. Reardon's project to kill the killers, to disavow death, has also been a project to kill 'The Killers', to put an end to Hemingway's incessant and interminable limbo. Rather than giving us too much, then, Reardon's mission leaves us with the sense of all that is missing, even though what is left out is not something that could ever have been put in.

In his efforts to placate death with analysis, Reardon demonstrates the reductive, rationalising response to the inconclusive, unfathomable

---

[13] Nick echoes how the Nick Adams of 'In Another Country' responds to news of death: ' "Oh –" I said, feeling sick for him' (1955, 50). In a film whose script pays extraordinary attention to detail, the echo may well be a debt.

[14] Far from coincidentally, the mother plays a crucial role in numerous Siodmak films, including *Criss-Cross*, the effective sequel to *The Killers*.

quality of 'The Killers' so well expressed by Paul Smith, for whom the story 'leaves us with the sense that something profoundly important, something elemental and enigmatic, has occurred and one life at least has been changed' (12). The life that has been changed in 'The Killers' is, as we see by his traumatised reaction, that of Nick Adams; in *The Killers*, we recognise by the end that Reardon's life has not been changed in the least. Rather than being represented within the film text, the life to be changed by this *Killers* is the object of its address – that is to say, the spectator. From here, it is a short step to projecting onto Reardon the identity of the analytical reader, to say that he holds up a harsh mirror to the critic carrying out 'the routine, rationalized business of interpretation' (Bordwell 255). And this is why it is so crucial to see that the film's overt project of investigation – 'there are some last words and a mysterious handkerchief, puzzles solved in due course' (Greco 88) – is completely undermined from within by its covert operations. Reardon's empty victory at the end, with a self-satisfied smile and flippant wave of the hand, and the ironic reward from his boss of a weekend off work, signals a critique of all his activity. Arriving at Hemingway's conclusion by the opposite route, the truth of *The Killers* turns, in effect, on exposing Reardon as no true story teller. It's as if the film's parting shot is to say, 'This is how Hollywood does it!' – where 'it' denotes both the act of adaptation and the treatment of death. As Reardon says with almost his last words, 'Ah, it's the job.'

Works Cited

Abbott, Megan, 2002. *The Street was Mine: White Masculinity in Hardboiled Fiction and Film*. New York: Palgrave.

Agee, James, 1983. *Agee on Film*, vol. 1. New York: Peregree Books.

Alpi, Deborah Lazaroff, 1998. *Robert Siodmak*. Jefferson, NC: McFarland.

Altman, Charles F., 1985. 'Psychoanalysis and Cinema: The Imaginary Discourse', *Movies and Methods*, vol. 2, ed. Bill Nichols. Berkeley: University of California Press, pp. 518–31.

Baker, Carlos, 1972. *Ernest Hemingway: A Life Story*. Harmondsworth: Penguin.

Benson, Jackson J., ed., 1990. *New Critical Approaches to the Short Stories of Ernest Hemingway*. Durham, NC: Duke University Press.

Borde, Raymond and Étienne Chaumeton, 2002. *A Panorama of American Film Noir 1941–1953*, trans. Paul Hammond. San Francisco: City Lights.

Bordwell, David, 1985. *Narration in the Fiction Film*. Madison: Wisconsin University Press.

Brenner, Gerry, 1990. 'From "Sepi Jingan" to "The Mother of a Queen": Hemingway's Three Epistemologic Formulas for Short Fiction', in Benson, *New Critical Approaches*, pp. 156–71.

Carter, Steven, 1998. 'Interrogating the Mirror: Double-crossings in Hemingway's "The Killers"', *Language and Literature*, 23, 13–18.

Clark, Miriam Marty, 2004. 'Hemingway's Early Illness Narratives and the Lyric Dimensions of "Now I Lay Me"', *Narrative*, 12.2, 167–77.

Clinch, Minty, 1984. *Burt Lancaster*. London: Arthur Baker.

Conley, Tom, 1991. *Film Hieroglyphs: Ruptures in Classical Cinema*. Minneapolis: University of Minnesota Press.

Conley, Tom, 1997. 'The Killers', in *International Directory of Films and Filmmakers*, eds Nicolet Elert and Aruna Vasudevan. Detroit: St James Press, pp. 523–4.

Crowther, Bruce, 1989. *Film Noir: Reflections in a Dark Mirror*. New York: Continuum.

Dittmar, Linda, 1989. 'Larding the Text: Problems in Filming *The Old Man and the Sea*', in Oliver, *A Moving Picture Feast*, pp. 54–63.

Fleming, Robert, E.. 1984. 'Hemingway's "The Killers": The Map and the Territory', *The Hemingway Review*, 4.1, 40–3.

Greco, Joseph, 1999. *The File on Robert Siodmak in Hollywood: 1941–1951*. Dissertation.com.

Harris, Oliver, 2003. 'Film Noir Fascination: Outside History, but Historically So', *Cinema Journal*, 43.1, 3–24.

Hemingway, Ernest, 1955. *Men Without Women*. Harmondsworth: Penguin.

Hemingway, Ernest, 1986. *A Moveable Feast*. London: Grafton.

Hirsch, Foster, 1981. *Film Noir: The Dark Side of the Screen*. New York: Da Capo.

Hotchner, A.E., 1967. *Papa Hemingway: A Personal Memoir*. London: Weidenfeld & Nicolson.

Johnston, Kenneth G., 1982. '"The Killers": The Background and the Manuscript', *Studies in Short Fiction*, 19.3, 247–51.

Kaminsky, Stuart, 1989. 'Literary Adaptation: "The Killers" – Hemingway, Film Noir, and the Terror of Daylight', in Oliver, *A Moving Picture Feast*, pp. 125–34.

Krutnik, Frank, 1991. *In a Lonely Street: Film Noir, Genre, Masculinity*. London: Routledge.

Kuhn, Annette, 1985. *The Power of the Image*. London: Routledge.

Lacan, Jacques, 1992. *The Ethics of Psychoanalysis, 1959–1960*, ed. Jacques-Alain Miller, trans. Denis Porter. London: Routledge.

Laurence, Frank M., 1981. *Hemingway at the Movies*. Jackson: University Press of Mississippi.

Laurence, Frank M., 1989. 'Hollywood's Publicity and Hemingway's Popular Reception', in Oliver, *A Moving Picture Feast*, pp. 19–25.

Lewis, R.W., 1989. Introduction, in Oliver, *A Moving Picture Feast*, pp. xi–xvi.

Luhr, William, 1991. *Raymond Chandler and Film*. Talahassee: Florida State University Press.

Marling, William, 1995. *The American Roman Noir: Hammett, Cain and Chandler*. Athens, GA: University of Georgia Press.

Mayer, Robert, 2002. 'Introduction: Is there a text in the screening room?' in *Eighteenth-Century Fiction on Screen*. ed. Robert Mayer. Cambridge: Cambridge University Press, pp. 1–15.

Munby, Jonathan, 1999. *Public Enemies, Public Heroes: Screening the Gangster from Little Caesar to Touch of Evil*. Chicago: University of Chicago Press.

Naremore, James, 1998. *More than Night: Film Noir in its Contexts*. Berkeley: University of California Press.

Oliver, Charles M., ed., 1989. *A Moving Picture Feast: The Filmgoer's Hemingway*. New York: Praeger.

Palmer, R. Barton, 2004. 'The Sociological Turn of Adaptation Studies: The Example of *Film Noir*', in *A Companion to Literature and Film*, eds Robert Stam and Alessandra Raengo. Oxford: Blackwell, pp. 258–78.

Phillips, Gene D., 1980. *Hemingway and Film*. New York: Frederick Ungar.

Porfirio, Robert, 1996. '*The Killers*: Expressiveness of Sound and Image in *Film Noir*', in *Film Noir Reader*, eds Alain Silver and James Ursini. New York: Limelight, pp. 177–87.

Schickel, Richard, 1992. *Double Indemnity*. London: BFI.

Selby, Spencer, 1984. *Dark City: The Film Noir*. Jefferson: McFarland.

Shadoian, Jack, 2003. *Dreams and Dead Ends: The American Gangster Film*, 2nd edn. New York: Oxford University Press.

Shaviro, Steven, 1993. *The Cinematic Body*. Minneapolis: Minnesota University Press.

Smith, Paul, 1998. 'Introduction: Hemingway and the Practical Reader', in *New Essays on Hemingway's Short Fiction*, ed. Paul Smith. Cambridge: Cambridge University Press, pp. 1–18.

Turim, Maureen, 1989. *Flashbacks in Film: Memory and History*. New York: Routledge.

Tusca, John, 1984. *Dark Cinema: American Film Noir in Cultural Perspective*. Westport, CT: Greenwood Press.

Walker, Michael, 1992. 'Robert Siodmak', in *The Movie Book of Film Noir*, ed. Ian Cameron. London: Studio Vista, pp. 110–51.

Žižek, Slavoj, 1997. *The Plague of Fantasies*. London: Verso.

Burning Too: Consuming Fahrenheit 451

MARK BOULD

> He loved the crisp feel of books, the supple shine of aged
> leather, the *snick snick snick* of flipped pages. But to *read*? No
> one did that anymore. And surely the value of a collectible did
> not depend on its mere use, not in this Tits 'n' Glitz age.
>
> Gregory Benford (1996: 28)

I

RECENTLY, HOLLYWOOD HAS DECIDED THAT certain pulp science fiction
(SF) authors and/or titles have sufficient cultural cachet – or familiar-
ity – to possess marquee value.[1] Following the eventual critical success of
Blade Runner (Scott 1982) and the commercial success of its so-called
Director's Cut (1991) and *Total Recall* (Verhoeven 1990), there has been
a cycle of adaptations of pulp SF not only by Philip K. Dick but also by
Isaac Asimov, Lester del Rey, Robert Heinlein and Frank Herbert.[2]
Therefore, despite the relative critical and commercial failures of two
recent remakes of SF films previously adapted from literary sources –
Planet of the Apes (Burton 2001), *Solaris* (Soderbergh 2002) – the currently in-production remake/adaptation of Ray Bradbury's *Fahrenheit 451*
(1953) makes (Hollywood) sense. It is a pre-sold title by a frequently

---

[1] The term 'pulp' is derived from the cheap paper upon which US fiction
magazines were published in the first half of the twentieth century. It is not
intended as a value judgement, but merely as a way of referring to a specific US tradition of magazine and paperback SF. See Ashley 2000; Carter
1977; Clareson 1990; James 1994; James and Mendlesohn 2003; and Landon
1997.

[2] For example, see *Minority Report* (Spielberg 2002); *I, Robot* (Proyas 2004);
Mimic (del Toro 1997); *Starship Troopers* (Verhoeven 1997); and the TV
miniseries *Dune* (Harrison 2000). This cycle of SF remakes and adaptations
extends beyond literary sources, with a number of films reworking successful
SF TV series, like *Lost in Space* (Hopkins 1998) and *Thunderbirds* (Frakes
2004). The success of the *Harry Potter* and *The Lord of the Rings* movies has
undoubtedly prompted further Hollywood interest in pre-sold fantastic titles,
regardless of genre.

adapted celebrity author,[3] and the original adaptation, François Truffaut's *Fahrenheit 451* (1966), not only looks dated but also fails to develop those potentially spectacular elements of the novel favoured by contemporary Hollywood. Moreover, screenwriter-director Frank Darabont's first two films as director, *The Shawshank Redemption* (1994) and *The Green Mile* (1999), were both adaptations scripted by himself; financially successful, especially on video and DVD, they also attracted eleven Academy Award nominations. It is, therefore, an apparently safe commercial package, and thus not too hazardous to speculate about: it will showcase CGI effects; the chase sequence will be extended, multiplied; some version of the Mechanical Hound, absent from Truffaut's version, will be reinstated; and so on. But beyond this it is difficult to imagine what a new version might offer. This is neither a reflex derogation of Hollywood nor a championing of source over adaptation. Rather, my concern (or failure of imagination) is that, with the exception of marginal elements concerned with homosexuality and race Darabont's film is unlikely to develop, the novel has already been exhausted: by Truffaut's complexly and critically faithful film; and, as my conclusion will suggest, by an unofficial adaptation, *Equilibrium* (Wimmer 2002).

This essay will consider the critical reception of both Bradbury's and Truffaut's *Fahrenheit 451*.[4] It will consider the novel as a quintessential product of the 1950s and as a rejection of Campbellian world-building; the nature of the film's 'faithfulness' to the novel, despite the changes it introduces to plot, characterisation, and *mise-en-scène*; and how the novel's incoherent conceptualisation of texts and textuality ultimately forces the film to break with it. In closing, this essay will demonstrate

---

[3] Other adaptations of Bradbury's fiction include *The Beast from 20,000 Fathoms* (Lourie 1953), *Icarus Montgolfier Wright* (Engel 1962), *The Illustrated Man* (Smight 1969), *Picasso Summer* (Bourguignon and Sallin 1969), *The Martian Chronicles* (Anderson 1980), *There Will Come Soft Rains* (Tulyakhodzhaev 1982), *Something Wicked This Way Comes* (Clayton 1983), *V'eld* (Tulyakhodzhaev 1987) and *The Wonderful Ice Cream Suit* (Gordon 1998), as well as various episodes of *The Twilight Zone* (1959–64, 1985–7) and *Ray Bradbury Theatre* (1985–6).

[4] Space prevents consideration of Bradbury's 'Bonfire', 'Bright Phoenix', 'The Exiles', 'Usher II', and 'The Pedestrian', short stories in which the novel germinated; Bradbury's 25,000-word novella 'The Fireman' (1951), which he expanded into the novel; Bradbury's 1979 stage adaptation; Walter M. Miller's *A Canticle for Leibowitz* (1960), which can almost be read as a sequel to Bradbury's novel; Gregory Benford's affectionate riposte, 'Centigrade 233' (1994); or Michael Carin's *The Neutron Picasso* (1989), and Terry Bisson's *The Pickup Artist* (2001), both of which offer variants on Bradbury's book-burning conceit.

how *Equilibrium* draws to the surface two elements of the novel that Bradbury himself could not express (although *Equilibrium*'s own understanding of them is problematic).

But first, a reminder of the novel's plot. Guy Montag is a fireman, but in this future USA all books are banned and the role of the fireman is to burn books, not extinguish fires. His wife, Mildred, spends her days watching the three wall-sized TV screens, which dominate their living room. Into Montag's affectless life comes sixteen-year-old Clarisse McLellan, who like her family rejects the high-velocity, media-saturated modern world, preferring conversation and the contemplation of nature. She and her family are soon made to disappear. For some time, Montag has been taking and hiding books. One day, he steals a book from a house whose owner commits suicide by igniting the kerosene the firemen have sprayed over her forbidden collection. This act of self-destruction, more than the book-theft, triggers a crisis in Montag. Fire Captain Beatty indicates that he is aware of Montag's crime and gives him the opportunity to return the book. Having failed to persuade Mildred that books must have some special worth, Montag seeks out Faber, a former English professor he suspects of being a reader, for advice. Montag is anxious about wanting to appear repentant when he returns the book, so Faber wires him so that he can hear everything Montag hears and advise him how to respond. Back at home, Montag confronts Mildred and her friends, and reads Arnold's 'Dover Beach' to them. The distressed women flee. Montag heads to the firehouse, to a confrontation with Beatty. A call comes in and the firemen, including Montag, race out into the night – to Montag's own house. Mildred leaves. Beatty insists that Montag starts the fire. Montag turns the flame-thrower on him and flees, pursued by a Mechanical Hound. Having escaped from the city, he joins a band of hoboes who, as Granger explains, are dedicated to memorising books. As the novel ends, a nuclear war, presaged throughout, breaks out, destroying the city from which Montag fled. (Truffaut's film more or less follows this plot, but expands Clarisse's role, renames Mildred as Linda and omits Faber, the Mechanical Hound and the nuclear conflagration.)

II

Truffaut's film rarely receives more than passing comment in academic and popular writing on SF cinema. Various reasons for this can be postulated. In academic criticism, discussions of Truffaut generally emerge

from a concern with auteurism rather than genre, constructing his melo-
dramas as a non-generic norm and considering his several crime films a
more significant engagement with genre than his solitary SF film. In
popular criticism, the situation stems from the specific history of pulp SF.
For many years, it was a commonplace of folk SF criticism[5] that SF films
were inferior to written SF, and inevitably so. The reason for this was
that during the 1950s boom in US SF cinema, most producers ignored
the written genre, instead churning out monster movies.[6] This was
particularly galling to a folk criticism that had witnessed the wartime
revolution in pulp SF spearheaded by John W. Campbell, Jr, editor of
Astounding from 1937,[7] and the refashioning of pulp SF in *Galaxy* and
The Magazine of Fantasy and Science Fiction in the 1950s. Thus deploring
SF film became the norm in certain SF circles. However, with regard to
Truffaut's film, this default position is complicated by folk criticism's attitude towards Bradbury. The only major pulp SF writer of his generation
unable to sell to Campbell's *Astounding*, he was also the first pulp SF
writer to appear regularly, although not necessarily with SF, in non-pulp
and middlebrow publications like *Collier's*, *The Saturday Evening Post*,
and *The New Yorker* and prestige anthologies like *The Best American
Short Stories of 1946* and *O. Henry Prize Stories of 1947*.[8] Consequently,
while the SF community frequently brandished Bradbury as exemplify-
ing SF's maturity (a posture made more credible by the praise lavished on
him by Christopher Isherwood and Kingsley Amis), it also considered

[5] 'Folk SF criticism' refers to the criticism by authors, editors, reviewers, readers,
and fans that was produced within the pulp tradition and the organised fandom
that grew up around and as part of it.

[6] It was, however, a pulp adaptation – *Destination Moon* (Pichel 1950), adapted
by the leading Campbellian SF author Heinlein from his own *Rocketship Galileo*
(1947) – that triggered the boom, and those 1950s SF films that have best stood
the test of time, like *The Day the Earth Stood Still* (Wise 1951) and *The Thing
(from another world)* (Nyby 1951), were adapted from pulp sources. (For a rather
different and more sophisticated discussion of the impossibility of SF cinema,
see Freedman 2002.)

[7] See Berger 1993 and Westfahl 1998.

[8] Bradbury's relationship with the genre in the early 1950s is perhaps best
exemplified by *Fahrenheit 451*'s publication history. The novella 'The Fireman'
was rejected by various SF magazines before being appearing in 1951 in the
second issue of *Galaxy*. In 1953, the newly founded Ballantine Books launched
its SF line with novels by Frederik Pohl and Cyril Kornbluth, Arthur C.
Clarke, Theodore Sturgeon, and Ray Bradbury, who was asked to expand 'The
Firemen'. The resulting novel was also serialised in issues 2–4 of the newly
launched *Playboy*.

him an author of SF 'for those who do not like sf' (Aldiss 1975: 296), as is evident in the suggestion by Damon Knight, writing in the mid-1950s, that 'To Bradbury, as to most people, radar and rocket ships and atomic power are big, frightening, meaningless things: a fact which, no doubt, has something to do with his popular success' (1967: 109). James Blish, writing in the early 1950s as William Atheling, Jr, repeatedly addressed this contradictory attitude towards Bradbury:

> The story is the thing; Bradbury writes stories, and usually remarkable ones; he is of course a scientific blindworm, but in the face of such artistry, it's dif- ficult to care. [...] Probably, I would add, Mr. Bradbury did us good: In the heyday of the scientifically accurate story, bus-bars often got substituted for plots, and more generally speaking respect for facts went hand in hand with ignorance of writing. As I say, the purists have lost that battle, and everybody benefits by the loss. [...] I have said enough about Bradbury at this juncture to make it plain that I am not unqualifiedly admiring of his work, and that in some respects I think he has been bad for the field. [...] Whatever you may think of Bradbury as a writer of *science fiction*, it's already plain that he's a superb technician, that he is also something of a poet, and that, above all, he almost always knows exactly what he's doing. (1973: 48, 87, 89)

This essay will argue that the basis for these criticisms lies in Bradbury's rejection of Campbellian world-building, but first it will consider the popular criticism of Truffaut's film in which a series of similar dichotomies and ambivalences can be observed.

Unsurprisingly, complaints that the film is insufficiently like the book dominate. Brosnan and Nicholls write that 'The film is more ambigu- ous than the book and, so to speak, lacks its fire; Truffaut seems not altogether to accept Bradbury's moral simplicity' (in Clute and Nicholls 1993: 401). Hardy bemoans the absence of Bradbury's 'polemical sharp- ness' in 'Truffaut's worst film', suggesting that it 'suffers from its director's commitment to character [...] at the expense of the novel's vision of life', but he also praises the depiction of the Fire Captain because, unlike the novel's Beatty, 'he is a rounded, sympathetic character rather than a mere functionary' (1995: 251, 252). Wright complains that 'the film is curiously flat and uneventful' (1983: 143). Baxter considers it 'a less than courageous failure', offering only 'a vague retelling of the original story' (1970: 202). Pohl and Pohl IV note that when Truffaut 'discussed the score with composer Bernard Herrmann, he concurred that "his score should not have any meaning" – and surely he got what he asked for' (1981: 192–3); moreover, had Truffaut possessed 'Kubrick's finicking and inventive attention to detail' the film might have obtained 'enough solidity to engage an audience's emotions. Bradbury's own poet's disdain for plausibility might have made it an allegorical delight' (1981: 193).[9] Wingrove concludes that the film

> should never have been made. Bradbury's tale worked because it was in the literary medium; transferred to another medium the whole tenor of its argument (for film is, to a greater degree than literature, a passive medium) crumbled. That's why Truffaut could not keep Bradbury's black-and-white argument: it argued against his medium. What resulted is occasionally beautiful but generally severely flawed. (1985: 90)

Arguably, these complaints about the film's failure to be like the novel mediate a dissatisfaction with the film's failure to be like a conventional action-adventure movie: it lacks moral simplicity, polemical sharpness, characters as plot-functions, eventfulness, a precise retelling of a familiar tale, unequivocal meaning, solidity, emotional appeal, allegorical transparency, a passive-viewing position, and a clear-cut argument, while demonstrating ambiguity, a commitment to characters, and an intellectual appeal. While these critics often seem to attribute qualities to Bradbury's novel that it does not possess,[10] only Brosnan and Nicholls seem uncertain as to whether the values of the novel are actually preferable to those of the film; but more significant is the extent to which these criticisms of the film mirror earlier folk criticism of Bradbury. For example, Atheling, who repeatedly admires Bradbury's 'poetic' style, mentions 'those who complain, of such writers as Ray Bradbury, that much recent science fiction isn't sufficiently realistic' (1973: 26); similarly, admiration for the film's cinematography (by Nicolas Roeg) often mitigates complaints about the film's lack of persuasive extrapolation and concrete detail. By transposing Bradbury's supposed faults on to the film, it is possible to recuperate him into the core of pulp SF.

III

Knight observed that Bradbury's usual 'subject is childhood and the buried child-in-man; his aim is to narrow the focus, not to widen it; to shrink all the big frightening things to the compass of the familiar: a

---

[9] Coincidentally, at one point Truffaut approached Pohl to write the screenplay.
[10] For example, Hardy seems to mistake passages of sharp polemic from various mouthpiece characters for a polemically sharp novel.

spaceship to a tin can; a Fourth of July rocket to a brass kettle; a lion to a Teddy bear' (1967: 110).[11] Here, as invariably elsewhere, criticisms of Bradbury's 'prepubertal' imagination are bound up in accusations of Luddism,[12] a critical tendency that is better understood as a reaction to his refusal of the kind of expansionist SF, rigorous SF world-building methodologies and varieties of 'cognition effect'[13] espoused by Campbell and exemplified by Heinlein.[14]

Campbell demanded that SF authors extrapolate in rigorous detail feasible and consistent worlds but only reveal those details important to the story – and that he or she do so not through exposition but through the skilful deployment, in passing, of telling detail from which the reader could construct the imagined social totality.[15] Heinlein's *Beyond this Horizon* (1948) opens as

> Hamilton Felix let himself off at the thirteenth level of the Department of Finance, mounted a slideway to the left, and stepped off the strip at a door [...]. He punched the door with a code combination, and awaited face check. It came promptly; the door dilated, and a voice inside said, 'Come in, Felix.'

Discussions of this passage focus on the dilating door and its ability to conjure a frisson of difference – as Harlan Ellison wrote, 'And no discussion. Just "the door dilated". I read across it, and was two lines down

---

[11] In his seminal theorisation of SF, Suvin twice dismisses Bradbury in a similar vein (see Suvin 1979: 68, 141). While (imagined) childhood is undoubtedly central to Bradbury's sentimentalism and nostalgia, both popular and academic criticism tend to conflate immaturity and irrationality with fantasy, and maturity and reason with SF – as if Bradbury's nostalgic reconstruction of 'childlike' simplicity are manifestations of something definitional of fantasy (as SF's Other). The gendered nature of this opposition is suggested by Watt's discussion of the characters around Montag: 'The men are the intellectual and didactic forces at work on Montag, while the women are the intuitive and experiential forces. Beatty articulates the system's point of view, but Mildred lives it. Faber articulates the opposition's point of view, but Clarisse lives it' (1980: 197).
[12] Bradbury's attitude towards technology is more complex than this characterisation allows; and as Bleiler 1998 demonstrates, pulp SF has a long history of anti-technological stories.
[13] See Freedman 2000: 17–19.
[14] Benford's 'Centigrade 233' fondly mocks this refusal: 'It was raining, of course. Incessantly, gray and gentle, smoothing the rectangular certainties of the city into moist matters of opinion' (1996: 24).
[15] See Westfahl 1998: 179–204.

before I realised what the image had been, what the words had urged forth. A *dilating* door. It didn't open, it *irised!* Dear God, now I knew I was in a future world' (quoted in Westfahl 1998: 223). However, by Campbell's standards, this ludicrous door should have provoked negative comment. The 'thirteenth' floor of a government building suggests massive bureaucracy (as well as ill-fortune). Slideways, keycodes, and automated ID verification evoke high levels of automation. But the door is a mere conceit. Increased automation and bureaucratisation could easily be extrapolated from contemporary trends, but while the door adds to the sense of an automated world (perhaps even suggesting an eye and, therefore, surveillance), the lack of a reasonable design-rationale makes it anomalous. Consequently, this frequently lauded moment actually represents a failure of technique – something evident, if not stated, in Ellison's account of its disruptive effect – which is significant in at least two respects. First, it indicates the epistemological shortcomings of an SF world-building predicated upon reducing complex multiple determinants to straightforwardly explicable causal chains, and to the necessity of breaking with this model, if only occasionally, to produce textured fictional worlds. Second, it indicates the extent to which Bradbury's world-building methodology – the introduction of the innovations necessary for the telling of a particular story into a represented world not unlike the extratextual present – might actually be superior because, by default, it allows for ambiguous determination and the differential temporalities of development.

The world of Bradbury's novel is an exaggerated Cold War suburbia. In the immediate postwar period, changes to the American urban landscape foregrounded the dialectical interaction of centripetal and centrifugal spatial tendencies.[16] While centripetal space is organised (and not just geographically) around a central business district, centrifugal space (along with the mass media) opposes centration, dispersing the city. Utopian and dystopian traditions in SF have often focused on centred cities,[17] but in *Fahrenheit 451* and other 1950s SF the centrifugal suburb becomes the key location.[18] Bradbury's novel gives very little sense of an urban centre: it might have sliding walks (13) instead of the

[16] See Dimendberg 2004.
[17] See, for example, *Metropolis* (Lang 1926), *Things to Come* (Menzies 1936), and James Blish's *Cities in Flight* novels (1955, 1956, 1958, 1962).
[18] See, for example, Clifford D. Simak's *City* (1952), Frederik Pohl and Cyril M. Kornbluth's *Gladiator-at-Law* (1955), *Invasion of the Body Snatchers* (Siegel 1956), and *The Incredible Shrinking Man* (Arnold 1957).

suburbs' 'unused buckling sidewalks' (12); it is found at the other end of a clean and efficient subway system and at the hub of 'wide empty thoroughfare[s] ten lanes wide' (131). Although these transport structures centre the city (Bradbury's use of 'boulevard' (132) evokes the Haussmannisation of Paris), they function in the novel, which opens with Montag travelling outwards, as dispersal routes.

Montag's house is full of modern conveniences, including an automatic front door, a robotic toaster whose 'spidery metal hand' (26) butters the toast, and doorbells and telephones that call the owner's name. Most significantly, giant TV screens have replaced three living room walls, and Mildred is anxious to get a fourth installed because then 'it'd be just like this room wasn't ours at all, but all kinds of exotic people's room' (28). Beyond their geographical features, centripetal and centrifugal space also constitute 'set[s] of cultural attitudes and beliefs' (Dimendberg 2004: 99). Much of the discourse around centrifugal space is concerned with establishing distance, whether between work and home, public space and private space, extended kinship networks and nuclear families, tradition and modernity, different classes, different ethnicities; it is about social atomisation, the replacement of community or collective identities with pseudo-individuated masses and privatised dissent valorised as individualism, self-determination, and privacy. *Fahrenheit 451* catalogues the stereotypical concerns such atomisation prompted in the 1950s: tranquillisers, sleeping pills, psychiatry, and counselling to enable individuals to 'fit in'; juvenile delinquency, drag-racing, rock'n'roll; the suburban housewife with nothing to do all day; kaffeeklatsches, cocktail parties, consumer durables, and credit-purchases; comic books, lurid paperbacks, pornography, advertising and other mass cultural debasements; a politics predicated on the personal grooming of rival candidates; censorship; abstract art; correct parenting; marriages, divorces, abortions, and Caesareans; martinis and misogyny. Montag himself resembles Ed Avery (James Mason) in *Bigger than Life* (Ray 1956), both of whom are employed by hierarchical corporate structures, vaguely dissatisfied, risking burn-out and nervous breakdown; and like Ron Kirby (Rock Hudson) in *All That Heaven Allows* (Sirk 1955), Montag breaks with that life and escapes into some version of the wilderness.[19]

---

[19] The flight from the domesticated masculinity required by postwar Fordist economic reorganisation represented by this nostalgia for an earlier form of masculinity – which can be understood as manifesting 'a desire to return to an earlier stage of capitalism before the rise of mass culture, when male subjectivity

Bradbury's metaphoric structures, which are generally based around simple dichotomies (heat/cold, light/dark, white/black, fire/water, organism/technology), help to generate the sense of atomisation that underpins his hyperbolisation of centrifugal attitudes and beliefs, while his explicit images of atomisation concern walls and bodily disintegration. Every house is sealed off from the world by a fireproof plastic sheath. Windows and, therefore, houselights are a rare sight because TV screens have replaced whole walls. Mildred's life revolves around these wall-screens: she visits friends and friends visit her to watch TV together; she believes that she shares a relationship with the regular TV characters, calling them her family and fearing for their safety if the firemen burn down her house. This cocooned existence has isolated her from any sense of the passage of time: she cannot believe that it is only a couple of months since the third wallscreen was fitted; and Montag himself needs Clarisse to remind him of the natural world and such markers of time's passing as the blooming of flowers, morning dew, seasonal weather, and the moon. As Montag and Mildred become increasingly estranged, he senses 'there [is] a wall between [them.] Literally not just one wall but, so far, three!' (51); he sees, or perhaps imagines, her 'eyes with a kind of cataract unseen but suspect far behind the pupils' (55–6); and he feels as if he is 'one of the creatures electronically inserted between the slots of the phono-colour walls, speaking, but the speech not piercing the crystal barrier. He could only pantomime, hoping she would turn his way and see him. They would not touch through the glass' (54).

Montag experiences his own body as a collection of fragments. His face is several times described as a mask; he has an 'other self, the subconscious idiot that ran babbling at times, quite independent of will, habit, and conscience' (18); when questioned by Clarisse, he feels 'his body divide itself into a hotness and a coldness, a softness and a hardness, a trembling and a not trembling, the two halves grinding one upon the other' (31); his hand seems to take on a life of its own when it steals the book (45); the book infects and possesses his hands and eyes (48); and he yearns to be given 'back the old face and the old hands' (85). This atomisation of the self culminates in his inability to decide whether it was his hands on the flame-thrower 'or Beatty's reaction to the hands [that] gave him the final push toward murder' (126), reducing his agency to a subsystem of a cybernetic loop.

had supposedly not yet been penetrated by the commodity form' (Corber 1997: 14) – is a vital component of the critique of commodities that Bradbury is unable to articulate but which runs through his novel.

This imagery of separation from a cold, distant and neglectful mother figure, and of a body possessed of an agency beyond conscious control, can, of course, be related to Bradbury's prepubertal imagination, just as the novel's articulation of urban space can be related to Bradbury's own contradictory attitude towards the city. The small town-as-utopia recurs in his fiction, in *Fahrenheit 451* representing what is absent from the superficially similar suburb:

> there used to be front porches. And people sat there sometimes at night, talk-ing when they wanted to talk, rocking, and not talking when they didn't want to talk. Sometimes they just sat there and thought about things, turned things over. My uncle says the architects got rid of the front porches because they didn't look well. But [...] that was merely rationalizing it; the real rea-son, hidden underneath, might be they didn't want people sitting like that, doing nothing, rocking, talking; that was the wrong *kind* of social life. People talked too much. And they had time to think. So they ran off with the porches. And the gardens, too. Not many gardens any more to sit around in. And look at the furniture. No rocking chairs any more. They're too com-fortable. Get people up and running around. (70)

This passage contravenes Campbell's injunction against explaining the differences between the extratextual world and the future extrapolated from it by reintroducing a variety of what Frye called utopian fiction's 'Intourist guide' (1973: 26). Here, Clarisse's textual analysis of her world highlights the relative inability of the Campbellian world-builder to express significant absences from the imagined world. It also points to the kinds of material intrinsic to Bradbury's novel that are most difficult to express in a specifically filmic manner.

Truffaut's solution to this particular instance is twofold. First, he follows the logic of Clarisse's argument and, rather than noting this absence, foregrounds the concomitant presence of television aerials. The title sequence *sans* titles, over which the opening credits are spoken, consists of a series of zooms in on shots of aerials, establishing their ubi-quity; simultaneously, the spoken word introduces the absence of the written word. Later, a neighbour informs Montag (Oskar Werner) that the McLellans were 'special', pointing to their house's lack of a TV aerial. Second, Truffaut's *mise-en-scène* does incorporate elements of Clarisse's exposition. The McLellans' basement does contain a discarded or, more likely, concealed rocking chair, which Clarisse (Julie Christie) explains to Montag in terms abbreviated from the novel. While it is unfamiliar to him, it is notable that when he first started to read, he selected a high-backed chair, not unlike a rocking chair (but minus the rockers), to sit

in. Although Truffaut is unable to make clear the absence of front
porches, something of the supposed naturalness of the rocking chair, an
image of the lost utopian home, is present in Montag's selection of this
chair; for viewers familiar with the novel, the later appearance of a rocking chair makes the general absence of rocking chairs and all that it
implies more pronounced. As this example suggests, Truffaut's attempts
to transpose Bradbury's words into filmic images are not always wholly
successful, and with regard to the polemical passages this is indeed, as
Hardy suggests, because Truffaut humanises Bradbury's mouthpieces and
dissipates some of their rhetoric into telling detail (introducing, in this
at least, some Campbellian discipline).

Truffaut's dependence on *mise-en-scène* to adapt Bradbury's words is
evident in his working through of this 'poetic' passage:

> How like a mirror, too, [Clarisse's] face. Impossible; for how many people did
> you know that refracted your own light to you? People were more often [. . .]
> torches, blazing away until they whiffed out. How rarely did other people's
> faces take of you and throw back to you your own expression, your own
> innermost trembling thought? (18)

Truffaut extends the infantile narcissism underlying Montag's conceptualisation of intersubjectivity throughout the society he depicts: on the
monorail, a young woman kisses her reflection in the window; other
characters caress themselves, stroking the fabric of their clothes with an
air of sensual distraction.[20] Integral to Truffaut's development of
Bradbury's imagery is the scene in which Linda (Julie Christie) packs her
suitcase before leaving Montag. In close-up, with her back to us, Linda,
reflected, regards herself in the mirror, caressing her cheek. The camera
pulls back as she moves to her left to lift down a framed black-and-white
photographic portrait – a more youthful, almost schoolgirl image of
herself – which she puts in her case. This sequence conveys in visual
terms not only Linda's narcissism but also that which is involved
in (Bradbury's) Montag's desire to see himself reflected back in the face
of an other. Such a reflection distorts the other, conforming it to the self,
or eradicates it completely, replacing it with a fantasy of other as self.

---

[20] The film's only sex scene comes when a blood transfusion arouses Linda from
her generally narcotised condition, giving her 'an appetite for all sorts of things'.
Later, we see her stroking her breast, with the front door apparently disabled so
as to prevent Montag entering the house – as if she has not yet returned to her
'normal' condition and finds her more solitary pleasure shameful.

It is typical of Truffaut to predicate his translation of specific passages into filmic images on a critical understanding of the novel. From the opening sequence, in which the firemen slide down the pole, board their bright red fire engine and race off into the countryside, accompanied by a lively musical evocation of youthful playfulness, it is evident that Truffaut has grasped Bradbury's prepubertal imagination. The infantilism infesting Truffaut's future world is best captured by the Fire Captain (Cyril Cusack), played as a slightly addled schoolmaster, who has a toy fire engine in his office and treats the firehouse rather like a public school. As Truffaut recorded in his journal:

> *Fahrenheit 451*, in script form, was a hard and violent film, inspired by worthy sentiments and altogether on the serious side. In shooting it, I realize that I have been trying to give it a lighter tone. [...] I have been viewing the script with a certain detachment, treating the future in the same way as I treated the past in *Jules and Jim* – not trying to ram it down the audience's throat or make them believe in it too deeply. If I had to start the film over, [...] I'd say to the art director, costume designer and cinematographer [...] 'Let's make a film about life as children see it, with the firemen as toy soldiers, the firehouse as a model, and so on.' (1972: 122–3)

Although Bradbury's 'childishness' only became clear during shooting, Truffaut clearly worked to preserve it, as is apparent in his treatment of Montag's relationships with Linda and Clarisse. Pruriently, Bradbury killed off Clarisse before, and because, her sensuous engagement with the world threatened to become an erotic involvement with a man twice her age. Her proximity to this transition can be observed in this sixteen-year- old's claims to be seventeen, and is nervously signalled when the sexually dissatisfied[21] Montag tells Clarisse she makes him 'feel very old and very much like a father' (36). By casting Christie as both Linda and Clarisse, by increasing Clarisse's age to twenty and by not killing her off, Truffaut could have explored the intersection of 'political subversion and erotic passion' (Suvin 2003: 70) typical of dystopian fiction; and the triangularity of Montag's relationship with Linda and Clarisse must have been intriguing to the director of *Jules et Jim* (1961). However, faithful to

---

[21] This dissatisfaction, suggested by descriptions of Montag's bedroom in terms of coldness and the tomb, is addressed directly when Montag turns the flame-thrower on the 'twin beds [which] went up in a great simmering whisper, with more heat and passion and light than he would have supposed them to contain' (124).

Bradbury's prepubertal imagination, Truffaut retained the superficial innocence of Montag's friendship with Clarisse, writing that 'I have desexed Clarisse to avoid involving her and Montag in the kind of adulterous situation which has had a thorough workout in fields outside science fiction' (1972: 123–4).

One aspect of this desexing begins to open up the novel's queerness: Clarisse's close-cut hair which, in contrast to Linda, lends her a boyish appearance. Strick's suggestion that the paternalism of Truffaut's Fire Captain is 'in keeping with one of Bradbury's most persistent themes, the adored but elusive father' (1979: 106) overlooks the homoeroticism of the homosocial worlds both Bradbury and Truffaut construct. Excluded from the homosocial firehouse, rejected by Beatty (whom, oedipally, he must kill), Bradbury's Montag seeks other fathers in Faber and Granger. Queer connotations surround the cloistered, perhaps closeted, Faber: an older, experienced man, he 'picks up' Montag in a park, mentors him and, courtesy of the communications device, enjoys a particularly intimate relationship with the younger man; he envisions himself as a 'Queen bee' (98) with similarly equipped men as his drones. Bradbury's exclusively male book people offer Montag a replacement homosociality, and the suppression of (hetero)sexuality elsewhere in the novel emphasises the queerness of this situation.

In the film, Montag's heterosexual dormancy does not necessarily signal queerness. However, Truffaut's firehouse betrays its homoerotic potential. Two trainee firemen are forbidden to sit together in the classroom. Summoned by the Fire Captain to be reprimanded for some unspecified mischief, they conspire, barely audibly, to tell the same story about having met by accident. After dismissing them, the Captain suggests that Montag 'increase the dosage, more sports for everyone. Hmmm? Strengthen the group spirit. Organise the fun. Hmmm? Just keep them busy and you keep them happy.'[22] Furthermore, Fabian (Anton Diffring) perceives Montag as a rival for the Captain's attention. In one very peculiar shot, when Montag accompanies Clarisse to the school from which she has been dismissed, Diffring briefly appears as a middle-aged woman. His cross-dressed appearance suggests something of Mrs Bates from *Psycho* (Hitchcock 1960), connoting queerness not just as effeminacy but also as menacing. By positing a queer threat, Truffaut foregrounds the occlusion

---

[22] This homophobia is developed by the conflation of long-haired men, intellectualism, and effeminacy apparent in the TV footage of a 'mop-up squad' detaining a long-haired young man, one of the 'messy know-it-alls' who still 'boycott the barbershops', and shaving his head in front of a laughing crowd.

of queer identity Bradbury's prepubertal imaginary must perform in order
to construct homosociality without the homoerotic.[23]

IV

Folk criticism often focuses on the film's concluding image of the book
people: in place of the novel's post-apocalyptic euphoria, with the book
people advancing on the devastated city, Truffaut closes with a static
view of a wintry lake, with the book people, passing back and forth in
front of the camera, muttering to themselves, memorising. While
Bradbury celebrates 'the book people's transformation of themselves
into a living library and arsenal for future revolutionaries', the film
'sees them as zombies' circling 'in the snow endlessly intoning the
world's literature', as 'brainwashed in their commitment to that which
they don't understand as [are] their book-burning persecutors' (Hardy
1995: 251). Fischer complains that Truffaut's book people are not a
'cohesive' community but 'a group of eccentric characters who recite to
themselves [...], each lost in their own little world' and 'as bereft of life
as the television watching drones' (2000: 701),[24] while Montag's rebel-
lion 'simply exchang[es] one authority for another' (Strick 1979: 106),
'one form of chilling pointlessness [...] for another' (Nicholls 1984:
55), or 'allegiance from one interest group to another, equally sterile

[23] Discussing his 'The Better Part of Wisdom', in which a dying man accepts of
his grandson's homosexuality, Bradbury said: 'We all have love affairs when we
are children that are never equalled in our late days ... where you walk through
the world transfigured by your friendship ... the love of being alive in the universe. You walk around, you look at the clouds, you lie on hills, you hold hands,
but you don't even know why you are holding hands – except this is your best
pal' (Johnson 1980: 129; ellipses in original).

[24] The figure of community and revolutionary collectivity provided by
Bradbury's book people is itself more problematic than these criticisms suggest.
As Zipes argues, 'The dystopian constellation of conflict in *Fahrenheit 451* is not
really constituted by the individual versus the state, but the intellectual versus
the masses. The result is that, while Bradbury does amply reflect the means and
ways the state endeavors to manipulate and discipline its citizens in the United
States, he implies that the people, i.e., the masses, have brought this upon
themselves and almost deserve to be blown up so that a new breed of book-
lovers may begin to populate the world. [...] This elitist notion ultimately
defeats the humanistic impulse in Bradbury's critique of mass technology and
totalitarianism [...]. Bradbury [...] exhibits no faith in the masses while trying
to defend humanity' (1983: 191–2, 194).

(if somewhat more romantic) group' (Wingrove 1985: 90). This apparent consensus – and Nicholls's suggestion that Truffaut's 'strange picture is the revenge of a film-maker upon literature' (1984: 55) – is misguided. Unlike Truffaut, it fails to interrogate the novel's own contradictory attitude towards books, and its emphasis on the ending of the film as the meaning of the film[25] detaches the closing sequence from Truffaut's critical reconceptualisation of textuality evident throughout.

Bradbury's Granger says of the book people:

> All we want to do is keep the knowledge we think we will need, intact and safe. We're not out to incite or anger anyone yet. For if we are destroyed, the knowledge is dead, perhaps for good. We are model citizens, in our own special way [...]. We'll pass the books on to our children, by word of mouth, and let our children wait, in turn, on the other people. A lot will be lost that way [...]. But you can't *make* people listen. They have to come round in their time [...]. The most important single thing we had to pound into ourselves was that we were not important [...]; we were not to feel superior to anyone else in the world. We're nothing more than dust-jackets for books, of no significance otherwise. [...] some day, some year, the books can be written again, the people will be called in, one by one, to recite what they know and we'll set it up in type until another Dark Age, when we might have to do the whole damn thing over again. (159–61)[26]

This self-effacement, this refusal of revolutionary consciousness, and this desire to fit into the cracks of the world-machine without disturbing it exemplify a debilitating passivity, which extends to their relationship with the books they preserve. Instrumentalists, they read only to memorise and then destroy the books they have memorised. The novel fetishises books – denies that they are mass-produced commodities and effaces the labour involved in their production – by distinguishing between them and 'dream[s] made or paid for in factories' (165) and mystificatorily evoking the author as solitary genius, as in Montag's realisation that 'a man was behind each one of these books. A man had to think them up. A man had to take a long time to put

[25] On the problems with this kind of reading strategy, common to neoformalist criticism, see Perkins 1990.

[26] A neglected context for Bradbury's novel can be found in the contemporaneous concern of Lionel Trilling and others about the possible death of the novel. See Klein 1969 and Trilling 1950.

them down on paper. [...] It took some man a lifetime maybe to put some of his thoughts down, looking around at the world and life' (59).[27] The book people conform to the new masculinity demanded by postwar Fordist economic reorganisation, replacing industrial capitalism's emphasis on the driven, ambitious, innovatory individual with corporate capitalism's 'personality market', in which 'personal or even intimate traits of the employee are drawn into the sphere of exchange and become of commercial relevance, become commodities in the labor market' (Mills 1956: 182). As Corber argues, this 'signaled the penetration of male subjectivity by the commodity form. The reorganization of work reduced men to instrumentalizing their own appearance in order to increase its exchange-value' (1997: 34–5).

The commodity form has penetrated the passive book people's subjectivity more thoroughly than the employee-commodities selling themselves on the personality market. They are not so much concerned about their appearance as in becoming the appearance – the jackets – for the books they memorise: 'I am Plato's *Republic*,' Granger boasts, 'And this other fellow is Charles Darwin, and this one is Schopenhauer, and this one is Einstein [...]. Here we all are, Montag. Aristophanes and Mahatma Gandhi and Gautama Buddha and Confucius and Thomas Love Peacock and Thomas Jefferson and Mr Lincoln, if you please. We are also Matthew, Mark, Luke and John' (158–9). Colonised by the commodity form, they have become other than themselves (as Granger's introduction of each book person as a mystificatory corpus/author suggests, evoking Marx's argument that under capitalism relations between people become confused with relations between things and its dialectical reversal, that the relations between things become confused with the relations between people). In becoming other than themselves, the book people reify and utterly subordinate themselves to the texts they memorise.

Bradbury's euphoric conclusion is far from unequivocal, in that it also describes Montag preparing for his first public performance of/as the commodity – *Ecclesiastes* – that has overtaken him. Truffaut's ending develops this contradiction by reintroducing the notion of labour. While Bradbury's Granger tells Montag, 'All of us have photographic memories [...] and now we've got the method down to where we can recall anything that's been read once' (158), Truffaut refuses to occlude

---

[27] See also Granger's identification of individual book people with authors rather than particular texts, quoted below. Truffaut's Granger, in contrast, introduces specific book people as specific books by specific authors.

the book people's labour, showing them in the process of memorising, and by doing so foregrounds Bradbury's contradictory attitude towards books, overlooked by so many of the film's critics in their haste to prefer the novel.

One of the epigraphs to Truffaut's *The Films in My Life* quotes Henry Miller's *The Books in My Life*: 'These books were alive and they spoke to me,' a sentiment expressing an active relationship with text (while betraying commodity fetishism). According to Faber, 'quality' books possess 'texture':

> This book has *pores*. It has features. It can go under the microscope. You'd find life under the glass, streaming past in infinite profusion. The more pores, the more truthfully recorded details of life per square inch you can get on a sheet of paper, the more 'literary' you are. That's *my* definition, anyway. *Telling detail*. Fresh detail. The good writers touch life often. The mediocre ones run a quick hand over her. The bad ones rape her and leave her for the flies. [...] now do you see why books are hated and feared? They show the pores in the face of life. The comfortable people only wax moon faces, pore-less, hairless, expressionless. (91)

This contradictory passage is indicative of, if not identical to, Bradbury's conception of the text. It defines quality in terms of an accumulated informational density and depth, *and* of rough edges that demand the reader's active involvement. The latter raises the possibility of the *scriptible*, but the novel's emphasis, evident in the book people's subordination, is on the *lisible*. Truffaut's epigraph implies that he prefers *scriptible* texts, which invite participation and creative dialogue, while his disdain for the *lisible* is clear in his reworking of the scene in which Mildred 'participates' in an interactive TV drama, rendering the invitations to Linda's participation deliberately awkward, stripping away the illusion of interaction. Similarly, while Bradbury presents 'Dover Beach' as an unquestionable work of genius, incomprehensible to Mildred and her friends, Truffaut selects a passage from *David Copperfield*, which speaks not only to Montag's situation but also to that one of Linda's friends, who is moved to tears by its invitation to participate in meaning-making. Truffaut's disruptions of the conventional, continuity-edited film extend a similar invitation.

Baxter's complaint that Truffaut was 'truer to his spiritual father Alfred Hitchcock than to Bradbury' (1970: 202), his homages to the former overwhelming his retelling of the latter, implies that Truffaut's film should, like one of the book people, have utterly subordinated itself to a written text. However, rather than merely memorise, Truffaut actively and critically engaged with Bradbury's novel. His historically and materially situated reading of the novel is manifested in his orientation of the film towards Hitchcock's work. The score, by long-time Hitchcock collaborator Bernard Herrmann, echoes his score for *Vertigo* (1958). Christie's double role recalls Kim Novak's, while Montag's dream recalls Scottie's (James Stewart) in *Vertigo*, even recreating Hitchcock's 'vertigo effect' shot. The long dissolve from Montag's face to Clarisse's face recalls the dissolve from wrongly accused Manny Balestrero (Henry Fonda) to the real criminal in *The Wrong Man* (1957). The book that falls from behind Linda's picture recalls the dead bird that falls from behind a picture in *The Birds* (1963). Baxter's criticism of such homages suggests that they detract from the film by distracting from Bradbury's narrative. However, their disruptions are central to the textuality with which the film replaces Bradbury's confused championing of the *lisible*.

When Clarisse tells Montag about the book people, he mishears her and asks, 'The good people?' 'No,' she replies, 'book. The book people.' In the screenplay, written in French by Truffaut and Jean-Louis Richard (then translated by David Rudkin), this dialogue puns, more effectively, on 'hommes livres' and 'hommes libres', but in either version Truffaut's desire to open up the paradigmatic axis rather than precipitate some headlong syntagmatic rush is clear. Foregrounded intertextuality functions in a similar way, introducing

> anomalies [...] in a text, blocking its development, [and] impel[ling] us toward an intertextual reading. This is because every 'normative' narrative text possesses a certain internal logic. This logic motivates the presence of the various fragments of which the text is made. If a fragment cannot find a weighty enough motivation for its existence from the logic of the text, it becomes an anomaly, forcing the reader to seek its motivation in some other logic or explanatory cause outside of the text. [...] Unable to find a motivation contextually, the reader looks outside the text. (Iampolski 1998: 30)

When the 'calm of mimesis' is thus disturbed, 'we witness the birth of meaning, which is normally transparent wherever mimesis remains untroubled, dissolving into the effortless movement from signifier to signified'; the quotation or allusion severs the 'mimetic link' between 'the sign and objective reality' and orients 'the sign toward another text rather than a thing' (Iampolski 1998: 30). Consequently, Truffaut's Hitchcockian intrusions function as an active remembering, rather than a passive memorisation, of Hitchcock's films, and, like the various enigmas the film poses,[28] as a means of opening a potentially closed text by demanding an active viewer. Contrary to Baxter, this represents a faithfulness to Bradbury: while Campbellian world-building tends towards the construction of hermetic explicable worlds, Bradbury's introduction of anomalies (like Heinlein's door) disturbs cohesion.

Truffaut, however, is committed to a more thoroughgoing disturbance of mimesis. He 'textures' the visual image: the quick cuts of the opening book-burning soon followed by the three-minute take of Montag and Clarisse walking home; the reversed footage when Montag dons the fire-proof suit; the superimposed close-up of Montag as he sits waiting while paramedics treat Linda; the repeated slow-motion close-up of Linda and Montag at the start of the sex scene; the negative film in the dream sequence; the various jump cuts. Truffaut's self-consciously outmoded cinematic grammar produces a similar texturing: the slow iris in onto a photograph of the back of Montag's head; the black vertical wipe that obscures half of the screen while Montag frisks a suspect[29]; and the repeated dissolves to black (and other colours) between sequences. These dissolves are also an homage to Hitchcock, who attempted to create the illusion of a single eighty-minute take by filming *Rope* (1948) in ten-minute takes, each of which ended on a close-up of a block of colour, with the next take starting with a close-up of the same object. Truffaut, in contrast, uses dissolves to blocks of colour to foreground artifice and disrupt normalised viewing. Consequently, these assaults on mimesis constitute Truffaut's greatest faithfulness to Bradbury: not by memorising and regurgitating his novel, but by being more than the mindless transposition its critics seem to want, something other than the kind of text Beatty describes:

> because they had mass, they became simpler. [...] Films and radios, magazines, books levelled down to a sort of paste pudding norm. [...] Books cut

[28] Why does the Fire Captain ask Montag the time, only to conceal, moments later, the wristwatch he is wearing? What are the trainee firemen actually guilty of doing? Why does the young man in the park pretend to be embracing someone? Why does the baby have a miniature book in its pocket? Why is such an emphasis placed on photographs of the back of Montag's head? Is it Fabian in drag who spies on Montag and Clarisse at the school, or is Diffring playing another – female – character in that shot? If the former is the case, why is he in drag? If the latter, why is he playing a female character for one very brief shot? And so on.

[29] This perhaps alludes to André Bazin's championing of deep-focus and long takes over conventional Hollywood shooting practices, which guide the viewer to the narratively important element of the shot rather than allowing the viewer to judge the relative importance of scenic elements.

shorter. Condensations. Digests. Tabloids. Everything boils down to the gag, the snap ending. [...] Classics cut to fit fifteen-minute radio shows, then cut again to fill a two-minute book column, winding up at last as a ten- or twelve-line dictionary résumé. [...] *Click? Pic? Look, Eye, Now, Flick, Here, There, Swift, Pace, Up, Down, In, Out, Why, How, Who, What, Where, Eh? Uh! Bang! Smack! Wallop, Bing, Bong, Boom!* Digest-digests, digest-digest-digests. Politics? One column, two sentences, a headline! Then, in mid-air, all vanishes! Whirl man's mind around about so fast under the pumping hands of publishers, exploiters, broadcasters, that the centrifuge flings off all unnecessary, time-wasting thought! (62; italics in original)

V

At first glance, *Equilibrium* is just another rather silly SF action movie – *The Matrix* (Wachowski brothers 1999) on a shoestring – but it is something more than that: a *Fahrenheit 451* for a post-literate generation. After a globally devastating Third World War, Libria took extreme measures to prevent a Fourth. Every few hours, its inhabitants inject 'intervals' of Prozium which, at the expense of positive emotion, suppresses negative emotions; and Libria is policed by the Grammaton Clerics, a paramilitary order 'whose sole task is to seek out and eradicate the true source of Man's inhumanity to Man, his ability to feel'.

Equilibrium draws out two submerged elements of Bradbury's novel. The first, undeveloped by Truffaut, might emerge in Darabont's adaptation; if so, it will probably be, as with *Equilibrium*, a consequence of casting rather than conscious critique. The second is only hinted at by Truffaut and again does not seem to be a conscious critical development in *Equilibrium*; and it is probably too complex a notion for contemporary 'high concept' filmmaking to pursue.

Bradbury's novel is haunted by the spectre of lynching. Bradbury once said, 'When Hitler burned a book I felt it as keenly, please forgive me, as burning a human, for in the long sum of history they are one and the same flesh' (quoted in Mogen 1986: 107), and has elsewhere claimed that book-burning has never happened in the USA. While the latter statement is simply not true, the former's logic of equivalence is surely unconscionable after the Holocaust, the nuclear- and fire-bombing of Japanese and German cities. Taken together, these statements can be seen to function not only as denial of US wartime atrocities but also, when the novel's treatment of race is taken into account, as a denial of lynching, in which African-American victims would also often be burned. This is peculiar, as the reader is presumably intended to deplore Beatty's failure to distinguish between the burning of *Little Black Sambo* and *Uncle Tom's Cabin*. Equally troubling is Bradbury's description of the soot-covered Montag as 'a minstrel man, burnt-corked' (11) and Montag's later observations about the firemen's shared blackness (40), which contrasts starkly with the emphatic whiteness of Clarisse ('her face was slender and milk-white [...]. Her dress was white [...] the white stir of her face' (13)) and Faber ('He and the white plaster walls inside were much the same. There was white in the flesh of his mouth and cheeks and his hair was white and his eyes had faded, with white in the vague blueness there' (88)). *Equilibrium* amplifies this familiar racist imagery of whiteness threatened by blackness by casting African-American Taye Diggs as Cleric Brandt, who closes in on white 'sense criminal' Cleric John Preston (Christian Bale). This conflict culminates with Preston, immaculate in white, killing darkly clothed Brandt, and thus overthrowing the totalitarian regime. Reading *Fahrenheit 451* after watching *Equilibrium*, one is immediately struck by the ways in which Bradbury conflates degraded mass culture with black(ened) men who must be eradicated.

But why burn books? During *Equilibrium's* opening raid on a rebel hideout, in which numerous paintings are stockpiled, the dissident source of emotion seems to be art; the sequence ends with a flame-thrower being turned on the Mona Lisa.[30] In Bradbury's *Fahrenheit 451* all books are burned, but only literary 'greats' are mentioned. *Equilibrium* follows the example of Truffaut, who cuts from the destruction of *The Brothers Karamazov* to *Lolita* to *No Orchids for Miss Blandish*, pushing Bradbury's logic even further than Truffaut takes it, arguing that 'sense offenses' are not just triggered by paintings or poems,[31] but 'all those things that might tempt us to feel again': records, films, 'two-dimensional

---

[30] This alludes to Bradbury's 'The Smile', in which a boy is only able to save a fragment of the Mona Lisa from destruction.

[31] It is tempting to read *Equilibrium's* foregrounding of Yeats's 'He Wishes for the Cloths of Heaven' as a response to Bradbury's claim to be a more significant poet than Yeats: 'Some of the poems that have popped out of my head in the last two years are incredible [...] – good god, they're *good*. I have written at least three poems that are going to be around 70 years, 100 years from now. Just three poems you say? But the reputation of most of the great poets are based on only one or two poems. I mean, when you think of Yeats, you think of *Sailing to Byzantium*, and then I defy you, unless you're a Yeats fiend, to name six other poems' (quoted in Platt 1980: 1987). Unfortunately, the interviewer did not conduct a survey to see whether anyone can name a single Bradbury poem.

illustrated material', 'discs of musical content', 'interactive strategy computer games', and so on. While Truffaut depicts a world obsessed with commodities,[32] in *Equilibrium* it is the commodity form itself that is problematic. During various raids on dissident hoards, we are presented with rooms full of posters, prints, cheesecake pin-ups, glitterballs, executive toys, stereos, gramophones, rocking horses, ornaments, jewellery, binoculars, paperweights, children's books, perfume bottles and all manner of bric-a-brac. In contrast, Cleric Preston's apartment is decorated with a minimalism designed to evoke mere functionalism (although it is too stylish to do this effectively). This contrast represents Libria's attempt to eradicate not emotion but an aspect of commodity fetishism. As the massed ranks of Librians' resemblance to *Metropolis*'s trudging proletarians demonstrates, Libria has no interest in restoring the human relationship between producers that the commodity obscures. Rather, Libria seeks to eradicate the process by which consumers over-invest in the commodity fetish because it prompts desire, jealousy, selfishness, anger, rage, war.

Beatty's speech quoted above contains a tantalising suggestion of a passage from *The Communist Manifesto*: 'All fixed, fast-frozen relations, with their train of ancient and venerable prejudices and opinions are swept away, all new formed ones become antiquated before they can ossify. All that is solid melts into air, all that is holy is profaned' (Marx and Engels 1992: 6). Beatty's description of endless disruption and distraction is not dissimilar to Marx and Engels's description of capitalism's energy:

> The bourgeoisie cannot exist without constantly revolutionizing the instruments of production, and thereby the relations of production, and with them the whole relations of society. [...] Constant revolutionizing of production, uninterrupted disturbance of all social conditions, ever-lasting uncertainty and agitation distinguish the bourgeois epoch from all earlier ones. [...] The need of a constantly expanding market for its products chases the bourgeoisie over the whole surface of the globe. It must nestle everywhere, settle everywhere, establish connections everywhere. (1992: 6)

This passage begins to suggest one function of book-burning in Bradbury's novel that he himself is unable to express clearly, but which

---

[32] This is evident in the decor of the Montags' house, which imagines a future of 1960s design, and foregrounded in the sequence in which Linda presents Montag with a cut-throat razor, saying 'It's the very latest thing, everyone's using them now. Can I throw your old one away?', and then drops his rather modern electric razor in the bin.

Equilibrium perceives: consumption. While Libria attempts to eradicate (excessive) commodity fetishism while leaving the commodity form intact, for Bradbury's bookburners books represent use-value in excess of exchange-value. Unlike the rapid, immediate, instant, and promptly forgotten gratifications of Bradbury's massified media and fashionable commodities, books are not used up as they are read. The first lines of Bradbury's novel suggest capitalism's rapacious creative destruction:

> It was a pleasure to burn
>   It was a special pleasure to see things eaten, to see things blackened and *changed*. With the brass nozzle in his fists, with this great python spitting its venomous kerosene upon the world, the blood pounded in his head, and his hands were the hands of some amazing conductor playing all the sym-phonies of blazing and burning to bring down the tatters and charcoal ruins of history. (11)

But the connection between burning and consumption, always present as a possible pun,[33] only comes into focus once, when Montag imagines Beatty coaching him to burn books:

> Watch. Delicately, like the petals of a flower. Light the first page, light the second page. Each becomes a black butterfly. Beautiful, eh? Light the third page from the second and so on, chain-smoking, chapter by chapter, all the silly things the words mean, all the false promises, all the second-hand notions and time-worn philosophies. (84)[34]

Only by destroying the syntagmatic chains, replacing history with the euphoric present, can the exchange-value's triumph over use-value be assured; but that is not how books work, as Truffaut demonstrates when Montag begins to read *David Copperfield*. The sequence starts with the book at three-quarters in close-up, before cutting to a close-up square-on to the book. Montag traces his finger beneath the lines of text, his voice pausing as he reaches the end of each line and returns to the start of the next. Cut to an extreme close-up of the page, and the camera

---

[33] It is also evident in the novel's 'distinctly oral images of happiness' (Touponce 1984: 108)—a different sense of consumption, but one that is nonetheless related to consumerism through Montag's complaint: 'I'm so damned unhappy, I'm so mad, and I don't know why I feel like I'm putting on weight. I feel fat. I feel like I've been saving up a lot of things, and don't know what' (71).

[34] For some suggestive comments on the significance of smoking in Bradbury's *Fahrenheit 451*, see McGiveron 1996: 253.

pans along each line of text (with the lines above and below always visible, and the lines printed on the other side of the page visible through it), before whip-panning back to the start of the next, an effect which, through the difference between camera-movement and eye-movement, accentuates the materiality of reading and the physical endurance of the text beyond the moment of reading-consumption. Thus it is necessary to burn books, and again Truffaut captures this logic visually: in one book-burning montage, a volume of Dali reproductions flicks, courtesy of jump cuts, from page to page, revealing each image before the page turns and is consumed.

VI

Capital always seeks to maximise exchange-value. One way to do this is through the logic of obsolescence, which prevents maximal use-value being derived from a commodity. While it would be appropriate to conclude with a discussion of how Darabont's movie demonstrates the tendency to maximise the exchange-value derivable from Bradbury's novel, this essay will instead draw attention to an alternative to Bradbury's book-burning proposed in Terry Bisson's *The Pickup Artist*: print John Grisham novels on acid-rich paper.

With thanks to Andrew M. Butler, Carl Freedman, Kathrina Glitre, David Seed and, of course, Fugazi.

Works Cited

Aldiss, Brian W., 1975. *Billion Year Spree: The History of Science Fiction*. London: Corgi.

Ashley, Mike, 2000. *The Time Machines: The Story of the Science-Fiction Pulp Magazines from the Beginning to 1950. The History of the Science-Fiction Magazine*, vol. I. Liverpool: Liverpool University Press.

Atheling, William, Jr, 1973. *The Issue at Hand*, 2nd edn, ed. and intro. James Blish. Chicago: Advent.

Baxter, John, 1970. *Science Fiction in the Cinema*. New York: A.S. Barnes & Co.

Benford, Gregory, 1996. 'Centigrade 233', *Matter's End*. London: Victor Gollancz, pp. 24–38.

Berger, Albert I., 1993. *The Magic That Works: John W. Campbell and the American Response to Technology*. San Bernadino, CA: Borgo.

Bisson, Terry, 2001. *The Pickup Artist*. New York: Tor.

Bleiler, Everett F. with Bleiler, Richard J., 1998. *Science-Fiction: The Gernsback Years*. Kent. OH: Kent State University Press.

Bradbury, Ray, 1993. *Fahrenheit 451*. London: Flamingo.

Carter, Paul A., 1977. *The Creation of Tomorrow: Fifty Years of Magazine Science Fiction*. New York: Columbia University Press.

Clareson, Thomas D., 1990. *Understanding Contemporary American Science Fiction: The Formative Period, 1926–1970*. Columbia, SC: University of South Carolina Press.

Clute, John and Nicholls, Peter, eds, 1993. *The Encyclopedia of Science Fiction*. London: Orbit.

Corber, Robert J., 1997. *Homosexuality in Cold War America: Resistance and the Crisis of Masculinity*. Durham. NC: Duke University Press.

Dimendberg, Edward, 2004. *Film Noir and the Spaces of Modernity*. Cambridge. MA: Harvard University Press.

Fischer, Dennis, 2000. *Science Fiction Film Directors*. Jefferson, NC: MacFarland.

Freedman, Carl, 2000. *Critical Theory and Science Fiction*. Hanover. NH: Wesleyan University Press/University Press of New England.

Freedman, Carl, 2002. 'On Kubrick's 2001: Form and Ideology in Science-Fiction Cinema', *The Incomplete Projects: Marxism, Modernity, and the Politics of Culture*. Middletown, CT: Wesleyan University Press, pp. 91–112.

Frye, Northrop, 1973. 'Varieties of Literary Utopia', in F.E. Manuel, ed., *Utopias and Utopian Thought*. London: Souvenir Press, pp. 25–49.

Hardy, Phil, ed., 1995. *The Aurum Film Encyclopedia: Science Fiction*. London: Aurum.

Iampolski, Mikhail, 1998. *The Memory of Tiresias: Intertextuality and Film*, trans. Harsha Ram. Berkeley: University of California Press.

James, Edward, 1994. *Science Fiction in the Twentieth Century*. Oxford: Oxford University Press.

James, Edward and Mendlesohn, Farah, eds, 2003. *The Cambridge Companion to Science Fiction*. Cambridge: Cambridge University Press.

Johnson, Wayne L., 1980. *Ray Bradbury*. New York: Frederick Ungar.

Klein, Marcus, ed., 1969. *The American Novel Since World War II*. Greenwich, CT: Fawcett.

Knight, Damon, 1967. *In Search of Wonder*, 2nd edn, rev. and enlarged. Chicago: Advent.

Landon, Brooks, 1997. *Science Fiction After 1900: From the Steam Man to the Stars*. New York: Twayne.

McGiveron, Rafeeq Q., 1996. 'What "Carried the Trick"? Mass Exploitation and the Decline of Thought in Ray Bradbury's *Fahrenheit 451*', *Extrapolation*, 37.3, 245–56.

Marx, Karl and Engels, Friedrich, 1992. *The Communist Manifesto*, trans. Samuel Moore, ed. David McLellan. Oxford: Oxford University Press.

Mills, C. Wright, 1956. *White Collar*. New York: Oxford University Press.

Mogen, David, 1986. *Ray Bradbury*. Boston: Twayne.

Nicholls, Peter, 1984. *Fantastic Cinema: An Illustrated Survey*. London: Ebury Press.

Perkins, V.F., 1990. 'Must We Say What They Mean?: Film Criticism and Interpretation', *Movie*, 34/35, 1–6.

Platt, Charles, 1980. *Who Writes Science Fiction?* Manchester: Savoy Books.

Pohl, Frederik and Pohl IV, Frederik, 1981. *Science Fiction Studies in Film*. New York: Ace.

Strick, Philip, 1979. *Science Fiction Movies*. London: Galley Press.

Suvin, Darko, 1979. *Metamorphoses of Science Fiction: On the Poetics and History of a Literary Genre*. New Haven: Yale University Press.

Suvin, Darko, 2003. 'Reflections on What Remains of Zamyatin's *We* after the Change of Leviathans: Must Collectivism Be against People?', in M.S. Barr, ed., *Envisioning the Future: Science Fiction and the Next Millennium*. Middletown, CT: Wesleyan University Press, pp. 51–81.

Touponce, William F., 1984. *Ray Bradbury and the Poetics of Reverie: Fantasy, Science Fiction and the Reader*. Ann Arbor, MI: UMI Research Press.

Trilling, Lionel, 1950. *The Liberal Imagination: Essays on Literature and Society*. New York: Viking.

Truffaut, François, 1972. 'From "The Journal of FAHRENHEIT 451" by François Truffaut', in W. Johnson, ed., *Focus on the Science Fiction Film*. Englewood Cliffs. NJ: Prentice-Hall, pp. 121–5.

Truffaut, François, 1982. *The Films in My Life*. Harmondsworth: Penguin.

Watt, Donald, 1980. 'Burning Bright: *Fahrenheit 451* as Symbolic Dystopia', in J.D. Olander and M.H. Greenberg, eds, *Ray Bradbury*. Edinburgh: Paul Harris, pp. 195–213.

Westfahl, Gary, 1998. *The Mechanics of Wonder: The Creation of the Idea of Science Fiction*. Liverpool: Liverpool University Press.

Wingrove, David, 1985. *Science Fiction Film Source Book*. Harlow: Longman.

Wright, Gene, 1983. *The Science Fiction Image: The Illustrated Encyclopedia of Science Fiction in Film, Television, Radio and Theater*. New York: Facts on File.

Zipes, Jack, 1983. 'Mass Degradation of Humanity and Massive Contradictions in Bradbury's Vision of America in *Fahrenheit 451*', in E.S. Rabkin, M.H. Greenberg and J.D. Olander, eds, *No Place Else: Explorations in Utopian and Dystopian Fiction*. Carbondale, IL: Southern Illinois University Press.

Updike's Golden Oldies: Rabbit as Spectacular Man

JUDIE NEWMAN

IN THE OPENING SCENE OF UPDIKE'S *In the Beauty of the Lilies* D.W. Griffith is filming a medieval costume drama in 1910, in which Mary Pickford gallops across a castle lawn in pageboy tights, supposedly bearing a momentous message, 'Sire, the king bids the troops to attack the Saracen infidels!' (Updike 1996: 4). Overcome by the weight of her costume and the torrid heat of Paterson, New Jersey, Pickford faints as the camera comes in for a close up – and simultaneously, in his rectory, Updike's pastor hero, Clarence Wilmot, loses his faith. It is an emblematic moment, as the crusading Pickford takes over the role of religious inspiration from Clarence, and as the visual image replaces the spoken word. Since *The Call to Arms* is a silent film, Pickford's message will be spelled out on the screen in white on black, ornately framed. Coincidentally Clarence develops a throat problem and becomes unable to preach, trading in his vocation for a job as an encyclopaedia salesman, and regular movie attendance. Clarence's granddaughter Essie Wilmot becomes a film star, Alma DeMott (the soul of the demotic), who ministers to far larger masses than Clarence ever did. The novel explicitly engages with the notion that churches have been replaced by movie houses as locations of mystery, passion, and spiritual renewal, with 'larger-than-life gods and goddesses, emanating as images of light moving across and conquering the darkness' (Schiff 62). As Jack De Bellis, almost the only critic of Updike to consider the role of cinema in his work, argues, Essie's vocation as a screen goddess connects with yearnings for perfection and immortality, and the escape from a flawed and meaningless reality. In the words of one reviewer:

> The cinematic close up marked a moment in history when the face of God was put in the shade by other divine faces who had the added advantage of being able to offer worshippers a signed photo. (Pearson)

Updike's works have of course multiple points of contact with the cinema, including inter-textual references and allusions in his novels, the construction of novels using cinematic devices (montage in *The Poorhouse Fair*, the present tense in *Rabbit, Run: A Movie*, that novel's original title), poems ('Movie House'), movie reviews, essays (on Doris Day, Gene Kelly, and Lana Turner) and reminiscences. A lifelong fan of Disney cartoons, Updike has rarely missed a Disney animation since he saw *Snow White and the Seven Dwarfs* in 1937. As a child Updike wanted to be an animator because 'To create motion, frame by frame, appeared Godlike' (Updike 1999: 642). Recalling the old movie houses of his youth, he described them as lifting men and women 'from their ordinary lives onto a supernatural level. . . . No wonder so many of the vacant theatres are now churches. We worshipped in those spaces' (Updike 1999: 643). What is most significant however, about the interface between film and Updike's fiction is not the various techniques or references drawn from individual films and deployed in specific novels, but the place of cinema in Updike's consideration of the overall relationship between American society and the visual. Updike, a would-be cartoonist, a trained artist, the author of *Just Looking*, a book of art reviews, and an authority on Vermeer, might be expected to be interested in our society's fascination with the eye. Indeed a recent novel, *Seek My Face*, forms an extended homage to American art, with its characters constructed as amalgams of key figures: Rauschenberg, Johns, Lichtenstein, Pollock, Warhol, and Indiana. Above all, it is the social impact of visual domination that most concerns him; cinema is only one strand in a wide-ranging exploration of the role of the spectacular in contemporary life. In focusing upon the opposition of cinema and church, in *In the Beauty of the Lilies*, Updike draws upon a long tradition of anti-ocular discourse, and a general ambivalence towards the spectacular in the West, as related to the fear of idolatry in the three major Western religions: the idea that what is 'real' is somehow not capable of representation. It is not for nothing that Judeo-Christian prophets, for example, tend to hear the voice of God without visible manifestation (Jay: ch. 7). The opposition between word and image, voice and vision is particularly acute in *Rabbit at Rest* and its sequel 'Rabbit Remembered'.

In contrast to the usual understanding of the neorealist as a policeman of the emotions and a disciplinary overseer engaged in ideological control, Updike is deeply concerned with the role of the instincts in American society.[1] Updike's *Rabbit* tetralogy draws quite clearly, though not naively, on Freud's analysis of society as founded upon repression, the idea that because the lasting interpersonal relationships on which

---

[1] For an excellent account of the relationship between realism and surveillance, see Seltzer.

society depends presuppose that the sex instincts are inhibited there is a high personal price to pay for the benefits of civilised life and techno-logical progress, and a fundamental opposition between sensual gratifi-cation and social utility (Newman 1988 and 1998). Updike introduces this conflict between work and play explicitly in *Rabbit, Run*; he pro-ceeds in *Rabbit Redux* to examine the potential McLuhanite sensual lib-eration of the individual, set free by new technology from the visual slavery of Gutenberg man; and, in *Rabbit is Rich*, analyses the ways in which society may deform and exploit the instincts by the creation of mass fantasy. In *Rabbit, Run*, Harry's indulgent holiday from virtue with Ruth is ended by the death of his daughter, and a return to family and repression. In *Redux* the excursion with Jill and Skeeter again closes with death, a return to the family, and a job in the family business. In *Rabbit is Rich* an actual excursion (to the Caribbean) brings Harry into metaphoric contact with death and returns him to the fold. So far, so disciplinary.

But in *Rabbit at Rest*, Updike changes direction. The novel begins on holiday (retirement in Florida), then makes a brief return to the world of work, only for Harry to restage his original 'run' once more, this time definitively, returning to die in Florida as the circle of the tetralogy closes upon him. In *Rabbit at Rest* desire is over-indulged, actively encouraged by a society more interested in consumption than produc-tion. Notions of play, games, leisure, and holiday occupy centre stage, together with their commodification in the leisure industries, whether official (Harry's golf and water sports, various films) or unofficial (Nelson's permanent holiday of crack addiction, which triggers Harry's return to the world of work). The family business comes under threat from Harry's own indulgence (overeating and adultery), Nelson's addic-tion, women (Harry's feminist wife), gays (Nelson's associates in embezzle-ment are AIDS sufferers trying to buy miracle drugs) and finally other races (the Japanese reassert the work ethic and pull the plug on the Toyota franchise).

It is easy to see a case for reading the novel as racist, homophobic, and sexist. Dilvo Ristoff, for example, views Rabbit as 'a prisoner of a nostalgic pull that brings to his mind images of a world that is grander and better, more glorious and more desirable than the drudgery and turmoil he now faces' (Ristoff 5). Even worse, Updike inscribes this particular discourse of indulgence in global, political terms, as the Cold War – the ultimate image of repression at home and abroad – comes to an end and America finds itself liberated into insignificance, consigned to the sidelines – 'like a big Canada' (Updike 1990: 352). For Harry,

'Without the Cold War, what's the point of being American?' (Updike 1990: 436), a suggestion reinforced by the plot. When his adultery with his daughter-in-law is discovered, Harry could make peace with his family. In choosing to flee to Florida instead, Harry creates his own personal Cold War, an icy, hostile stand-off. The problem posed by Harry's identification with an older ideal is the extent to which Updike is guilty of a similar nostalgia for the repressive Cold War certainties of an older America – a time when the family business, and by extension the American economy – was less vulnerable to the threats of women, gays, and racial 'Others'. Importantly, Harry's final run has a soundtrack – a long sequence of golden oldies played on the radio, which Harry listens to as he heads South to death. Superficially a nostalgic celebration of an earlier America, both in the songs themselves and in the nostalgic associations with radio (as an older medium than, for example, an in-car sound system), the sequence is crucial to Updike's engagement with techniques of demystification of the spectacle and of resistance to visual domination.

At the risk of digression, an example from contemporary film forms a useful jumping-off point for discussion of these songs and their relationship to the politics of *Rabbit at Rest*. In *Reservoir Dogs*,[2] in one of the nastier images of violence in recent film, the Michael Madsen character (Mr Blonde) becomes nostalgic about a golden oldie and plays it while torturing a young cop and cutting off his ear. The song is 'Stuck in the middle with you', performed by Stealer's Wheel in 1974 and including the lines:

> Clowns to the left of me, jokers to the right,
> Here I am, stuck in the middle with you.[3]

It is a scene that exposes the evocation of a supposed past middle ground as a killer nostalgia, a surface celebration that overlays and obscures the violence beneath. It is an image that highlights one of the major issues in approaching *Rabbit at Rest* – the opposition between a story of middling, average Americans, and the damage caused by their unrepressed gratifications. Above all, it is a scene of such sickening violence that it calls our spectatorship into question. The viewer becomes uneasy with

---

[2] *Reservoir Dogs*, directed by Quentin Tarantino, Dog Eat Dogs Productions, 1991.
[3] The song was written by Gerry Rafferty and Joe Egan (EMI Music Publishing Company, 1974).

the fact of viewing, precisely because the scene separates the visual spectacle – torture – from the soundtrack in a fashion designed to create a disjunction between the two, undermining the seamless nature of what Guy Debord has termed the 'society of the spectacle'.[4] In what follows I shall argue that Updike proceeds to a similar analysis and demystification of the spectacle, in surprising agreement with one of the more radical thinkers of the French left, particularly in his employment of nostalgic popular song in opposition to the dominance of the visual.

In *Rabbit At Rest* leisure has become society's tool. Play and work have been collapsed into each other. The image presented here is entirely consonant with that presented by Debord in *The Society of the Spectacle*: the analysis of a society that has been turned into a gigantic spectacle, in which the visible form of the commodity totally occupies everyday life, uniting production and consumption in one monstrous system. Critics have made a similar point about the world of the Rabbit novels, brimming with brand names and products. (For the curious it is worth noting that there are 871 brand-name mentions in *Rabbit at Rest*.) As Martin Jay has argued, Debord's critique employs familiar motifs from other anti-ocular discourses. In particular it builds upon the opposition between (on the one hand) lived, temporally meaningful experience, immediacy of speech (the word). and collective participation, and (on the other hand) dead spatialised images, the distancing effect of the gaze, and the passivity of individuated contemplation. In Debord's words,

> The whole life of those societies in which modern conditions of production prevail presents itself as an immense accumulation of spectacles. All that once was directly lived has become mere representation. (Debord 12)

Debord particularly homes in on notions of play, as opposed to modern 'leisure' practices, which are in fact penetrated by and subordinated to the world of work. In the view of Debord and his fellow Situationists, what is referred to as liberation from work, increased leisure time, is a liberation neither within labour itself nor from the world labour has

---

[4] See Debord 1975 and also McDonough, ed., 2002, particularly Greil Marcus, 'The Long Walk of the Situationist International', pp. 1–20; Thomas Y. Levin, 'Dismantling the Spectacle: The Cinema of Guy Debord', pp. 321–454; and Jonathan Crary, 'Spectacle, Attention, Countermemory', pp. 455–66. Levin's account of Debord's films is invaluable, given that Debord withdrew them all from exhibition after the murder of his friend Gérard Lebovici in 1984.

brought into being (Debord 22). In a description that chimes uncannily with Nelson's addiction and Harry's final morphine heaven, the spectacle has become 'a permanent opium war waged to make it impossible to distinguish goods from commodities, or true satisfaction from . . . survival' Debord 30).

Debord is, of course, merely one of a whole series of modern thinkers who have homed in on the dominance of Western culture by the visual. As Michel de Certeau puts it:

> from TV to newspapers, from advertising to all sorts of mercantile epiphanies, our society is characterized by a cancerous growth of vision measuring everything by its ability to show or be shown and transmuting communication into a visual journey. (de Certeau xxi)

Vision has been understood as implicated in the surveillance central to repressive power in the modern world, as Michel Foucault argues in *Discipline and Punish* (1975). Foucault's argument that the eighteenth-century focus on visible surfaces gave way to a penetrating gaze into the body itself (notably in the dissection of corpses), with the result of more visual penetration being a focus not on life but on death, on the body as a dominated object, is exemplified in the novel in Harry's angioplasty, a heart operation under local anaesthetic, which he is able to watch on a monitor, during which he has a heart attack on screen. Film critics have been much exercised by the power of the gaze, particularly as it positions the male as the gazer, the woman as the object of the gaze, with predictable sexist consequences. Where most thinkers, however, focus on the disciplinary and repressive effect of being the object of the gaze, Debord stressed the dangers of being its subject – of being the person who does the gazing, rather than the person gazed at. In his view seduction by the spectacle of modern life was more nefarious than Big Brother's omnipresent watchfulness. Orwell envisaged the TV screen in the corner of the room as watching us. Updike follows Debord in being more alert to the dangers of us watching the screen, and, as in the case of Harry's angioplasty, of us watching our lives rather than living them.

Debord's term 'spectacle' implies in French a theatrical presentation of commodities, in which commodities are like idols worshipped in lieu of gods. Debord understood alienation not as rooted in production (as in the nineteenth century) but in consumption. As a left-wing theorist, Debord was intent on creating a movement that would help the masses unmask the illusions that enslave them. Like most radical movements, the Situationists' heyday was brief, flourishing from 1966 to 1968, and then declining, though their influence has been detected in the punk movement, in which deliberate ugliness and ripped clothing undercut the seamless illusion of the consumer dream. Stavros comments in the novel on the politicisation of consumption by punks: 'Pain is where it's at for punks . . . For these kids today, ugly is beautiful. That's their way of saying what a lousy world we're giving them' (Updike 1990: 237). *Rabbit at Rest* is notable for its interest in passive spectatorship, and the fashion in which human beings become subordinate to images. Harry, in the hospital, lives only through the TV screen, quite literally. A machine is doing the living for him – he is watching The Harry Angstrom Show, his own heart. Judy, possessed by a gluttony for images, channel-surfs continually, offering an image of technological short-circuiting of emotional affect as whole families become interchangeable on screen:

Faces, black in *The Jeffersons*, white in *Family Ties*, imploringly pop into visibility and then vanish. (Updike 1990: 77)

Pru orchestrates a seduction from television scripts, Janice becomes a business woman after watching *Working Girl*. Harry's obsession with the Lockerbie bombing focuses on an event that appeared to watchers as the disappearance of a dot from a screen. When Harry scares his family by getting lost, Nelson emphasises invisibility as death. 'Suddenly we *looked* around and you weren't there. Like Pan-Am 103 on the radar screen' (Updike 1990: 25). Harry is later drawn to the image of the Challenger space rocket disaster, in which the death of the astronauts is a national spectacle, watched live on TV. When Nelson hits Pru, he feels as if he was 'standing outside watching and felt no connection with myself. Like it was all on television' (Updike 1990: 258). When Harry watches a football game on TV the game is almost invisible as the result of a sudden fog. Television coverage has been reduced to the sideline cameras; nobody knows what is really going on; there is an unbridgeable gap between real action and media image. The crowd 'rumbles and groans in poor sync with the television action, trying to read the game off the electronic scoreboard' (Updike 1990: 161). The crowd are actually present, but their understanding and reaction is attuned only to the visual media. As an image of American politics it could hardly be more telling.

For Debord, 'The spectacle is capital accumulated to the point where it becomes image' (Debord 24). The commodity takes over social life. Similarly Updike's characters don't dominate the products – the products dominate them. Even when he is lusting after Pru in a bathing costume, Harry registers a brand name – it is her 'Spandex crotch' that fills his eye. Nelson does not run his habit; cocaine runs him. This is a novel in which we are bombarded with images through the mass media, with advertising invading everything. Reality has become nothing more than a simulation. When Harry marches in a Fourth of July parade as Uncle Sam, liberty is converted into the spectacle of liberty. Some are excluded from the celebration. Judy's Girl Scout troop mounts a display in which one girl features as the Statue of Liberty, surrounded by others whose faces are painted brown, black, red or yellow to represent the races of mankind. Representation is all. The girls have to be painted, since there are no Asian or black girls in the troop. The parade itself clearly represents an older America replete with nostalgic soundtrack, a medley of half-heard snatches of music, incongruously mixing a pipe band wailing forth 'Highland killing songs' (Updike 1990: 365), a local rock singer impersonating Presley, Lennon and Orbison, together with 'American Patrol' and 'Yesterday'. Leading the parade, Harry finds the main street (cleared for the event) eerily empty. Normal life has been put on hold, replaced by the spectacle. The scene is followed by the funeral of Harry's lover, Thelma Harrison. Looking for her 'no-brand-name church' (Updike 1990: 366), Harry and Janice get lost and end up instead in a shopping mall with six-screen Cineplex. Nobody there has any idea where the church might be. The real priorities of American society are not in much doubt here.

Debord, of course, wrote without reference to Disneyland. But it is not coincidental that Updike sets his novel in Florida, surrounded by spectacle-worlds, theme-parks and pseudo-realities – spectacles that hardly seem any different from the world surrounding them. Leisure time tends to be considered as our 'real' life, those authentic moments away from work. But in Florida the leisure is completely commodified by tourism. Wherever they are, the Angstroms are effectively tourists on their own lives, watching rather than living, taken over by the images and the commercial brand names. In Valhalla Village, family dinner is dominated by bingo numbers blaring from a loudspeaker. Harry can *see* Judy speak, and Pru's mouth move in response, but the soundtrack is that of the bingo caller, in a commercial game. The Angstroms' words have been lost. When Harry is fighting for his life having a heart attack, he encourages Judy to sing, to keep him conscious and to keep her occupied. Judy runs out of nursery rhymes and can only sing snatches of television commercials, McDonalds, American Airlines, 'like switching channels back and forth' (Updike 1990: 138), and 'Coke is it!' followed by jingles from the movies. A cheerful Disney soundtrack accompanies Harry's agonising pain – a disjunction between sound and image akin to that in *Reservoir Dogs*.

In what precedes Harry's final run, therefore, the novel foregrounds the passivity of a spectacular society, implicitly contrasting it with Harry's nostalgia for the Cold War world of an older America. Importantly. the Florida to which he returns (in the off season) is no longer the world of permanent holiday, but a nostalgic time warp. On his daily walks Harry moves away from the mass vacation locale to an older community. The main sound coming from the houses is that of scratchy radio music mixed with human voices. This area of town, with its old-fashioned wooden houses, chicken coops, and general stores reminds him of the town of his childhood

> in the days of the Depression and distant war, when people still sat on their porches and there were vacant lots and odd-shaped cornfields. (Updike 1990: 471)

In 'Reflections on Radio' Updike noted that 'In my childhood and youth, radio was everywhere' (Updike 1999: 803) and applauded its appeal to the imagination. 'Freed from the tyranny of visual mimesis' radio liberated its hearers, as opposed to the 'image-saturated modern consciousness which has pre-experienced everything' (Updike 1999: 804). The nostalgia, however, is shadowed by the fact that this is a black community. The scene offers an implicit critique of nostalgia by displaying the economic underpinnings, the labour for the hotels, theme parks and condos, which make the permanent holiday possible. In *Rabbit, Run* Harry had begun a similar trip, also listening to songs on the radio (Updike 1964: 26). When he tries to reenact this journey, however, he finds the original country garage, bathed in nostalgia in his own mind, now engulfed in 'sulfurous illumination' (Updike 1990: 431). On the radio Harry hears a news item concerning Jim Bakker, a disgraced TV evangelist, the embodiment of the Word as dominated by the visual medium. Further South news comes of preachers declaiming prayers to sports crowds through bullhorns, the Word writ large, in protest against the attempt to remove organised prayers before football games (Updike 1990: 442). Harry is not religious, however, and turns off the Bible stations in favour of a long sequence of songs on the radio. Superficially the songs (and the fact that they are in the 'older' medium of radio) suggest a nostalgia for the past. They are golden oldies, 'the music of your life' (Updike 1990: 452) in the presenter's phrase, heavy on crooners and songs of love, 'the sweet old tunes, the tunes he grew up by' (Updike 1990: 430). Many of the songs apparently evoke personal events. Johnny Ray's 'Cry' recalls the moment when Harry's sweetheart *did* send him a letter of goodbye, for example. Dean Martin's 'That's Amore' recalls early sexual experiences. 'It's a rare song that doesn't light up some of his memory cells' (Updike 1990: 452). In symbolic terms also the songs tend to have relevance to Harry's own life. 'A-Tisket, A-Tasket', with its second line 'I've lost my yellow basket', evokes Harry's decline from his former stardom as a basketball hero. Ella Fitzgerald's heart attacks may also be relevant. 'Love Me Tender' recalls Presley's death from overindulgence; Frankie Laine ('Mule Train') had bypass surgery for the second time in 1990. Several songs make explicit reference to impending death: the black-bordered letter in 'Mule Train', 'Vaya Con Dios', and 'Just a Gigolo', which closes 'Life goes on without me'.[5] 'The Wayward Wind', 'On the Road Again', and 'Rambling Rose' remind us that Harry has wandered off the straight and narrow in erotic terms and is now literally on the move away from his wife and family. It is tempting to read this as irresponsible flight, the nostalgic staging of a personal Cold War. Certainly the song 'Wheel of Fortune' suggests that Harry is in some way coming full circle.

On the car journey, however, Harry is entirely alone, free, and above all invisible. Nobody knows where he is, nobody is watching. He is not under surveillance. Invisibility, like the dot disappearing on the screen, is either death or freedom. Potentially, then, the songs offer access to a non-homogenised, individualised history beyond the realm of the spectacular, a space where the whole texture of Harry's personal history overlays 'Love Me Tender'. Most readers will be familiar with the experience of suddenly hearing a song that recalls emotional scenes from earlier periods of our lives. Musical references of this type are essentially inter-textual, with specific but transmutable memories, both private and public, attached to them by time. We can attempt to hang on to the original context and meaning of the song (nostalgically) or transmute it by adding other memories or placing

[5] Louis Prima, the singer, starred as the voice of King Louie in Disney's *The Jungle Book*, before spending years in a coma after a major operation. I am grateful to Jon Bennett, Hugh Brogan, and Warren Chernaik for assistance in identifying and commenting on particular songs. Other details are drawn from the following websites: http://www.songlyrics4u.com26/0604; http://www.lyricsfreak.com26/0604; http://www.oldies.com; and from the individual singers' websites.

the song in a new context. In general, we tend to resent it if a popular song is transferred from our own private memories to a commercial frame, as for example Marvin Gaye's 'I heard it on the grapevine' suddenly became the soundtrack for a scene involving Levi jeans in a laundrette. Ad agencies have been quick to realise the added value a great rock song can add to their products, by conjuring up a particular mood and time. Can one now hear 'Search for the hero' without thinking of a Peugeot 406 commercial, or 'He ain't heavy, he's my brother' independently of Miller Lite beer? Subconsciously we think of these songs as part of our individual lives, as if we are having the emotions, not having them supplied by a commercial song. But is this the case? Harry comments bitterly (on Connie Francis's 'Where the boys are'), that it came out in the 'beach-party era', when the songs celebrated a leisure fun time of barbecues and parties. Harry, however, was working as a linotyper by then, 'no more parties for him' (Updike 1990: 453).

So 'whose life are these songs?' (Updike 1990: 453). The songs selected also glorify a cheerful ethnic mix in a schmaltz of emotion that papers over political dissent – invoking an earlier American ideal of the 'melting pot'. They include Latin American, Israeli, African-American, Italian, and other immigrant groups, featuring Sinatra, Dean Martin, the Three Caballeros, Nat 'King' Cole, Ella Fitzgerald, and 'Oh My Papa!' Some of these songs are 'classics'. But the tenuousness of this political harmony may be indicated by the inclusion of 'Tzena, Tzena', an Israeli hora issued in 1950 as the B-side to the Weavers' first big hit, 'Goodnight Irene'. It is not an obvious candidate for inclusion in a roll call of golden greats, though it is a song that remains popular at Jewish weddings, and might well feature on the radio in Florida. Harry, however, has not heard it in years. As he comments, 'The music doesn't come ethnic any more' (Updike 1990: 452). As a folksong (if a somewhat packaged one) it was part of the agenda of a group that performed political and union songs, and was blacklisted and put out of business in 1952, as part of the McCarthy witch-hunts. The cheerful dance music ('Tzena, Tzena, can't you hear the music playing?') and Utopian lyrics ('Pioneering all together, come and lend a hand, Tzena, Tzena, building a new nation') are thus out of sync with an era of political oppression. Ethnic or racially 'other' performers were tolerated – and exploited – in the entertainment business only as long as they did not rock the political boat. To a lesser extent the songs also call into question authoritative gender constructs. Neither racial nor gender categories are really as stable as an earlier America would have had it. Sound allows a freedom that scopic discipline does not. It is not an accident that Harry listens to Orbison's falsetto and to Johnny Ray. Ray was billed as the next Sinatra but assumed by some listeners to be black and/or female.[6] In the 1950s people could not necessarily see the singer on screen. Sound was more important than the visual message. Connee Boswell ('Say It Isn't So') was crippled by polio and usually appeared seated in an elevated wheelchair with a gown designed to make it look as if she was standing. Few of her fans knew that she was wheelchair-bound.

In its bricolage of song excerpts, memories, and titles the sequence asks whether there is a free space for the individual – a space in which authentic personal experience can take precedence over media substitutes – or whether the individual's life is scripted and programmed by the media, the emotions exploited and the personality 'scored' for the right performance in the spectacle. In this respect it is striking that Updike indicates the sounds of the songs, not just the words: Patti Page's 'Never let me gooooo, I love you sooooo', Kay Starr's 'Puleazzze let it be now' and Ray Charles's 'yesterdayssss' are spelled out quasi-phonetically. Although readers may have their own memories of these songs we remain programmed to perform in only one way – just as the performers themselves were tolerated as ethnic performers, only within the bounds of commercial culture, contributors to the spectacle that holds them captive. The text thus confronts its readers with the constraints upon our freedom. We will all remember or ignore the songs to different degrees, connect them to different experiences and be informed to varying degrees about the fate of the Weavers or the gender and race of Johnny Ray. We have a degree of reader-freedom in how we remember these songs, connected to our own individual histories. On the other hand, the songs can only be performed in one way. The reader is firmly 'cued' into the correct performance, by a medium that cuts every 30 minutes to news bulletins, in the usual 'infotainment' sequence of international, national and local items, reinforcing the sense of human experience as firmly under the control of dominant cultural programming. Even if we do not know the songs at all we will be forced to recognise that their very alien quality in itself suggests

[6] David Chappell, University of Arkansas, Fayetteville, 'Hip Like Me: Racial Cross-Dressing in Popular Music before the Advent of Elvis', paper presented on 9 May 1998 at the Martin Luther King Memorial Conference, University of Newcastle upon Tyne.

that the same will be true of today's songs in 40 years' time. As Harry recognises,

> the songs of his life were as moronic as the rock the brainless kids now feed on . . . it's all disposable, cooked up to turn a quick profit. (Updike 1990: 454)

Yet the songs have a politically effective result nonetheless. The long musical excursus takes place in almost complete absence of any external visual scene. The reader has almost no visual cues at all to the outside world. Instead Harry focuses on visual images from his childhood – Kroll's department store with its 'otherworldly displays' (Updike 1990: 454) of goods. In his youth Harry had been an ardent believer in capitalism, as represented by Kroll's. When Kroll's closes, he realises that 'the world was not solid and benign, it was a shabby set of temporary arrangements rigged up for the time being, all for the sake of money' (Updike 1990: 455). The immersion in sound and the separation from the visual scene has led Harry to the perception that the political landscape is not geology, an unchanging background against which life takes place, but stage scenery, 'spectacle', painted hardboard.[7] When he does focus once more on his surroundings he finds that he is approaching Disneyworld. For miles a succession of amusement and theme parks go rolling by – Wax Works, Circus World, Sea World – as the spectacular nature of his society is finally revealed to him, without its illusory mystifications. In this technique of setting the spectacle against itself Updike invites comparison with the strategies of the Situationists in their critical separation of word and image. Debord, for example, made a film (*Hurlements en faveur de Sade*) in which the sound dominated vision and for four-fifths of the film the screen was completely blank (Jay 423). The film caused riots among spectators, forced to endure twenty minutes of final silence to boot. Later Debord realised that the refunctioning of the image could serve political ends better than its obliteration – visual material was ironically undercut by sound commentary, or hijacked for illicit purposes to strip away enslaving illusion. He proposed that rather than censoring *Birth of a Nation* for its racism, for example, a soundtrack should be added, denouncing the horrors of American Imperialism. Characters from *True Romance* were given different cartoon balloons, and made to declaim revolutionary sentiments. In this way it was possible to confront the spectacle with its own effluvia and to reverse the usual ideological

---

[7] Ascherson makes this point about the Situationist legacy.

format, in order to disrupt a society organised as appearance on the field of appearance itself. Similarly Updike mounts a spirited resistance to the hegemony of the visual, and deploys the word in favour of a penetrating critique of American society. What the novel demonstrates is that seduction by the spectacle may be resisted without surrendering to punishment from the panopticon.

On his deathbed, Harry had tried to tell Nelson the secret which he has kept up to this point – that Nelson has an illegitimate sister, Annabelle Byer, the product of one of Harry's liaisons. But his voice has failed. The existence of the sister is (Updike 1990: 275) 'an old story, going on and on, like a radio nobody's listening to' – a secret personal story that has never been part of the social script. The radio is silent. It appears that Nelson will now never know of her existence. As readers, of course, we do – we have access to a personal, individual history outside the norms of the social spectacle. The ending of the novel, therefore, confronts us again with the disjunction between authentic, lived experience – a personal history – and the loss of that experience along with the loss of the voice. As Maurice Blanchot put it:

> the everyday loses any power to reach us; it is no longer what is lived, but what can be seen or what shows itself, spectacle and description, without any active relation whatsoever. The whole world is offered to us, but by way of a look. (Blanchot 14)

Yet there is a postscript to *Rabbit at Rest*, the novella 'Rabbit Remembered', in which Annabelle Byer, Harry's daughter, plays a leading role. The years have passed and Nelson can hardly remember his father, though his description of him reminds the reader of Harry's immersion in the norms of his society:

> Time has turned *the spectacular man* to powder in just ten years. (my emphasis) (Updike 2000: 255)

At first it appears that Harry's life remains framed in irony and loss, and that his own late-gained understandings have simply disappeared with him. On his run South, Harry had, if only fleetingly, located a site of potential resistance to the domination of the visual, but the next time the reader encounters him in his car, he is going in reverse direction, as Nelson and Janice reenact his journey, carrying his cremated remains back to Pennsylvania for the funeral. When Judy weeps in a motel at the thought of Grandpa's ashes, alone in the trunk of the car, the family place the urn reverently on top of the television set, as if Harry were part of the picture gazed at. Even worse, at the following stop, they man-age to forget the urn in the bathroom of a Comfort Inn. Nelson under-stands this 'unconscious vengeance in their leaving Dad behind, as he had more than once left them behind' (Updike 2000: 271). When Annabelle contacts the family, she apparently offers a chance for Nelson to reconnect with his father. At Thanksgiving, however, she inadvertently triggers an orgy of revenge on Harry by proxy. While Georgie Harrison enthuses about Broadway shows and offers free tickets, the family put on a show of their own. Ostensibly discussing President Clinton, the assembled relatives overlay the public figure with their own lived experiences. Annabelle defends Clinton for his love of people, his gambler's nerve, and the inability to hold a grudge, but the appeal of a reckless, greedy charmer is lost on the others. Ronnie Harrison, now married to Janice, takes revenge on the man who slept with both his wives, and his mistress (Annabelle's mother) describing Annabelle as the daughter of 'a hooer and a bum' (Updike 2000: 300). Nelson's stepbrothers join in the fray, avenging their seduced mother by describing Clinton in terms which are wincingly apposite to Harry ('He's dead meat. He's a leftover going fuzzy at the back of the fridge' (Updike 2000: 297)), and take an implicit sideswipe at Janice via the First Lady 'She's been enabling his affairs for years' (Updike 2000: 293). An infuriated Nelson defends his father against the loathsome Ronnie, demanding of his mother: 'Why did you marry him? How could you do that to us?' The 'us', he realizes, must include his dead father' (Updike 2000: 301).

A final car journey establishes the extent to which Harry's influence lives on. At the close of the novella Nelson, his wife Pru, Annabelle, and Billy Fosnacht go to see the film *American Beauty,* on millennium eve. As in the car trip in *Rabbit at Rest*, external visuals are muted. Leaving Instant Classics, the aptly named second-run, cut-price cinema, Nelson loses his way and ends up heading for outer darkness, missing the dazzling displays of millennial fireworks, and narrowly avoiding a fatal car crash right beside the site of Kroll's department store, as a computer glitch extinguishes the lights of Brewer. Despite the millennial date, the scene could not be less spectacular. The disjunction between lived temporally meaningful experience and the illusory satisfactions of a spectacular soci-ety is highlighted in the general sense of anti-climax, of people staying home with their families, and in Ronnie's observation that the millen-nium has already dawned in Fiji, Australia, and Japan. 'For most of the world the millennium is already history! Time is relative' (Updike 2000: 340).

Similarly, *American Beauty* is relayed to the reader only through the words of the characters, collectively discussing it in the car. Just as their personal histories dominated the public story of Clinton, reinterpreted through their own hostilities, so the film is subordinated to the Angstroms' personal concerns. Significantly *American Beauty* is a film about perception, exploring the disjunction between projecting an image and being true to oneself.[8] Much of the action of the film is seen through a window or a camera lens, allowing the reader to step back and watch without quite surrendering to the image. At one point a character, Jane, accuses the video-wielding Ricky, of being 'like any other dweeb who worships Quentin Tarantino for the same reason you can't let go of that camera: because you don't know how to be a real person in a real life'. Ricky, however, uses the camera to reveal real beauty in the everyday, as in girl-next-door Jane, for example, as opposed to the commercially perfect Angela, a nubile would-be starlet. Ricky, a former drug addict and mental patient, uses the camera therapeutically to help set everyone in the film free from their old selves, and to allow them to face death, a constant fascination in the film, in which a car wreck allows a teenager to stare into the eyes of a corpse and claim to have seen God. The overall moral is that if we 'look closer' (a tag in the film) there is beauty and joy in ordinary things, as opposed to the artificial images of perfection cultivated on screen and in a spectacular, consumerist society.

Ricky's experience clearly chimes with that of Nelson, himself a former drug addict, now a therapeutic counsellor, who understands very clearly the problems of the 'perfect' image. One of his clients, Michael DiLorenzo, son and heir to the firm of 'Perfect Cleaners', has recently killed himself, unable to live up to his parents' expectations that he would become Mr Perfect. Michael's schizophrenia is described as a fatal disjunction between word and image. While voices hammer inside his head urging him to kill, 'Things up close look far away; there is no clear depth in which to locate himself' (Updike 2000: 232). If Nelson is Ricky, Janice corresponds to Carolyn Burnham, a failed mother, adulteress and real estate agent, and Harry is Lester Burnham, whose midlife crisis and flight from his job plunge the family into chaos. Lester's fresh

---

[8] *American Beauty* (1999) was directed by Sam Mendes and written by Alan Ball. Ball's screenplay, available at http://scifiscripts.name2host.com/msol/A_B.html, is much less sentimental than the finished film. Jane and Ricky are convicted erroneously of murder and jailed; Carolyn marries her lover after Lester's death, and Angela becomes a film actress.

start ends in death, illustrating for Nelson that there can be 'No fresh start, no mercy.' For Nelson, death is just a 'freeze-frame' (Updike 2000: 343), an arrest, a final stop light. *American Beauty*, however, is narrated by Lester from beyond death, most memorably at the close when he recalls the magic of the stars and of his grandmother's hands. The Angstroms' reactions are mixed, displaying some desire to believe in the film's transcendent message, combined with a healthy scepticism for its more transcendent excesses. The film certainly assists Billy Fosnacht in feeling less afraid of mortality ('Didn't Kevin Spacey look happy dead?' (Updike 2000: 343)) but he is upset by the gay subplot (as a dentist he is afraid of contacting AIDS from his gay patients). Pru is dismissive: 'that guy never acted like a man who had ever noticed his grand-mother's hands or anything else except his own selfish itches and threatened ego' (Updike 2000: 343). The alert reader will remember at this point Harry's frequent memories of his mother's large hands as opposed to his son's 'little Springer hands', recreated in Judy (Updike 2000: 356), and will qualify Pru's dismissal. Unlike Annabelle, who applauds Lester, Pru also dismisses the scene in which Lester, propos-itioned by Angela, refrains from taking sexual advantage of her: 'I think that was unrealistic, too. Most men would have just screwed her any-way. I mean, he'd been dreaming about nothing else' (Updike 2000: 346). Ten years ago Pru had propositioned Harry, who had not resisted temptation. In the novella alternative constructions of Harry are offered – vilified as Clinton, idealised as Lester.

Nelson, however, finally conjures up and exorcises the loved-but-abusing father, in a scene that privileges voice, immediacy of speech and collective participation over the spatialised images that the foursome have just contemplated on screen. At Thanksgiving Annabelle had identified with Clinton as 'poor in a crummy town with an abusive step-father' (Updike 2000: 295), a comment that gains full relevance only in the final scene of the novel. Remembering Pru's adultery with her father-in-law, Nelson skilfully opens Annabelle up, forcing her to con-front the sexual abuse she had suffered at the hands of her stepfather. In *American Beauty* Lester's daughter, Jane, hates her father and asks Ricky to kill him ('Kill my father. Do it.' (Updike 2000: 344)). Indeed, the film plays with the spectator's assumptions, suggesting at various points that Jane, Ricky, Carolyn, or Ricky's rebuffed gay father may have shot Lester. Annabelle does not endorse Jane. 'I didn't like her. I identified with the other one, the pretty one who acted like a tramp but turned out to be a virgin' (Updike 2000: 344). Annabelle is desperate to hang on to innocence, to rewrite a painful history (mother as 'Savvy old tramp' (Updike 2000: 346), father as abuser), but Nelson will have none of it. 'What do you think, Annabelle? How far would the older man have gone? The father figure? . . . How far did Mr Byer go with you?' (Updike 2000: 346). It is Nelson's 'inner ear' (Updike 2000: 252) as a counsellor that had previously alerted him to the falsity of Annabelle's glowing descriptions of Frank Byer. In the car he is alert to the tone of Annabelle's 'childishly trusting' (Updike 2000: 345) voice, and picks up her emphasis on innocence and youth in her delight in the schoolkids' routine as cheerleaders (Updike 2000: 344). Brutally, he forces her to admit that her stepfather's death was a relief: 'I felt I'd killed him! Good for me!' (Updike 2000: 347). It is at this point that Harry becomes an almost palpable presence in the car. Nelson dare not turn his head to look at the backseat, where his sister is being comforted by Billy: 'his sensation of a fifth person in the car is so strong he needs to strengthen his grip on the steering wheel' (Updike 2000: 347). For the reader the sense of impending disaster, engineered from beyond the grave, is teasingly evoked. Moving forward, Nelson refuses to yield at the intersection to a larger vehicle, and narrowly avoids a fatal accident. As he squeaks past the other car, Christian rock-music bursts upon him from a concert, and he feels as if 'a contentious spirit is leaving him' (Updike 2000: 353). Death is no longer a freeze-frame. As Billy says, 'It's funny about death. When you actually face it, it's kind of a rush' (Updike 2000: 353). The implication is that the characters have now integrated a realistic image of Harry into their lives, recalled him and exorcised him. Nelson recommits to Pru. Ronny and Janice move to Florida. Annabelle and Nelson enjoy a final telephone conversation in which he assures her that 'The very motion of our life is towards happiness' (Updike 2000: 357), and she reminds him that nobody is perfect (Updike 2000: 358). In the final lines Annabelle reveals her intention to marry Billy in church, and Nelson agrees to give her away. The collective discussion in the car, the primacy of the word, the rejection of the perfect, transcendent image, have delivered the Angstroms back, if not into the arms of religion, at least into the arms of each other.

Works Cited

Ascherson, Neal, 1998. 'Comment', *The Observer*, 3 May.
Blanchot, Maurice, 1987. 'Everyday speech', *Yale French Studies*, 73, 14.
De Bellis, Jack, 1955. '"It Captivates . . . It Hypnotizes." Updike Goes to the Movies', *Literature/Film Quarterly* 23, 3, 169–87.

Debord, Guy, 1995. *The Society of the Spectacle*, trans. Donald Nicholson-Smith. New York: Zone Books. [First published as *La société du spectacle*. Paris: Buchet-Castel, 1967.]

de Certeau, Michel, 1984. *The Practice of Everyday Life*, trans. Steven F. Rendall. Berkeley: University of California Press.

Jay, Martin, 1993. *Downcast Eyes: The Denigration of Vision in Twentieth-Century French Thought*. Berkeley: University of California Press.

McDonough, Tom, ed., 2002. *Guy Debord and the Situationist International. Texts and Documents*. Cambridge, MA: MIT Press.

Newman, Judie, 1988. *John Updike*. London: Macmillan, and New York: St Martin's Press.

Newman, Judie, 1998. '*Rabbit at Rest*: The Return of the Work Ethic', in Lawrence R. Broer, ed., *Rabbit Tales: Poetry and Politics in Updike's Rabbit Tetralogy*. Bowling Green, OH: State University Popular Press, pp. 189–206.

Pearson, Allison, 1996. 'Honest John', *Observer*, 5 May, p. 14.

Ristoff, Dilvo I., 1990. *John Updike's Rabbit at Rest. Appropriating History*. New York: Peter Lang.

Schiff, James A., 1999. 'The Pocket Nothing Else Will Fill: Updike's Domestic God', in James Yerkes, ed., *John Updike and Religion: The Sense of the Scared and the Motions of Grace*. Grand Rapids, MI: William B. Eerdmans, pp. 50–63.

Seltzer, Mark, 1982. '*The Princess Casamassima*. Realism and the Fantasy of Surveillance', in Eric J. Sundquist, ed., *American Realism. New Essays*. Baltimore, MD: Johns Hopkins Press, pp. 95–119.

Updike, John, 1964. *Rabbit, Run*. Harmondsworth: Penguin.

Updike, John, 1990. *Rabbit at Rest*. London: André Deutsch.

Updike, John, 1996. *In the Beauty of the Lilies*. London: Hamish Hamilton.

Updike, John, 1999. *More Matter. Essays and Criticism*. London: Hamish Hamilton.

Updike, John, 2000. 'Rabbit Remembered', in *Licks of Love*. New York: Knopf .

Updike, John, 2002. *Seek My Face*. New York: Knopf.

On Conversation

CAROL WATTS

THE MUTUAL INFORMING OF FILM AND LITERATURE has long been a commonplace, the histories of their crossings tracked and anticipated, from the dioramas mimicked in Balzac's novels and Griffith's fascination with Dickens, to the intermedial passages that define what came to be called postmodernism, now finding new digital fields. In fact, the relation between cinema and the novel, as such, might now appear a largely anachronistic consideration, since the mediated nature of culture and its cannibalisms have long superseded such a supposed discrete interrelationship between forms. The question at root here concerns the shifting relations between emerging visual and writerly technologies and the textual word, and the aesthetic transformations that arise from them. Such a mapping can produce curiously deterministic kinds of synchrony in critical terms, as Fredric Jameson describes in his discussion of technological explanation in *Signatures of the Visible*, a form of reduction by which 'aesthetic features begin to coincide with descriptions of the objects of other forms of historiography (including the technological ones)' (Jameson 181).

Jameson is thinking of cinema here in particular, the way in which a periodising account of its development segues smoothly into the documenting of the rise of television and other media, all to be explained 'in the unity of a single historical process, whose parts condition each other reciprocally, but also "reflect" each other in curious and aleatory parallel spirals': an assertion of 'unity' that he argues needs to be 'earned' by much more careful 'local' critical work given a 'desperate lack of perspective' (Jameson 182). Yet something similar might be noted in the tracking of the processes of contemporary writing, marked, despite lags and persistences, by the timelines of new mediated forms and activities like a series of identifiable thresholds or horizons: from cinema to television to video, to the zapping between multiple satellite channels, the computer screen, gaming, hypertext, e-mail, mobile texting, and the interactive possibilities of digitalisation. How far these inform the practices and discourse of the contemporary novel as its very *thought* (beyond the sometimes market-driven and piecemeal recognition of themes and tropes that suggest that the writing is in touch with the times) is interesting to consider, and will become part of my object here.

142

The problem of assessing the impact of technological encounters on aesthetic form is, as Jameson explores, an interpretative one, confronted in the relation between *techne* and text sometimes as moment of material defamiliarisation – the explanation of form through external technological facts – or internally as an Adornian 'deep content'. It risks at its loosest tempting homologies of mutual 'reflection', the conflation of 'methodological moments', the premature closing down of 'dilemmas and antinomies' (Jameson 182). It would seem to be useful to note where these antinomies exist, and how generative they prove to be both in terms of the encounters and crossings between cultural forms and their insertion in wider historical shifts and meanings. If literary language absorbed the tactics of cinematic form for its own aesthetic ends, for example, not least within the moment of modernism as I've argued elsewhere, the literary desire called film was also about the encounter with a radically different and in some respects incommensurable medium. A medium that was, in fundamental ways, non-linguistic, despite discussions of its languages and syntax, and their transmutations into the fields of philosophy and psychoanalysis at the time. Filmic techniques of construction lent themselves in the modernist novel to a seemingly shared lexicon of formal creative strategies – the foremost of which might be said to be montage – yet the perceptual experience of cinema and its hieroglyphics remained very different from reading a book, intertitles notwithstanding.

Chris Marker's point in his CD-ROM *Immemory* records a later moment of intermedial encounter, but holds true in broader literal terms: 'Cinema is that which is bigger than we are, what you have to look up at. When a movie is shown small and you have to look down at it, it loses its essence. . .What you see on TV is the shadow of a film, nostalgia for a film, the echo of a film, never a real film' (Marker, quoted in Bellour 56). If this is about loss, a moment in one of the many deaths of cinema heralded over the last century, it also articulates a specificity of the experience of cinema – 'that which is bigger than we are' – which underlined its distinction to earlier modernist eyes. 'Looking up' in the moment before the coming of the talkies meant, in the words of Dorothy Richardson, the acknowledgement of a new perceptual arena – 'the gift of quiet, of attention and concentration, of perspective', which was at one with 'the social gifts: the insensibly learned awareness of alien people and alien ways', 'the living news of the changing world' (Richardson, quoted in Watts, 77, 78). The impact of that world suggested new roller-coaster forms of intensity. But it also carried a utopian dimension, evident in Richardson's rather more contemplative celebration of cinema, which sensed the democratising and internationalising potential of the largeness of the medium, in her case wrapped in a vision of an ideal (and no doubt imperialising) salvation to be found in the picture house as cathedral. It held out nonetheless a virtual mass public, or publics, not to be recognised in the horizon of the modernist novel, and it is arguably the 'echoes' of this desire 'shown small' in its pages, in tandem with the mobile impressionism incorporated from film aesthetics, which mark one dimension of the antinomies of cultural form at that time.

My point here is simply that it seems important to think about ways in which intermedial crossings involve elements and materials that do not add up, or synchronise expressively – the word antinomy serves here to mark that incommensurability – even as they modulate through the circuits of their very difference into new forms. Indeed, critical work may require an inhabiting of those gaps and transitions where moments of translation take place. The attempt to think the specificity of a cultural form – Marker's auratic 'essence' – while often inflected sometimes conservatively in terms of a mourning or loss (the death of cinema, the end of the novel), is here a means of signalling something wider at stake in the practice of what has now become, in the words of Gilles Deleuze, the 'internal struggle with informatics' (Deleuze 1989: 270). And thus it may be possible to reveal how these disjunctures become generative in the making of as yet unarticulated subjectivities and collective languages, a making that itself has a number of histories. In this essay I'll be sketching one of them, using montage as an Ariadne's thread, and Deleuze's account in his cinema books of the shift from the movement to the time image as a periodising guide. The aim of the whole is ultimately to explore several novels, loosely grouped – by Kazuo Ishiguro, Haruki Murakami and David Mitchell – and offer a view of their formal novelistic incorporation of intermedial thought. I want, though, to begin by thinking about my title – on conversation – as a filmic framing device for the whole.

A Conversational Gambit

In Francis Ford Coppola's 1974 film *The Conversation*, the audience experiences what might be seen as a moment of transition between visual technologies that carries with it a latent moment of shock. Gene Hackman's bugging specialist, Harry Caul, trained in cutting-edge security methods at the height of the events of 1968, is now working for private corporate clients rather than the state, not questioning the reasons for his surveillance. He has recorded and filmed at their behest a conversation between a young couple walking through Union Square, in San Francisco. The sound is distorted, and like a film director and sound editor, he must cut and coordinate the sound to bring it into focus, and the action with it. The sound 'noise' has to be rendered intelligible by tapes and feedback loops, continuously repeated in the movie as a mode of technological attention, and picked up as it seems to escape into Harry's life as fragments of song and paranoid possibility. The film is centrally about the witnessing and decoding of visual and aural information, and carries with it from the outset a certain interpretative idealism, as if the truth of this scene, once synchronised, might be available to audience and surveillance team alike. A private intimate truth, it would seem, of a love affair at mortal risk from the mechanisms of corporate and technological control, which the specialist begins to question, concerned to protect the wellbeing of his 'victims'.

Yet his decoding of the situation is fundamentally mistaken. Not only does he get it wrong, his methods suddenly outmoded, as the 'victims' themselves turn out to be the murderous perpetrators within the corporation, but the audience also inhabits a certain loss of innocence. By the end of the film the steady serenity of the frame and the spectatorial gaze are the same, and as we watch the specialist in his apartment, a scene we have experienced before, it dawns on us that our line of sight is that of a bugging device planted by unknown others, which he is now destroying his own apartment to find. The conversation, repeated now in all its clarity, is suddenly revealed as wholly strategic, its emphases transformed. The film is marked by its Nixonian *mise-en-scène*, a post-68 'fall' into the murky dealings of privatised control and paranoia. What makes it remarkable is the way viewers find themselves in a new spectatorial environment by the end of the film – at one (and colluding) with an emerging technological milieu – when they had started out innocently enough, albeit with the naturalised innocence of an interpretative trust in the ways of the state, somewhat against its grain.

Kaja Silverman has explored the way in which the camera and tape recorder 'make possible a certain anthropomorphism of the cinematic apparatus' because of their close and 'harmonizing' association with human vision and hearing (Silverman 11). If this anthropomorphism is in play in *The Conversation*, it also undergoes a defamiliarisation, in that not only are sound and sight out of synch, but once produced, their synchronies turn out to be open to falsification and strategy. Rather than emphasising the truths of the coherence of actions and words in an identifiable – because crucially legible/audible – public realm, these techniques undermine belief in that milieu altogether. It would be possible to mount an argument here about a self-reflexivity on the part of the cinematic apparatus encountering for the first time the ramifications of that privatised small screen of video, its potential for repetition and rerecording, and also for the modes of public surveillance whose grainy images are, in the twenty-first century, second nature in the documentary registering (and 'protection') of the patterns and silent conversations of everyday life. And to reinforce the historical import of this encounter, to note that it is at this time in the 1970s that there is 'a massive diffusion of technology in commercial and civilian applications', as Manuel Castells details in his The *Rise of Network Society*: Sony producing VCR machines commercially for the first time, the industrial production of optic fibre, the development of the electronic communications network by the research arm of the US Defense Department that would later become the Internet (Castells 1996: 47). To which we might want to add the imminent arrival of the Dolby system, which would transform the technologies of sound available to specialists like Walter Murch, who was responsible for the sound editing of Coppola's film and his later *Apocalypse Now*.[1]

This would be to 'explain' the film in terms of a wider technological environment, to discover that techne as its object. Yet if *The Conversation* opens up what might be seen as a *habitus* of technological transition, felt in its generation of free-floating sensations of obsolescence, or the mysterious disenfranchisements of new kinds of intellectual capital that others seem effortlessly to possess (like the pure gaze of the bugging device), it also reflects in its own terms on a certain cinematic loss, in touch with the antinomies of that encounter. Key here is the notion of conversation, which is marked by a disjuncture between sound and image that the action of the film apparently aims to overcome, like cinema itself, only to discover that its universe has mutated, and the meaning of such an overcoming has shifted even as the fundamental disjuncture remains. Sound is abstracted, experienced in the process of a kind of autonomising, either floating in aleatory ways, cut loose from the visual image it might be expected to reinforce, or joining with it cynically. It is at this point that Deleuze's account of cinematic conversation provides a useful, if undoubtedly idiosyncratic, long view.

---

[1] See in particular the section on 'Contemporary Innovators' in Weis and Belton for a brief take on Walter Murch and his methods, and the later impact of the Dolby system.

The 'Triumph' of Sound Conversation

For Deleuze, reflecting in *Cinema 2: The Time-Image* on the 'break' between silent cinema and the coming of the talkie, it was the 'triumph' of cinema to invent 'the sound conversation'. Unlike the novel and theatre, he argues (allowing some exceptions for those influenced by or contemporary with cinema: Proust, James, Dos Passos), cinema captured the speech-acts central to human interaction, pragmatic forms of sociability passing through conversation that are 'never identical with society' (Deleuze 1989: 231). In his account, the coming of sound 'denaturalizes' the visual image of silent cinema, which had presented 'the natural being of man in history or society' (226) alongside its indirect 'read image' of intertitle speech. When discourse is heard directly, a new visual dimension of the image is brought into play:

> when speech makes itself heard, it is as if it makes something new visible, and the visible image, denaturalized, begins to become readable in turn, *as something visible or visual*. The latter, from this point, acquires problematic values or a certain equivocal quality which it did not have in the silent cinema. What the speech-act makes visible, interaction, may always be badly deciphered, read, seen; hence a whole rise in the lie, in deception, which takes place in the visual image. (229)

If speech becomes visible, in the movement of voices in action and in the absences implied by the use of voice-off, the legibility it brings to the visual image requires more complex kinds of decipherment. And there is a performative dimension to this speech, in which, for example, 'interests, feelings or love no longer determine conversation' but 'themselves depend on the division of stimulation in conversation, the latter determining relations of force and structurations which are particular to it' (230). In conversation, cinema reveals the constitution of a 'sociology of communication':

> interactions are established in the margins or at the crossroads, constituting a whole *mise-en-scène* or dramaturgy of daily life (uneasinesses, deceptions and conflicts in interaction), opening up a field of special perception, of specific visibility, and provoking a 'hypertrophy of the eye'. Interactions *make themselves seen* in speech-acts. Interactions do not simply concern the partners in a speech-act precisely because they are not explained through individuals, any more than they derive from a structure: rather it is the speech-act which, through its continuous circulation, propagation and autonomous evolution, will create the interaction between individuals or groups who are far away, dispersed, indifferent to each other. (227)

Such a 'dramaturgy' works in the classical cinema of the movement-
image along behaviourist lines, locating the stimulations of affective
material in a wider organic whole, embodying them in the movement
of specific behaviours and their interaction with and transformation of
milieux. As D.N. Rodowick describes, its

> sensorimotor schema limits movement to a physical trajectory or transfor-
> mation in space, giving a restricted sense to the image and to the narrative
> logic deriving from it. Affections must be translated into spatial images con-
> stitutive of a mise-en-scène. These in turn create the possibility of situations
> requiring series of actions and reactions, conflicts and resolutions. The
> whole of the sensorimotor schema unfolds as organic composition where
> commensurability is the rule: on the one hand, movement between parts of
> the whole; on the other, montage within which the web of actions and reac-
> tions is woven. Each requires connection through rational intervals.
> (Rodowick 74)

The place of the 'sound continuum' – broken down into audible and
inaudible words, noises, music, phonations, 'jargons', silences – within
this sensorimotor schema is thus to maintain 'communication between
the image and a whole which has become increasingly rich and complex'
(Deleuze 1989: 241).

If classical Hollywood narrative is the model for the cinema of the
movement-image, the prime example of 'sound conversation' for
Deleuze is prewar American comedy. Its crazy, quick-fire exchanges,
rapid reversals and stammerings hint at the social content lacking in the
abstraction of his account: conversation as a popular discourse promised
by American democracy, 'mobilizing nations . . . regions, classes and
also all those outside classes'. In enunciating its 'patchwork' of collective voices (exemplified in fictional form for Deleuze in the potential of
Melville's writing[2]), American discourse reveals a people in the process
of becoming. It appears though to take on in this mode a statist form.
Conversation can move from interactionist routine to propaganda predicated on the 'we' as actant:

> it is understandable that discourse as cinematographic object could make Capra
> go from comedy to the series 'Why we fight', in so far as the very form of socia-
> bility, despite its relations of forces and the cruelty essential to its stakes, appears
> in democracy, defined as 'artificial world' where individuals have abandoned

[2] See for example the chapter on Melville's *Bartleby* in *Critique and Clinique*
(Deleuze 1993: 89–114).

the objective aspects of their situation and the personal aspects of their activity in order to produce a pure interaction between themselves. (232)

It is seemingly this 'pure interaction' that *The Conversation* will later
reveal as a zone of distortion and falsifying, in the aftermath of 1968 and
the Vietnam war and during the Nixonian fall from grace; its democratic
potential mired in forms of strategy that invade even the most intimate
exchanges. The dislocation of sound and image, rather than confirming
the ability to act and react within an identifiable milieu, underlines its
loss, and with it the break from the realm of the movement-image:

> the speech-act is no longer inserted in the linkage of actions and reactions,
> and does not reveal a web of interactions any more. It turns in on itself; it is
> no longer a dependant or something which is part of the visual image; it
> becomes a completely separate sound image; it takes on a cinematic auton-
> omy and cinema becomes truly audiovisual. (243)

With the crisis of the movement-image arrive new forms of cinema, and
a mode of montage that articulates this sense of disjuncture.

Conversation in the Reign of 'Incommensurables'

The post-1945 break from the realm of the movement-image transforms
the uniformity of its milieux into 'a proliferation of empty, disconnected,
abandoned spaces', 'any-space-whatevers', through which characters
move not as actants – able to contest and transform their environment –
but as 'seers', confronted with a devastated world where 'the intolerable is
no longer a serious injustice, but a permanent state of a daily banality'
(170). The cinema of the time-image, mapped in the affective cartographies of Italian neorealism, the French New Wave, new American
cinema, and first developed earlier and intensified in later postwar work
by the Japanese director, Ozu, responds to a landscape shaped in the aftermath of Auschwitz and Hiroshima by flows of geopolitical – and
psychological – remaking. Wandering characters are immersed in 'purely
optical and sound situations' without the comfort of their resolution or
control, lacking trust 'that a global situation can give rise to an action
which is capable of modifying it' (Deleuze 1986: 206), and in search of a
belief that might connect them to the world at all. Such characters

> are in the grip of a mutation, they are themselves mutants . . . Mutation of
> Europe after the war, mutation of an Americanized Japan, mutation of

France in '68: it is not the cinema that turns away from politics, it becomes completely political, but in another way. (Deleuze 1989: 19)

Conversation – understood in terms of 'the web of interactions' constituting the mass promise of the cinema of the movement-image – has been shattered, having 'degenerated into state propaganda and manipulation, into the kind of fascism which brought together Hitler and Hollywood, Hollywood and Hitler' (164). But new forms of conversational discourse emerge that are in many ways realisations of the creative pragmatism Deleuze espouses, mutating through a mode of montage-cut, which works the asymmetrical and irrational rhythms of the direct presentation of time into the interstices between the visual image and sound image, in a continual deframing. In Ozu's films, for example, scripts are famously built up from 'any dialogue whatever' that has no recognisable subject matter, and rather than being linked organically within a sensorimotor schema or even by the associations of story, visual images and sound images remain dissociated, bringing 'emancipated senses into direct relation with time and thought' (17). In such modern(ist) cinema, Deleuze suggests,

> the ethereal speech-act creates the event, but always placed crosswise over tectonic visual layers: there are two trajectories crossing each other. It creates the event, but in a space empty of events. What defines modern cinema is a 'to-ing and fro-ing between speech and image', which has to invent their new relationship. (247)

The pedagogies of this relationship are in significant ways 'novelesque' for Deleuze. Novelesque, but not pertaining to narrative. This relates in part to the freeing of the creative act of storytelling – 'the pure speech act' – in the incommensurability of sound and visual images, a free indirect relation that reminds him of Bakhtin's account of the novel:

> Bakhtin defined the novel, in contrast to the epic or tragedy, as no longer having the collective or distributive unity through which the characters still spoke one and the same language. On the contrary, the novel necessarily borrows sometimes the everyday anonymous language, sometimes the language of a class, a group, a profession, sometimes the particular language of a character. To the extent that the characters, classes and genres form the free indirect discourse of the author, as much as the author forms their free indirect vision . . . In short, it is reflection in genres, anonymous or personified, which constitutes the novel, its 'plurilingualism', its speech and its vision. Godard gives cinema the particular powers of the novel. He provides

himself with the reflexive types as so many interceders through whom I is always another. (187)

Such an account of the novel dovetails with the auteurism privileged in Deleuze's approach even as it allows for what he calls 'the diversity, the deformity, the otherness of a free indirect discourse' (184). If television is deemed the bad instance of a form whose techne might be said to 'kill cinema' while feeding on it, having 'abandoned most of its own creative possibilities' (though nonetheless *the* explanation for the second stage of the talkie and its irrational cuts) (251–2), the novel as he defines it is paradoxically a means of thinking intermedial passages in the richest terms. Paradoxically, because of the limitations of novelistic form whatever its open-field plurilingualism, one might think, but then limits are what interest Deleuze here. The Bakhtinian movement of images of discourse, of categories known as 'genres', relates to his sense of the creative possibilities of film that are continually advanced in new forms of montage; genre understood not as 'the subsuming [of] images which naturally belong to it', but as the constitution of 'the limit of images which do not belong to it but are reflected in it' (184). By genres Deleuze is referring to categories that 'are never final answers but categories of problems which introduce reflection into the image itself' (186). These can mean psychic categories like imagination or memory, or kinds of singularity exhibited through individuals or actions, or specific feelings like surprise or the 'absence of passion', or phenomena like noise or silence. He also is thinking about the passage of other cultural forms:

> It is characteristic of cinema to reflect itself, and reflect the other genres, without the visual images referring to a pre-established dance, novel, theatre, or film, but themselves setting out to 'do' cinema, to do dance, to do novel, to do theatre, throughout a series, for an episode. (186)

In what follows I want to reflect on some contemporary novels and the way that they might be said to 'do film' in the broadest sense of the term. But at the same time I want to think about the way they also 'do novel' in an environment saturated by the intermedial passages attendant on the 'internal struggle with informatics' (270), a struggle anticipated for Deleuze in the cinema of the time-image. I want to continue an encounter with his work by focusing in particular on three aspects relating to the incommensurability of the sound image and visual image: the notion of a falsifying narrative, the cartographies of the brain-city, and fabulation. And the novels themselves might be reinvented as a series whose cuts and interstices have something to say: Kazuo Ishiguro's *The Remains of the Day* (1989), Haruki Murakami's *Hard-Boiled Wonderland and the End of the World* (2003; published 1985; first translated into English in 1991), and David Mitchell's *Ghostwritten* (1999), *number9dream* (2001) and *Cloud Atlas* (2004).

The Remains of the Day and the Time of Falsifying Narrations

What makes Ishiguro's novel remarkable in its transformation of an English novelistic tradition is its sustained literary rendering of a voice. Stevens, a butler or 'gentleman's gentleman', tells in the first person his recollections of his time as a butler at Darlington Hall. Central to Stevens's narrative is a concept of professional service, and its dignity, which he is keen to extol: a form of class 'sympathy' in which the values of a Tory aristocracy and its traditions are held in place through the rituals and felt 'privilege' of the household servant. Stevens's voice is a seemingly assured act of testimony, in which he recalls, with the cadences and mannered control of the gentleman butler, what such 'dignity' meant to the service class of his father's generation. In the noted story of the tiger under the imperial dining table, dispatched by three shots of a twelve-bore gun by a butler who calmly goes on to refresh the tea with the announcement to his employer and assembled guests that 'Dinner will be served at the usual time and I am pleased to say there will be no discernible traces left of the recent occurrence by that time' (Ishiguro 36) is Stevens's treasured example of the polite circumlocution and understatement that marks the novel as a whole.

Through its dramatising of voice the novel keys into a Englishness constructed from stereotypical tonalities and class accents. Like the conversational interaction made visible in the speech acts I discussed earlier, there is a performative dimension to such a speech, bringing 'interests, feelings and love' into play through its adjustments and stammerings rather than the other way around. Brecht would have called this a form of gest – social attitude expressed through the gestural behaviour of the voice and body.[3] If there is a pantomimic

---

[3] 'By social gest is meant the mimetic and gestural expression of the social relationships prevailing between people of a given period.' Bertold Brecht, 'Short Description of a New Technique of Acting' (in *Brecht on Theatre*, ed. and trans. John Willett. New York: Hill & Wang, 1992 (1964), p. 139).

quality to it – which means that Stevens can be mistaken for a gentleman by acting out visual and verbal cues – it is not unlike the discourse
of British movies in the period in which the novel is set, when characters were assigned a now fossilised register of language according to
their social class positioning. This gest is marked by crisis and mutation
in Ishiguro's novel, a source of humour, such as when Stevens tries desperately to learn how to 'banter' to suit the more relaxed style of his
new American employer, but one nonetheless given devastating social
content.

Irony in *Remains of the Day* seems commensurable with the sometimes mercurial inflexions of voice, like the tain of a mirror, making
readers work to make out the complex collusions and denials at stake,
as well as their own identifications with a naturalised image of a
social landscape. At the same time the tain is actually a tear or cut,
which sets the storytelling loose to follow its own wandering as if the
'web of action and reaction' that would govern it is weak and uncertain. The meaning of action in such an environment is thrown into
question, either subject to impossible waiting and anticipation (as in
the ever-deferred romance with Miss Kenton), or as the physical and
mental automation required of servitude and by the manipulations of
fascism. The weight of the narrator as perceiver, never actant (it
would seem), shifts as the novel advances, its optical and sound situations generating uncertainty, denaturalising. This is a revisiting of
that postwar crisis of the movement-image from a later 1980s
moment that attempted to resurrect its certainties as 'heritage', a
novelistic 'doing film' in which montage marks the text with the dis-
locations of a post-imperial melancholy, sending the testifying voice
into confessional spirals, like an admission of false consciousness that
buffers itself in the telling.

As Homi Bhabha describes, the splicing of different historical times –
'the authoritarian populism of the Thatcherite late 1980s (the moment
of authorship) restaging the Suez-centred mid-1950s with its post imperial "confusions" (the historical "present" of the narrative) which, in
turn, frames the country-house fascism of the fellow-travellers of the late
1920s and 1930s' (Bhabha 210) – introduces a contingency into a naturalised past and present, turning the 'nationalism of the silver service
into the "anxiety" of the past' (Bhabha 211). Another facet of this montage might now include the present moment of reading, in which the
Iraq war of Bush and Blair reworks the moment of Suez in particular, and
where the discourse of 'appeasement' has been employed in rather

different terms.[4] Bhabha grasps the novel's montage effect in psychoanalytical terms, quoting John Forrester:

> The present of the nation, which appears through Ishiguro's temporal montage, signifies a historical intermediacy intrinsic to the psychoanalytic concept of *Nachträglichkeit* (differed action or retroactivity). It is a transferential function, 'whereby the past dissolves the in the present, so that the future becomes (once again) an *open question, instead of being specified by the fixity of the past*'. (my emphasis) (Bhabha 212)

In this account montage disassembles the boundaries of the nation in the trajectories of colonialism and in the presences of racialised others, unravelling the violences of its seemingly quiet causalities: the dismissal of the Jewish maids, the price of working-class deaths. The future anterior – what will have happened – is broken open, rendered 'intermediate', and other potential communities, democratic possibilities, glimpsed in its 'disjunct differences' (Bhabha 216).

The voice of the butler, set loose from the 'trust' it invested in, comes to contemplate time, what 'remains', at the end of the novel. 'As if it were necessary for the world to be broken and buried for the speech-act to rise up', writes Deleuze of the cinema of the time-image that pursued the dissociation of voice and the visual, voice and body (Deleuze 1989: 268). These 'remains' are transformed, at an English seaside where people cheer as the evening lights go on, to become the rubble of an 'anyspace-whatever' even as they suggest an open future that might undergo mutation – where he might learn to 'banter' like an American. *Remains of the Day* revisions the limits of the English novel by deframing it, introducing a contingency that resembles a Deleuzian 'falsifying narration': where 'what is known is no longer anchored in a sure link between present and past, perception and memory' (Rodowick 96). Like the crisis of truth telling where the butler's conversation claims veracity yet also lies – a condition experienced as shame, embarrassment, anxiety, but also in the same politely sustained timbre of voice as 'a slightly misleading picture' (Ishiguro 124) – the effect of this is to generate a virtual disturbance around events, choices, decisions, actions, as if in a parallel universe other scenarios are simultaneously possible. Or even in the same world, writes Deleuze, reflecting on the paradox of 'contingent futures', since

---

[4] Thanks to Matthew Wraith, who made this point during an MA seminar discussion of the film adaptation of the novel.

nothing prevents us from affirming that incompossibles belong to the same world, that incompossible worlds belong to the same universe: 'Fang, for example, has a secret; a stranger calls at his door . . . Fang can kill the intruder, the intruder can kill Fang, they can both escape, they can both die, and so forth . . . you arrive at this house, but in one of the possible pasts you are my enemy, in another, my friend . . .' This is Borges's reply to Leibniz: the straight line as force of time, as labyrinth of time, is also the line which forks and keeps on forking, passing through *incompossible presents*, returning to *not-necessarily true pasts*. (131)

In this sense 'doing film' in *Remains of the Day* becomes a means of grasping the possibilities of this fictional 'falsifying' and thus the limits of 'doing novel'. These 'forking' contingencies are *read* rather than seen in the 'silent' interstices of the textual voice, as a condition of its historical deframing.

Hard-Boiled Wonderland and the Brain-City

In the opening sequence of Haruki Murakami's novel the sound has been turned down, to the disorientation of the narrator who is travelling in a lift. His cough 'seemed flat, like clay thrown against a slick concrete wall. I could hardly believe that dull thud issued from my own body.' He has no sense of the elevator's velocity or direction. 'Maybe I'd gone up twelve stories, then down three. Maybe I'd circled the globe. How would I know?'(Murakami 1). 'The doors showed no sign of ever opening. Stationary in unending silence, a still life: *Man in Elevator*' (3). After a while, the narrator finding a means of diverting his boredom by calculating the change in his pocket, the doors open. '(M)y eyes had seen the opening doors, but I didn't fully grasp the significance of the event. Of course, the doors' opening meant the linking of two spaces previously denied accessible continuity by means of those very doors. And at the same time, it meant the elevator had reached its destination' (6). A conversation with a young woman in a pink suit ensues, which I want to quote at length:

> She gave me a brisk I-know sort of a nod. A hint of *eau de cologne* drifted from her neckline. A scent reminiscent of standing in a melon patch on a summer's morn. It put me in a funny frame of mind. A nostalgic yet impossible pastiche of sentiments, as if two wholly unrelated memories had threaded together in an unknown recess. Feelings like this sometimes come over me. And most often due to specific scents.

'Long corridor, eh?' I tried to break the ice. She glanced at me, but kept walking. I guessed she was twenty or twenty-one. Well-defined features, broad forehead, clear complexion.

It was then that she said, 'Proust.'

Or more precisely, she didn't pronounce the word 'Proust', but simply moved her lips to form what ought to have been 'Proust'. I had yet to hear a genuine peep out of her. It was as if she were talking to me from the far side of a thick sheet of glass.

Proust?

'*Marcel* Proust?' I asked her.

She gave me a look. Then she repeated, 'Proust.' I gave up on the effort and fell back in line behind her, trying for the life of me to come up with other lip movements that corresponded to 'Proust'. *Truest? . . . Brew whist? . . . Blue is it? . . .* One after another, quietly to myself, I pronounced strings of meaningless syllables, but none seemed to match. I could only conclude that she had indeed said 'Proust'. But what I couldn't figure out was, what was the connection between this long corridor and Marcel Proust? (Murakami 9–10)

The disjuncture of sound image and visual image – its technological manipulation – is experienced here in a habitus whose topographies appear radically new. If the textual joke about lipsynching the voice plays with a notion of involuntary memory, that 'Proustian dimension where people and things occupy a place in time which is incommensurable with the one they have in space' (Deleuze 1989: 39), it is a notion that seems broken into its contituent parts, like a montage-circuit that demands logical disassembly, comprised of indiscernible connections and junction boxes. Perception can't authenticate what it sees. Memory can't testify to recollections. The senses don't function reliably, but present contingent propositions that suggest new kinds of geometry – like the doors opening to bring together 'previously denied accessible continuity'. Scrambled sounds can't be rendered commensurable with the movement of the lips, but might nonetheless generate possible sound images in which corridors are as long as Marcel Proust. Mental cartographies then, which map 'a funny frame of mind'.

'Doing film' in *Remains of the Day* seems in this light a form of nostalgic relation to a world that could still be read in terms of the cinematic taming of space, not least in terms of the upright positioning of the frame, 'bigger than we are' in Marker's words. The disorientations of *Hard-Boiled Wonderland and the End of the World* twist the spatial coordinates of time and space according to other informational logics, like the labyrinths of a computer game. In Deleuze's account of cinema, the time-image anticipates new forms of electronic imaging 'whose relation to the cinematographic image remains to be determined':

> a new image can arise from any point whatever of the preceding image. The organization of space here loses its privileged directions, and first of all the privilege of the vertical which the position of the screen still displays, in favour of an omni-directional space which constantly varies its angles and co-ordinates, to exchange the vertical and the horizontal. And the screen itself, even if it keeps a vertical position by convention, no longer seems to refer to the human posture, like a window or painting, but rather constitutes a table of information, an opaque surface on which are inscribed 'data', information replacing nature, and the brain-city, the third eye, replacing the eyes of nature. (265)

Murakami's novel sketches the circuits of a 'brain-city' as if Kafka had entered the information age, with the narrator caught up as a 'Calcutec' pawn in a battle for the ownership, control, and decoding of data by faceless forces and thugs – the competing organisations of the System, Semiotecs, and the underground INKlings. These are, and are not, the byways of the 'culture of real virtuality' associated with 'the frontier of Japanese social life', which cannot now be understood 'in isolation from the global alleys of the virtual hypertext', as Castells discusses (1998: 241). If this is the social content of Murakami's 'hardboiled' world that flows under and through contemporary Tokyo, it is cut through alternately with what appears at first to be a disconnected narrative based in an imaginary walled – 'fortress' – city, where unicorns are protected beasts, and the narrator is a Dreamreader drawing out memories from their skulls, archived in the Library: a 'timeless' virtual parallel to that actual world, rendered archaeological, as if there is a 'hidden language of bones' that might decode its connections (Murakami 28).

These formal montage-cuts between incompossible worlds may mark disjunctures internal to the Japanese modernity that first generated the notion of an 'Information Society'.[5] They are also, it transpires, a

---

[5] The emergence of the notion of an 'Information Society' in Japan – to be understood 'not as a society that uses information technology' but as the 'specific social structure, associated with, but not determined by, the informational paradigm' – is discussed by Manuel Castells (1998: 236–43). First proposed in 1963, it was a concept popularised by futurologists and adopted in the late 1960s in government strategic thinking both in terms of a new phase of global competition – particularly with the US and in Asian markets – and internally as a 'profound transformation of Japan through the diffusion of information technology', accompanied by a 'new

reflection on time. Their cuts are internal to the brain-wiring of the narrator himself, who is the creator of this mythic 'End of the World', as well as existing as a decoder in Wonderland; possessor of an extraordinary facility in the scrambling and unscrambling – 'shuffling' – of data between the right and left hemispheres of his brain. The Professor who has engineered this capacity in the narrator's neural and cognitive pathways has been aided by skills acquired before 'the War' as an assistant film editor. Finding the mind's 'black box' central to the mysterious 'factory floor' of the cognitive system, he has worked out a means of harnessing it. But he needs to control the impact of 'random chance' and new experiences by 'flash-freezing' the system at one point in time, in a state that can be recalled, while allowing another ongoing system to coexist within the same person. A series of parallel circuits that the mind can switch between: memory, in this light, is a cartographic 'membrane', one that can be deframed, re-edited.

Videoing the 'core consciousness' of his subject, the Professor constructed a third circuit: ' "cuttin' and pastin', tossin' out some parts, resequencin', exactly like film editin'. Rearrangin' everything into a story." "A story?" "That shouldn't seem so strange," said the Professor. "The best musicians transpose consciousness into sound; painters do the same for colour and shape. Mental phenomena are the stuff writers make into novels. It's the same basic logic" ' (262). This is the edited 'story' of the End of the World, a 'sealed' mental environment that the narrator finally elects to inhabit as his other circuit closes down, one that begins to be interrupted by forms of the involuntary memory previously 'taken out' or controlled – 'the air, the sounds, the light. I am reawakened by songs' (386) – thus beginning, in aesthetic and temporal terms, to change its state.

In what ways might Murakami's novel seem to anticipate new pathways for cinema's afterlife, figuring the limits of what it means to 'do film' or 'do novel' in the light of the 'struggle with informatics' (Deleuze 1989: 270)? In a sense it reveals as story another technological trajectory also present in Deleuze's account, now culminating in the future prospect of a 'cinematic experience without light and eyes . . . images without perception conveyed by the direct stimulation of neural networks': a 'neurocinema' in which the 'brain, as opposed to the eye, would become the screen' (Weibel 599). But it also returns to the question of technological

mythology . . . which actually tried to replace social thinking and political projects with images of a computerized/telecommunicated society' (237, 238). It would be interesting to explore Murakami's work further in this (and other) contexts.

transformation and aesthetic form. What does it entail to inhabit this environment, the interstices of its falsifying narrations, its data overloading, the indistinctness of the relations between the actual and the virtual: psychic automation, or the release of new creative possibilities?:

> cerebral creation or deficiency of the cerebellum? The new automatism is worthless in itself if it is not put to the service of a powerful, obscure, condensed will to art, aspiring to deploy itself through involuntary movements which nonetheless do not restrict it. An original will to art has already been defined by us in the change affecting the intelligible content of cinema itself: the substitution of the time-image for the movement-image. So that electronic images will have to be based on still another will to art, or on as yet unknown aspects of the time-image. (266)

The poetic culmination of the *Hard-Boiled Wonderland and the End of the World* might seem to recapitulate this will to art, in Deleuze's words, though in terms of a creative authorship: as if to 'do novel', even at the limits of the brain-city, is to retain its immanent hope.

Serial Fabulations: Towards a Conversational Conclusion

Intermedial passages and technological transformations are often accompanied by a sense of an ending. In David Mitchell's *number9dream* (the dream that comes after an ending, we are told) a 'goatwriter' chooses a fountain pen and his own stammering language over the digital seductions of a website diva who offers to 'download you to the side of the screen where the future awaits! Link up with cyberagents, the e-bookshops! The paper book is dying!' If there is something maniacal (and market driven) projected in the voice of the apparatus – 'film rights and book deals in twenty-seven languages . . . will be mine! Mine! Miiiiiiiiine!' (247) – such that the imperatives of new technology might resemble a state of 'siege' (Bellour 56), these are also interstitial kinds of encounter where the telling of stories is a new intensive form of thought, a performative act. *number9dream* declares via its goatwriter that 'Reality is the page. Life is the word.' But its free indirect relations with genres – in the Deleuzian sense of the term – play out alternatives to the literary page: in the speed of the video games that short-circuit the narrative action, in the identity imaging of a society of control, in the hardboiled Yakuza thriller whose action takes place via the screen of the cash machine or through a deadlier video violence, in the wartime journal of the *kaiten* torpedo-man, who aims to ride its technology against American ships to his death. The story of the goatwriter is written by a self-appointed 'fabulist', but the fabulation of the novel itself is of another order.

It may be that Deleuze's account of cinematic thought reaches a limit at this point in what it can offer as a new analytic of the image, an analytic that may find its limits reflected in 'doing novel'. But the dissociation between sound and visual images that I have been tracking in the moment of the time-image, an 'irrational' and 'non-totalizable relation', continues to generate potential: 'here where a musical speech rises and is torn away, there where the visible is covered over or buried' (Deleuze 1989: 261). David Mitchell's work is interesting in this regard. If in their performance of the 'pure speech act' of storytelling – Deleuze's fabulation – his books touch on the crises and deframings discussed in the *Remains of the Day*, the buried trajectories of other histories; or if in their play with the temporal crossings of the past and future in an open present, they explore the virtuality that is the formal and aesthetic conundrum of Murakami's novel; they also return to a mode of *conversation* once more.

For Deleuze there is a democratic potential in interactive performativity, the conversational 'patchwork' of dispersed and indifferent voices. It is a potential betrayed by fascism in the cinema of the movement-image, a loss explored in *The Conversation*. If there is to be 'creation beyond information' in Deleuze's terms (270), it is one that revisits this potential. In *Ghostwritten* and *Cloud Atlas* in particular, animate and inanimate voices rise like musical speech, sometimes creolised, affirming, played out in the 'otherness' of free and indirect relations such that the narration is coextensive with their processes of becoming: like the 'rogue soul' in *Ghostwritten* who shorts through the bodies of hosts, discovering 'the imprint of a undecidability which was just the passing of life' (Deleuze 1989: 203). In these novels conversation takes place in series form – as if the montage-cut has become an 'irrational interval that . . . now exists as a force encouraging a change of state', as D.N. Rodowick explains. 'One kind of becoming is the force of time as change; another is becoming-other, the pure form of time as the (un)founding of subjectivity whose formula is "I is an other" . . . as *Zarathustra* exclaims, it is to "create itself the freedom for new creation", to affirm the ever-recurring possibility for change' (Rodowick 150, 151).

In his discussion of Ozu's cinema, Deleuze had described the 'violent interruption' of American colours (Coca-Cola red, plastic yellow) in postwar Japanese life – 'the clash of two everyday realities' – repeating the words of the character in *The Flavour of Green Tea over Rice* who had asked 'what if the opposite had occurred, if saki, samisen and geisha wigs had suddenly been introduced into the everyday banality of the Americans. . .?' (Deleuze 1989: 15). If the mutations of modernisation are 'always imagined', as Naoki Sakai describes, 'as a concrete transfer from one point to another on a world map' (Sakai 98), the novels I have touched on ask what crosses to and fro in the banalities and buried histories of much more complex and globalising geoinformational image flows.[6] In *Ghostwritten*, the shifts between East and West mobilise voices – electronic, radio, terroristic – caught up in those mutations, and the violences which accompany them. The force of fabulation in this light is to 'free fiction from . . . a fiction of the truth which is always that of the colonizer' (Rodowick 160). An ambition that animates the series of chronicles, legends and tales from different temporal moments in *Cloud Atlas*, where the storytelling function ostensibly frees voices to speak against the historical grain of violence and disenfranchisement. In a sense the wandering attempt to restore a *belief* in the world with which the novel ends, is also that of Deleuze's cinema of the time-image. The novel's declaration, both political and aesthetic, 'that this is the hardest of worlds to make real', is not uncomplicated or lightly made (Mitchell 2004: 528).

Works Cited

Bellour, Raymond, 2003. 'Battle of the Images', in *Future Cinema: The Cinematic Imaginary After Film*, eds Jeffrey Shaw and Peter Weibel. Cambridge, MA: MIT Press, pp. 56–9.

Bhabha, Homi, 1994. 'Anxious Nations, Nervous States', in *Supposing the Subject*, ed. Joan Copjec. London: Verso, pp. 201–17.

Castells, Manuel, 1996. *The Information Age: Economy, Society and Culture. Volume I: The Rise of the Network Society*. Oxford: Blackwell.

Castells, Manuel, 1998. *The Information Age: Economy, Society and Culture. Volume III: End of Millennium*. Oxford: Blackwell.

Deleuze, Gilles, 1986. *Cinema 1: The Movement-Image*, trans. Hugh Tomlinson and Barbara Habberjam. London: The Athlone Press.

Deleuze, Gilles, 1989. *Cinema 2: The Time-Image*, trans. Hugh Tomlinson and Robert Galeta. London: The Athlone Press.

[6] I am conscious too that a much more careful engagement with Japan's historical and changing position within an understanding of global modernity, requiring more expertise than I have, would be of benefit here.

Deleuze, Gilles, 1993. *Critique and Clinique*. Paris: Les Éditions de Minuit.

Ishiguro, Kazuo, 1989. *The Remains of the Day*. London: Faber & Faber.

Jameson, Fredric, 1990. *Signatures of the Visible*. New York and London: Routledge.

Mitchell, David, 1999. *Ghost Written*. London: Sceptre.

Mitchell, David, 2001. *number9dream*. London: Sceptre.

Mitchell, David, 2004. *Cloud Atlas*. London: Sceptre.

Murakami, Haruki, 2003. *Hard-boiled Wonderland and the End of the World*, trans. Alfred Birnbaum. London: Vintage.

Rodowick, D.N., 1997. *Gilles Deleuze's Time Machine*. Durham, NC and London: Duke University Press.

Sakai, Naoki, 1989. 'Modernity and its Critique: The Problem of Universalism and Particularism', in *Postmodernism and Japan*, eds Masao Miyoshi and H.D. Harootunian. Durham, NC and London: Duke University Press, pp. 93–122.

Silverman, Kaja, 1988. *The Acoustic Mirror: The Female Voice in Psychoanalysis and Cinema*. Bloomington and Indianapolis: Indiana University Press.

Watts, Carol, 1995. *Dorothy Richardson*. Plymouth: Northcote House.

Weibel, Peter, 2003. 'The Intelligent Image: Neurocinema or Quantum Cinema?', in *Future Cinema: The Cinematic Imaginary After Film*, eds Jeffrey Shaw and Peter Weibel. Cambridge, MA: MIT Press, pp. 594–601.

Weis, Elisabeth and Belton, John, eds, 1985. *Film Sound: Theory and Practice*. New York: Columbia University Press.

Transcendence through Violence: Women and the Martial Arts Motif in Recent American Fiction and Film

DEBORAH L. MADSEN

Introduction

RECENT HOLLYWOOD MOVIES SUCH AS *Crouching Tiger, Hidden Dragon* (2000), *Kill Bill, Volume One* (2003), and the two *Charlie's Angels* movies (*Charlie's Angels* 2000, *Charlie's Angels: Full Throttle* 2003) have been characterised by the use of martial arts violence in place of earlier uses of guns and shooting as the primary vehicle of screen violence.[1] The 'shoot-em-up' has become the 'kick-em-up', and notable agents of this violence are women and specifically Asian women. In this essay I want to explore the connections between Asian femininity and the spectacle of Oriental violence in these movies and in Chinese American literary texts such as Maxine Hong Kingston's *The Woman Warrior* and *China Men*. Kingston's work is foundational both in terms of the subsequent development of Asian American literature and the ethnic women's movement. Kingston's popularity has been explained as the result of historical coincidence, which saw the publication of *The Woman Warrior* at a time when the feminist movement was beginning to make a widespread impact on American society. Kingston told American women what they wanted to hear, so this argument goes. But what of the representation of warrior women in a post-feminist age?[2]

---

[1] The action choreography of these movies is, in fact, the work of two brothers: Yuen Wo-ping (*Kill Bill*; also *The Matrix*, an important precursor, which uses martial arts but no female Asian warrior figure) and his brother Yuen Cheung-yan (*Charlie's Angels, Charlies Angels: Full Throttle*; also the two *Matrix* sequels: *The Matrix Reloaded* and *The Matrix Revolutions*). The Yeun brothers are responsible for bringing into the Hollywood mainstream the Hong Kong practice of 'wirework' to enable actors to leap and fly during action sequences.

[2] There is a connection between feminism and martial arts going back to Edith Garrud and the Suffragettes. The wife of noted martial artist William Garrud, Edith, who was also an expert in jujutsu, is reported as having achieved 'considerable notoriety both as a suffragette and as a trainer of "fighting suffragettes," the bodyguard unit for Mrs Pankhurst. Edith, after breaking with her husband,

Violence is stereotypically gendered as 'masculine' while femininity is symbolised as passive and pacific. Violent women then cross over into masculine territory, potentially to challenge patriarchal gender boundaries. This transgression can be figured as empowering of women or as sexually appealing to men. Lucy Liu, interviewed by Sean Chavel about her role in *Kill Bill, Volume One*, was asked, 'What's so sexy about girls fighting?' to which she replied:

> You know what it is? I don't see it as sexy, because it's more that women like to watch women fight because it makes them feel sort of empowered physically and mentally, internally, emotionally they feel kind of jazzed and excited by it. And men like to see it because two women fighting, men see women as a very different entity altogether. So to see that entity doing what men generally do is kind of an exciting thing. I'm not saying that women going out there and playing football is a hot thing, too, but you never know what's going to happen if you sort of turn things on its head, it always makes it more interesting, I think.

However, women adopting 'masculine' forms of violence also risk emasculating themselves, rendering themselves 'female eunuchs' of a new variety. Are, then, the violent Asian women of recent Hollywood cinema progressive or conservative representations of women's use of violence?

The emphasis upon powerful feminine martial artists in recent fiction and film (especially the latter) has coincided with a cultural moment that is variously described as post-modernist and post-feminist. In both cases, one might legitimately inquire into the significance of the cultural motif of the violent woman as a strategy for women's empowerment. Alice A. Jardine argued in *Gynesis* (1985) that the process named by her study represents the displacement of post-modernist anxieties concerning the instability or dissolution of the once-unified subject on to 'the feminine'. The feminine comes to represent the undesired knowledge of death, figured as the dissolution of the sovereign self, as a force akin to Freud's 'uncanny' (*unheimlich*): the repressed, the alien; 'something which ought to have remained hidden but has come to light' (Freud 1919: 241). In a post-modern age, the dissolution of stable categories of being – among them gender divisions and boundaries – gives rise to

opened a dojo close to Oxford Circus. This was used as a base for suffragettes to sally forth, break a few windows, rush back and be engaged innocently in jujutsu training when the police arrived' (http://www.budokwai.org/history_vol_i.htm).

the appearance of images of 'monstrous' women, which crystallise these anxieties. But this post-modern era is also the period of social, economic, and political advances made by the Women's Movement. These same cultural anxieties are given shape (and feminine form) by the patriarchal perception of feminine threat and female aggression. The image of the warrior woman or the militant female can be seen as American patriarchy's attempt both to express and to contain male anxieties about the restructuring of gender roles in the post-feminist age. I want to suggest that contemporary images of the Oriental warrior woman are far from subversive of patriarchal hegemony and in fact work to reassert conventional positioning of feminine sexuality.

Hollywood Oriental

Midway through *Charlie's Angels: Full Throttle* (2003) there comes a crucial confrontation between the dynamic trio and their nemesis, the 'fallen' Angel, Madison Lee (Demi Moore). They meet on one of the terraces of Los Angeles' Griffith Observatory, high above the city, and it is in this quasi-celestial location that Madison Lee's identity is revealed as the mastermind behind the crimes that the Angels have been engaged to solve.[3] Lee mocks what she calls the Angels' 'ass-kicking pose' and, as she sneers, she brandishes two outsized pistols, declaring 'back then, we used guns'. She then shoots them, knocking each in turn off the Observatory parapets so they 'fall', presumably to their deaths. The importance of this scene lies not only in its function as a turning point in the storyline. This confrontation underlines the absence of hardware, and specifically guns, in this action movie in favour of martial arts.

---

[3] The Griffith Observatory is a perceptive choice of location if only because of the commanding aerial context that is established for the confrontation between Angels. The Observatory is a well-known movie location, having functioned as a movie set (Gene Autry's *The Phantom Empire* [1935]) even before it was officially opened as an observatory in 1935. Later film and television roles include *Rebel Without a Cause*, *The Twilight Zone*, *Logan's Run*, and *Star Trek Voyager*. In this respect, the Observatory forms a part of the texture of simulacra that characterises this movie and its predecessor. The reality portrayed by the *Charlie's Angels* movies is that of the simulacra; the cinematic images refer to other cinematic images from which conventional understandings of reality are divorced. Below I will argue that the world of simulation, of the hyperreal, is key to an understanding of the representation of femininity and violence in these movies.

Kung-fu, kickboxing, or 'ass-kicking' as Madison Lee calls it, is the preferred form of violence in this twenty-first-century rendering of the 1970s drama series. The 'Orientalisation' of *Charlie's Angels* in these movies is represented powerfully by the substitution of kicking for shooting but is crystallised perhaps most clearly by the casting of Lucy Liu as an Angel. She becomes the only ethnic minority Angel (the others are played by Cameron Diaz and Drew Barrymore and are distinguished on the grounds of class). This casting of an ethnic Angel breaks the emphatically Caucasian feminine stereotype of the original TV series, which featured then-models of feminine perfection: Farrah Fawcett, Jaclyn Smith, Kate Jackson and, later replacing Farrah Fawcett, Cheryl Ladd, women who were to be distinguished from each other primarily according to hair, not skin, colour. Why, one must ask, is an Asian American actress cast alongside Cameron Diaz and Drew Barrymore?

I want to suggest that the inclusion of an Asian Angel has nothing to do with any kind of attempt at multicultural representation and everything to do with the sexualisation of the *Charlie's Angels* story. The explicit sexual dimension of both *Charlie's Angels* movies is expressed in myriad ways: from the sustained sexual innuendo of the dialogue, the inability of Dylan (Drew Barrymore) in both movies to resist the sexual attraction of the villain (in the first movie she explains this by describing hers as 'a full service job'), through to the comic subplot of the second movie where the father of Alex (Lucy Liu) is mistakenly led to believe that his daughter is a prostitute who, with her two close colleagues specialises in group assignments, and that Charlie is her pimp. It is this character of Lucy (despite or perhaps because of her unlikely Caucasian father, played by John Cleese) that provides a site for the playing out of a complex interplay between feminine (Oriental) sexuality and feminine (Oriental) violence.

Passive/Aggressive Women

In the case of the character portrayed by Lucy Liu, the militant woman is represented as sexual spectacle. The character of Alex in fact parodies the S&M figure of the Oriental dominatrix, the Dragon Lady. In the first movie she appears at one point clad in skin-tight black leather, wielding a whip, which she cracks periodically to assert her violent authority over a roomful of bureaucratised engineers. In the burlesque scene of the second movie, she again appears with a whip, which this time is used to remove Natalie's (Cameron Diaz) clothes. In both cases, the camera adopts the perspective of the male gaze, appropriating the spectacle of sexualised feminine violence as male entertainment. The masculine cooptation of Alex's aggression in such scenes is reinforced by those scenes that take place in the private domain. Here, apart from Charlie, the agency and her co-Angels, Alex's sexuality is defined by her relationship with Jason (played by Matt LeBlanc, reprising his role as the inept post-adolescent Joey of the TV series *Friends*). In the scenes with Jason, Alex is represented as passively engaged in traditional feminine activities (primarily cooking) and agonising over her inability to tell him her true profession. As if to emphasise the sexualisation of this character, Jason believes that she is a bikini-waxer and admits he finds this idea 'a turn-on'. Alex works at baking and roasting while practising potential confessional speeches, though she has talent for neither. Her culinary ambitions and her lack of talent form the basis for numerous incidental jokes, like the blueberry muffins, the 'Chinese fighting muffins', which when thrown in mock-battle become embedded in the door. Later in this movie, the trailer in which she is cooking is raked with automatic gunfire but Alex becomes concerned only when a bullet causes her perfect soufflé to deflate. The point of emphasising the conflict between Alex's professional talent as a private detective and warrior woman and her comically desperate attempts at conventional domestic femininity is to underline Alex's passivity in her relationship with Jason. She may represent pure aggressive sexual spectacle in her professional role but her private self is revealed to be passive and unthreatening. Any threat that the aggressive woman may represent is effectively defused by her private willingness to subordinate herself to one man and his appetites.

Much the same kind of scenario is represented in Maxine Hong Kingston's *The Woman Warrior* (1975), specifically in the 'White Tigers' section, which ends with the return of the victorious, crusading woman to a life of conventional femininity. She returns to her husband's parents with the promise that she will devote herself to work and the production of more sons. Her story concludes with the hopeful anticipation of legends that would be told of her perfect filiality. But we might interpret this filiality as perfect obedience and passivity, reasserted in place of the aggression she has demonstrated throughout her military career. In this story, women cannot be assertive both publicly and privately; public achievement must be compensated for with private humility and passivity. The choice between female militancy and female domesticity is a recurring theme in martial arts movies. The gifted female martial artist is plagued with doubts about the effect of

her physical prowess and her capacity for 'masculine' violence on her
ability to attract a husband. Wendy Arons argues, in her essay on
women in Hong Kong kung-fu movies, that 'even as such films depict
women as strong, independent, and capable fighters, they continue to
embed such images of women within a context that defines femininity
in terms of physical beauty and sexual attractiveness to men, and that
draws on traditional misogynistic stereotypes that reduce femininity to
a figure of "fascinating and threatening alterity"' (Arons, in
McCaughey & King 2001: 27).

The character Yu Shu Lien (played by Michelle Yeoh) in *Crouching
Tiger, Hidden Dragon* could be described as a female eunuch of this variety. She chooses honour and the discipline of the warrior's code over
romance. The opening sequence of the movie reveals the tension of her
undeclared passion for Li Mu Bai (Chow Yun Fat). This love must
remain unspoken, on both sides, because Shu Lien was once betrothed
to Li Mu Bai's dead friend. They must then resist this shared passion and
in fact transform this effort into of denial into an aspect of warrior discipline. Shu Lien is seen to make a choice between her feminine desires
and her fighting self, and her prowess is attributed in part to her choice
of asexuality. The feminine threat represented potentially by Shu Lien's
martial artistry is then defused by her choice to renounce her feminine
sexuality.

Of course, not all women warriors represent this reassuring passivity.
The authority over men asserted by the militant or violent woman is, in
patriarchal terms, an illegitimate authority. The female usurper of male
authority is, as a consequence, pathologised and then violently
destroyed. The connection between violence and the illegitimate feminine claim to authority is dramatised by the character of Jade Fox
(Cheng Pei Pei), in *Crouching Tiger, Hidden Dragon*. Cornered by the
hero, Li Mu Bai, Jade Fox is accused of stealing the master's book of
secret martial arts teachings. Her access to this restricted knowledge is
the result of murder, theft, and usurpation. In response to this accusa-
tion, Jade Fox replies that she killed him because he had 'no respect for
women'. She had possessed an honest desire to learn the martial arts but
the master had only sexual desire for her. She was regarded as good
enough to seduce but not good enough to teach. This injustice she
avenged by killing him and stealing the book of his teachings. Being
illiterate, however, she must entrust the book to her own protégé, Jen
(Zhang Ziyi), the governor's daughter who is herself struggling against
the arranged marriage that has been made for her father's benefit. The
pathological quality of Jade Fox's desire for martial skill is represented

through her unhealthy obsession with Jen. Jade Fox is represented as the corrupting force upon the young girl to whom she can teach technique, but this is skill devoid of the necessary discipline and ethics that makes a warrior great. Consequently, Jen steals the famous and magical sword, the Green Destiny; because she knows no honour, she is ignorant of the warrior's code. Jade Fox is ignominiously dispatched by Li Mu Bai, but for Jen is reserved the ambiguous ending of the movie, to which I will return below.

Feminist Fatales

In *Charlie's Angels: Full Throttle*, the usurping female warrior, Madison Lee, is represented as the *femme fatale*, poisonous to all the men she touches yet irresistible in her domineering sexuality. When Madison Lee first enters the action she is filmed in slow motion, walking out of the sea, clad in a skimpy black bikini (in contrast to Natalie's white counterpart), like a post-modernist parody of Botticelli's Venus. This slow-motion walk across the sand carrying her surfboard emphasises her almost masculine musculature but this is a physical strength transformed into an image of sexualised aggression. The nature of her femininity is also placed into question by the flashy red sports car (popular image of male ego-projection) in which she departs with an aggressive squeal of the tyres. It is not only in the role of the sexualised female aggressor that Madison Lee assumes the role of the *femme fatale*. As Elisabeth Bronfen observes, 'the classic *femme fatale* has enjoyed such popularity because she is not only sexually uninhibited, but also unabashedly independent and ruthlessly ambitious, using her seductive charms and her intelligence to free herself . . .' (Bronfen 2003). Madison Lee wants to liberate herself from the authority of Charlie, to stop 'taking orders from a speaker box' and become her own authority. But she does not want to become Charlie. Her ambition is much greater than that. 'Why be an Angel when you can be God?' she asks immediately before shooting each of the Angels, in the Observatory scene discussed above. The *femme fatale* is ambitious, independent, ruthless and, above all, dangerously sexual. However, as Bronfen incisively argues, she also embodies a will to death. The *femme fatale* uses her sense of her own personal destiny, which inevitably includes the knowledge of her own death, as the source of her power. Madison Lee tells the disembodied voice of Charlie, with a single tear trickling slowly down her face, 'I was never good. I was great' – before shooting the speaker box with her outsized gold pistol and turning to face the conclusion of this destiny that has been her obsession. The significance of that single tear lies precisely in her acknowledgement that the fulfilment of her destiny will also be her death. This is why she refers to herself in the past tense: 'I was great.' Mortality and triumph are inextricable. Precisely to the degree that Madison Lee, like all *femmes fatales*, exceeds the masculine fantasy of the tameable violent woman she risks her own mortality.

Violence and the Uncanny

If we return to Alice A. Jardine's argument that woman represents the uncanny, the frightening irruption of the repressed in everyday life, we can see how it is that the alien and alienated *femme fatale* in fact represents the irruption of mortality into the comfortable textures of everyday life. Madison Lee, like Jade Fox, makes present an image of femininity that is threatening because it represents that undesired knowledge of death. These characters accept the fact of their own mortality as a consequence of their pursuit of personal destiny. Destiny for these characters involves the dissolution of conventional gender boundaries – Jade Fox wants to possess knowledge that is prohibited to women; Madison Lee wants to become the Boss of all crime bosses. The post-modern, post-feminist anxieties concerning a perceived lack of stable gender and ego boundaries are dramatised by *femmes fatales* such as these. Eros and death are brought together with postmodernism, by Jean Baudrillard in *Symbolic Exchange and Death* (1975):

> Eros in the service of death, all cultural sublimation as a long detour to death, the death drive nourishing repressive violence and presiding over culture like a ferocious super-ego, the forces of life inscribed in the compulsion to repeat; all this is true, but true of our culture. Death undertakes to abolish death and is haunted by its own end. [. . .] Stage of the immanent repetition of one and the same law, insisting on its own end, caught, totally invested by death as objective finality, and total subversion by the death drive as a deconstructive process – the metaphor of the death drive says all of this simultaneously, for the death drive is at the same time the system and the system's double, its doubling into a radical counter-finality. (Baudrillard 1988: 152)

In Baudrillard's terms, the culture of the hyperreal is motivated by the desire to escape or repress or at least to efface knowledge of death but as a result becomes deeply imbricated in the fact of mortality ('all cultural sublimation as a long detour to death').[4] Eros, 'the forces of life', are pressed into the function of death-denial but the consequent reign of arbitrary semiotic signs, alienated from representation, is deathly ('Death undertakes to abolish death and is haunted by its own end'). However, the repression of death is never complete because the death drive is at the same time both the system of the hyperreal and also the repressed that will not remain repressed, which compulsively repeats its own sublimation, which irrupts into and shatters the hyperreal as *das unheimlich*, the uncanny. The spectacular violence of our post-modern screens (movie and TV), perhaps epitomised by the violent terrorist spectacle of 9/11, is the return of the repressed – the fact of death. This is the violence of the symbolic, which Baudrillard describes as 'haunting' modern social institutions as 'the prospect of their own demise' (1975: 120). The metaphor of haunting is reminiscent (probably deliberately so) of Freud's image of the uncanny as a haunting, symbolised by the haunted house. In his essay on the uncanny, Freud observes that: 'Many people experience the feeling in the highest degree in relation to death and dead bodies, to the return of the dead, and to spirits and ghosts. . . . Some languages in use today can only render the German expression "an *unheimlich* house" by "a *haunted* house"' (Freud 1919: 241; italics in the original).

It is the violence of the symbolic alone that has the power to break through or subvert the banality of the semiotic codes that constitute post-modern culture. These codes of the hyperreal – like CNN news, banal advertising, movies like *Charlie's Angels* that refer only to other movies – are susceptible only to spectacular violence that instantiates the fact of death in the midst of those codes designed to obscure and deny mortality. In Baudrillard's words, 'Only symbolic disorder can break the code' (1988: 122). Tarantino's *Kill Bill, Volume 1* demonstrates this breaking of banal semiotic codes through acts of extreme, spectacular violence. The irruption of death into the fabric of everyday

---

[4] Baudrillard defines the 'hyperreal' as 'the meticulous reproduction of the real, preferably through another, reproductive medium, such as photography'. This reproduction of the real refers to no reality beyond or outside itself and the free play of arbitrary signs. 'It becomes *reality for its own sake*, the fetishism of the lost object.' In the era of the postmodern, the real is defined as that which possesses not the capacity to be reproduced but which is 'always already reproduced' (Baudrillard 145–6; emphasis in original). See Richard J. Lane, *Jean Baudrillard: Routledge Critical Thinkers* (London: Routledge, 2000) for an excellent explanation of these concepts.

life is dramatised in the confrontation between 'the bride', (Uma Thurman) codenamed 'Black Mamba', and the second victim of her vengeance, Vernita Green (Vivica Fox). The suburban house in southern California before which she pulls up in her (misappropriated) car is filmed so that the pastel colours of the building, its spacious lawn strewn with children's toys, is more vivid than in any real American suburb. The house itself is a cliché of American sit-com TV, with cute gables and wide windows painted in contrasting pastel colours. Into this suburban calm bursts the violence of the bride's revenge. Again the contrast is heightened when Vernita Green's four-year-old daughter returns from school, bringing her mother's knife fight to an abrupt pause. The banal questions asked by the mother ('Did you have a nice day at school, sweetheart?') are posed by a woman caked in her own blood, standing in a room of shattered glass and trampled knick-knacks. This sequence culminates in Vernita's attempt to shoot Black Mamba with a gun hidden in a cereal packet. The packet, banal and ordinary as is the packaging of all children's cereals, is emblazoned with the word 'Kaboom'. We are back in the world of the simulacra where objects in the 'real' world imitate fantasy objects of television (like the house itself). But this hyperreality has been shattered, momentarily, by the violent killing of Vernita, by the intrusion of death in this spectacularly violent way and in a symbolic environment conventionally figured as 'safe'.

Baudrillard's theory of the symbolic expression and repression of death through code-violating acts of spectacular violence (note the emphasis on spectacle as constitutive of this violence) can be useful as a strategy by which to insert a feminist agenda into otherwise closed systems of representation, through the reappropriation of representations of violence. This happens through the identification of cultural constructions that equate feminine sexuality with death. Baudrillard's 'uncanny' as the irruption of violence as death and Jardine's description of the 'uncanny' quality of post-modern feminine sexuality are linked through Freud. Freud's essay on the uncanny constructs a link between the uncanny and woman precisely through the repressed knowledge of death.

In Freud's essay on 'The Uncanny', he observes that neurotic men have been observed to experience as uncanny the female genital organs. Freud interprets this experience to be the result of the return of repressed memories of inter-uterine fantasies. He links this to the image of the uncanny as attached not to the image of the house or home but to the haunted house, the home inhabited by death: 'The *unheimlich* place, however, is the entrance to the former Heim [home] of all human beings, to the place where each one of us lived once upon a time and in the beginning. . . . In this case, too, then, the *unheimlich* is what was once *Heimlich*, familiar; the prefix "un" ["un—"] is the token of repression' (Freud 1919: 245; parentheses in original). The return of repressed memories of death is intimately associated with feminine sexuality. Freud's explanation of the uncanny is primarily interested in the connection between the uncanny and death, not the uncanny and femininity. He observes that many people experience the uncanny in relation to the return of the dead, through spirits or haunting. But death is inseparable from life, and knowledge of mortality is inseparable from living. So long as we are living we know that we may die. And so the female – but specifically female sexuality, the female genitals, the locus of new life – is inscribed with death. She always already represents the return of repressed knowledge of death.

Baudrillard's 'uncanny' is the irruption of violence as death; but if the agent of that violence is feminine and her message is the inescapable fact of death, which post-modern culture has tried to efface through the hyperreal, then how can the violent woman achieve anything more than the reinscription of the category of woman as 'death'? Alice A, Jardine's image of post-modern woman as the 'uncanny' site for the expression of male anxieties about the breakdown of stable gender boundaries offers greater potential for the redefinition of femininity in a post-feminist (as opposed to post-modern) age. In the breakdown of stable gender boundaries there lies at least the potential to recreate gender in such a way that 'woman' is no longer identical to 'death'.

Death, Mortality, and Mastery

In the *Charlie's Angels* movies, as in *Crouching Tiger, Hidden Dragon*, the human capacity to fly is represented as a consequence of strict martial arts discipline and training. Only through discipline is it possible to transcend the limitations of the mortal body and fly. In *The Woman Warrior*, Kingston's heroine recalls the Chinese martial arts movies she saw as a child: 'on Sundays, from noon to midnight, we went to the movies at the Confucius Church. We saw swordswomen jump over houses from a standstill; they didn't even need a running start' (19). Young Maxine remembers the swordswomen who could defy gravity, who possessed the power to transgress the laws of nature. In the narrative that follows, 'White Tigers', she imagines herself as the warrior woman, Fa Mu Lan. Her training in the arts of war involves primarily learning to control and so transcend bodily, corporeal, and natural forces: muscular reflexes, noise, hunger. Eventually, she can control the movements of her irises; she can 'point at the sky and make a sword appear, . . . and control its slashing with [her] mind' (33). The ability to fly is a measure of her progress: after six years she can leap like the swordswomen of the movies ('I could jump twenty feet into the air from a standstill, leaping like a monkey over the hut' [23]), but still she says, 'I could not fly like the bird that led me here, except in large, free dreams' (24). However, the white horse that appears magically to carry her into battle bears on its hooves the ideograph 'to fly' (35). Insofar as she can fly, she describes how, high on the mountain, she runs but does not fall over the cliff edge, '[a] wind buoyed me up over the roots, the rocks, the little hills. We reached the tiger place in no time' (24).

This description is reminiscent of the sequence in *Crouching Tiger Hidden Dragon* when Li Mu Bai chases Jen to regain possession of the Green Destiny sword. They fly among the treetops, briefly touching down on each, and travelling very quickly as a result. When the sword falls into the mountain waterfall, Jen does not jump after it, rather she flies down the mountain until her flying becomes a dive down to the riverbed. The ability to fly is here represented as the characteristic skill of warriors trained in the Wu Dang method. Jen has learned this method illicitly from Jade Fox, and so although she possesses skill, she lacks the warrior's code and martial discipline. Her lack is represented as poison in the scene where the film reaches a climax: Li Mu Bai engages with Jade Fox over possession of Jen. Both wish to be her teacher and guide but both fail. Li Mu Bai kills Jade Fox, avenging his murdered master, but is poisoned by one of her darts. As she dies, Jade Fox tells Li Mu Bai the true meaning of poison: staring at Jen with unwavering eyes, she declares that poison is a young girl with eyes full of deceit. Both Jade Fox and Li Mu Bai are poisoned by their relationship with Jen. In the case of Li Mu Bai, there is a subtle yet powerful sexual dimension to this relation. Jen embraces the warrior's life because she wants to escape the arranged marriage that would sacrifice her to her father's political ambitions. But when Li Mu Bai pursues her after her flight down the mountain she asks him, which does he want, the sword or the girl? He has no answer to this question. He wants her as his pupil, ostensibly, but in his relation with Shu Lien he has been sublimating sexual passion into martial artistry for many years. Jen is seeking a kind of freedom that is not resolved by the role of female warrior eunuch, such as Shu Lien embraces. Jen is seeking a different way to be an assertive, even aggressive, sexual woman.

This quest is clearly revealed in the sequence in Mongolia, after she is taken captive and falls in love with the Mongolian bandit Luo (Chang Chen). This relationship is doomed, however, by the competing claims of civilisation and wilderness: she must return to her family in the city yet he cannot renounce his nomadic ways. She tries to live with him in the desert; he tries to prove himself a worthy, 'civilised' match for her. In the ambiguous concluding scenes of the movie, she meets him briefly at a monastery, high atop Wu Dang Mountain. Earlier, Luo has told of the legendary qualities of this mountain: how once a man whose children were ill jumped from the mountain and so brought his wishes true. He did not die, says Luo, but floated away happily knowing that his children were well again. The moral of this story, as Luo tells it, is the importance of a trusting heart. As Luo searches for Jen at the monastery through the morning mist, the camera leaves him peering over the parapets, over the cliff edge, and shifts to the image of Jen flying down the mountain. Her face is serene and confident; she is not falling, she is not frightened. She is flying towards some destiny (not this time the Green Destiny) that only she can see. No longer must she choose between the roles of patriarchal wife and sexless warrior woman, but what this alternative feminine destiny, this new definition of femininity, might be is not revealed.

Jen faces her own death and embraces that knowledge. Her ability to fly has granted her the power to transgress the law of gravity as her martial prowess has granted her an alternative to the social law of patriarchal marriage. Whether she achieves transcendence or simply transgression is ambiguous. Kingston's heroine, however, quite clearly achieves transcendence through her discipline and training. On the mountaintop, she faces death through exposure, hunger, wild animals: she describes being 'unable to sleep for facing my death – if not death here, then death someday' (25). But after she enters 'the dead land' her vision changes. She sees the ancient couple who have trained her, but now they are young, now they are angels. In her vision, they transcend time and mortality. It is not only death that the young warrior woman must confront and master; as I argued above, the connection between femininity and death is made through the life-giving properties of feminine fertility. By bringing babies into world where they will die women are dealers of death as well as bringers of life. Initially, Maxine's fantasy life as a woman warrior involves postponing the desire to have children in order to fight and win her martial victories. When she does fall pregnant, her armour transforms her appearance from vulnerable woman to 'a powerful, big man' and later to 'a fat man', as when the infant rides into battle inside his mother's armour (39). The baby is, significantly, a boy for whom all the full-month ceremonies (denied to girls, as Kingston points out elsewhere in the narrative) are performed. At this point, the woman warrior is certainly a devoted soldier and leader. But we must ask to what extent is she a *woman* warrior? Even through this most feminine of experiences – childbirth – she continues her masculine performance unabated. Except for the time of giving birth she boasts never to have absented herself from battle and, after her baby is sent to be with his father to stay with his grandparents, she is transformed once more into a 'slim young man' (41). The performance of masculinity is so complete that she effectively remains a man, a male warrior in her violent confrontations with death. Though she is a violent woman, she is much more a perfect filial daughter who, after avenging her family's grievances, returns to a life that is undisturbed by her violent achievements:

> Wearing my black embroidered wedding coat, I knelt at my parents-in-laws feet, as I would have done as a bride. 'Now my public duties are finished,' I said, 'I will stay with you, doing farmwork and housework, and giving you more sons.' (45)

The paradigm for femininity remains unchanged by this story of female filiality. Gender roles and boundaries are unchanged, and the conclusion of the story asserts the primacy of feminine passivity over female aggression. This is underlined by the contrast drawn between the filial and obedient warrior woman and a group of women she liberates from the clutches of the evil baron. The narrative suggests that these women become themselves a band of swordswomen, devoted to the liberation of all women. The warrior woman tells how: '[t]hey did not wear men's clothes like me, but rode as women in black and red dresses. They bought up girl babies . . . When slave girls and daughters-in-law ran away, people say they joined these witch amazons' (45). The difference between 'witch amazons' and the 'warrior woman' lies in the extent to which the former assert a violent femininity that is not disguised by the naturalising performance of masculinity. The amazons are said to kill boys and men – an unnatural practice in a culture which, according to this narrative, kills only girls and women. These witch amazons embrace the power of death to assert a form of femininity that is unacceptable and unknown, which consciously defines femininity in terms of death and embraces the power to challenge normative gender boundaries with which that endows them. Death alone permits them to transcend the confinement of patriarchal feminine identities.

Conclusion

As Imelda Whelehan and Esther Sonnet have argued, following Camille Paglia,

> the 'post-feminist' heroine is regarded as transgressive and challenging for depicting a woman 'in control'. We are encouraged to position gender politics on an account of 'control' that rests solely on the view that a certain female style and set of behaviours can operate as ironic and knowing, which can celebrate pre-feminist feminine identity with a playfulness which is both performative and transgressive. There is, of course, a degree of debate about what would constitute a transgressive image, but presumably it must in some way dismantle gender binarism without reviving its essential dynamics. (Whelehan and Sonnet 1997: 42–3)

The Woman Warrior does not dismantle this gender binarism, as I have argued above. Kingston's young protagonist confuses the masculine armour and military successes for victory as a woman. She imagines herself as transgressive because she transgresses the patriarchal taboo against women 'passing' for men, but she willingly embraces this patriarchal orthodoxy when her brief career as a warrior woman has passed. Kingston's woman warrior is 'performative and transgressive', but she performs and transgresses masculine codes, not the codes of femininity. She is mistaken for a man. Only at the moment when she kills the evil baron does she reveal her gender, by exposing her breasts as she displays her parents' grievances which are carved into her back: 'When I saw his startled eyes at my breasts, I slashed him across the face and on the second stroke cut off his head' (44). This revelation of femininity at the moment of death reinscribes the feminine within the sphere of death. Again, femininity becomes inextricable from death, but this is death in the service of patriarchal filiality, not in the service of female liberation (as is the death-dealing of the 'witch amazons').

In Charlie's Angels: Full Throttle, Alex represents an Asian woman in control of her destiny, but this representation is a pastiche drawing upon the 'Dragon Lady' stereotype, which brings together the combined influences of racism and patriarchy. She is in control insofar as she wields a whip; like the other Angels she takes her orders from Charlie and, as I

argued above, retreats into domestic passivity in private. The cabaret
scene in the first *Charlie's Angels* movie attempts an 'ironic and knowing'
representation of pre-feminist roles, aiming to 'celebrate pre-feminist feminine identity with a playfulness which is both performative and transgressive'. However, this German-style burlesque (which nods towards the
Liza Minelli movie *Cabaret*) is more like a strip-show, as the name by
which it goes indicates: 'Pussycat Dolls'. These women are acting out
masculine fantasies of the aggressive yet sexually available woman: the
dominant and violent woman in Alex's case. The audience should make
a distinction between the role we have seen these women play as strong
and competent detectives and the image they create as dancing sex
objects. However, the point of this sequence is to distract the male audience with the spectacle of female sexuality while stealing keys and a security pass from one of them. In this scene, as in the movie as a whole (and
its sequel) feminine sexuality is represented as manipulative; as a substitute for feminine strength. Here, as in *The Woman Warrior*, femininity is
placed in the service of patriarchy. The cabaret scene is playful and performative, but it is 'transgressive' only insofar as the male fantasy played
out is coded as 'transgressive' within patriarchal culture. The performance
serves the interests of, and is possessed by, the male gaze. The essential
dynamics of gender binarism remains undisturbed.

In Kingston's writing and in the recent movies discussed above, the
martial arts theme functions as spectacle, as a choreography of violence that displays the female body and the Asian female body specifically as strong, aesthetically pleasing yet violent. The motif of flying,
which is used in *The Woman Warrior*, the *Charlie's Angels* movies and
Crouching Tiger, Hidden Dragon, hints at the possibility of transgression through the image of violent women, who transgress the law of
the fathers, of patriarchy, literally or physically transgressing the law
of gravity. But the possibility of liberation from the confinement of
patriarchally defined gender roles is not realised. Kingston's heroine,
like the Asian Angel, retreats into domesticity and is unable to rec-
oncile her femininity with her 'masculine' capacity for violence. In
Crouching Tiger, Hidden Dragon, the ambiguous conclusion hints at an
alternative subject position for the warrior woman, but the reality is
that the audience is left with the image of her body suspended in air,
destined perhaps for transcendence of conventional masculine/femi-
nine identities or destined perhaps only for death. The image of the
violent female in recent filmic and literary texts can then be seen as
American patriarchy's attempt to express and to contain male anxieties about the restructuring of gender roles in the post-feminist age.

The objectification of the feminine body in combination with the spectacle of physical power is reassuring to male audiences who possess the privilege of the objectifying gaze. Contemporary images of the Oriental warrior woman, then, are far from subversive of patriarchal hegemony, working instead to reassert conventional positionings of feminine sexuality.

Works Cited

Abbas, M.A. and Ackbar Abbas, 1997. *Hong Kong: Culture and the Politics of Disappearance*. Minneapolis: University of Minnesota Press.

Baudrillard, Jean, 1988. *Selected Writings*, ed. Mark Poster. London: Polity.

Bronfen, Elisabeth, 2003. 'Femme Fatale: Negotiations of Tragic Desire'. http://www.bronfen.info/writing/texts/2003_07_femme_fatale.html

Brownell, Susan, Jeffrey N. Wasserstrom and Thomas Laqueur, eds, 2002. *Chinese Femininities/Chinese Masculinities: A Reader*. Berkeley and London: University of California Press.

Desser, David, 2000. 'The Martial Arts Film in the 1990s', in Wheeler Winston Dixon, ed., *Film Genre 2000*. Albany, NY: SUNY Press, pp. 77–109.

Early, Francis H., Kathleen Kennedy and Rhonda V. Wilcox, eds, 2003. *Athena's Daughters: Television's New Women Warriors*. Syracuse, NY: Syracuse University Press.

Freud, Sigmund, 1919. 'The Uncanny', in the *Standard Edition of the Complete Psychological Works of Sigmund Freud*, trans. James Strachey. London: Hogarth Press, XVII, pp. 218–56.

Heinecken, Dawn, Cameron McCarthy and Angharad N. Valdivia, eds, 2003. *The Warrior Women of Television: A Feminist Cultural Analysis of the New Female Body in Popular Media*. New York: Peter Lang.

Inness, Sherrie A., ed., 2004. *Action Chicks: New Images of Tough Women in Popular Culture*. Basingstoke: Palgrave Macmillan.

Jardine, Alice A., 1985. *Gynesis: Configurations of Women and Modernity*. Ithaca, NY: Cornell University Press.

Kang, Laura Hyun Yi, 2002. 'Cinematic Projections: Marking the Desirous Body', in *Compositional Subjects: Enfiguring Asian American Women*. Durham, NC: Duke University Press, pp. 71–113.

Kingston, Maxine Hong, 1975. *The Woman Warrior*. New York: Vintage.

Liu, Lucy, interview with Sean Chavel. http://www.ugo.com/channels/filmtv/features/killbill/lucyliu.asp

Lu, Sheldon Hsiao-Peng, ed., 1997. *Transnational Chinese Cinemas: Identity, Nationhood, Gender*. Honolulu: University of Hawaii Press.

McCaughey, Martha and Neal King, eds, 2001. *Reel Knockouts: Violent Women in the Movies*. Austin: University of Texas Press.

Morris, Meaghan, 2001. 'Learning from Bruce Lee: Pedagogy and Political Correctness in Martial Arts Cinema', in Matthew Tinckcom and Amy Villarejo, eds, *Keyframes: Popular Film and Cultural Studies*. London and New York: Routledge, pp. 171–86.

Whelehan, Imelda and Esther Sonnet, 1997. 'Regendered Reading: *Tank Girl* and Postmodernist Intertextuality', in Deborah Cartmell et al., eds, *Trash Aesthetics: Popular Culture and its Audience*. London: Pluto, pp. 31–47.

Yoshioka, Marianne R. and Quynh Dang, 2000. *Asian Family Violence Report: A Study of the Cambodian, Chinese, Korean, South Asian, and Vietnamese Communities in Massachusetts, 2000*. Boston, MA: Asian Task Force Against Domestic Violence. http://www.atask.org/Resources_AFVR.htm

Index

[Films marked with asterisk]